Nawãr (Savages): Transformation of Individual and Collective Consciousness in Totalitarian Regimes in Syrian Society

Nawãr (Savages): Transformation of Individual and Collective Consciousness in Totalitarian Regimes in Syrian Society

By

Abdullah Chahin

Translated by Reham Selim

Cambridge
Scholars
Publishing

Nawăr (Savages): Transformation of Individual and Collective Consciousness in Totalitarian Regimes in Syrian Society

By Abdullah Chahin

This book first published 2024

Cambridge Scholars Publishing

Lady Stephenson Library, Newcastle upon Tyne, NE6 2PA, UK

British Library Cataloguing in Publication Data
A catalogue record for this book is available from the British Library

Copyright © 2024 by Abdullah Chahin

All rights for this book reserved. No part of this book may be reproduced, stored in a retrieval system, or transmitted, in any form or by any means, electronic, mechanical, photocopying, recording or otherwise, without the prior permission of the copyright owner.

ISBN (10): 1-0364-0678-4
ISBN (13): 978-1-0364-0678-3

To Salma and Alia, the apples of my eyes.

TABLE OF CONTENTS

Prologue viii

Chapter 1 1
The Making of Savagery: "The Context"
    Escaping failure 2
    Civilization 7
    The Un-Civilization 37

Chapter 2 75
The Caravan
    The ugly Nawāri and high society! 75
    The Nawāri and the legend 81
    Landmarks on the road 104

Chapter 3 132
The Intellectual Aspects of the Oppressed in the Nawāri Society: "Belongings"
    1- Ignorance 138
    2- Indiscretion 155
    3- Totalitarianism 174
    4- Exclusionism 199
    5- Isolation 208
    6- In conclusion: the non-self 232

Chapter 4 237
Behavioral Aspects of the Nawāri Community: "Litter"
    1- Tanbal (Sloth) 240
    2- Infallible 250
    3- Selfish 254
    4- Harbouk (Sly) 259
    5- Mkoleck (Sycophant) 267
    6- Antar 273

Conclusion 280
The One Nawāri I Know Well

Prologue

Bringing one's work to life in a different language requires more than mere translation, especially for such a book. When I wrote it in my native tongue, Arabic, I addressed peers and comrades sharing the same struggle. In the English version, I am speaking to a different audience, my examiners. The English version of the book attempts to give an inside perspective on the struggle and dynamics of a particular group under an unusual regime of totalitarianism at a highly exceptional moment in its history. I considered localizing some parts of the content to make it relevant to the Western reader and was tempted to address them directly. Instead, I thought I would just give them the space to unrestrictedly hear our internal conversation about our shared experience for the last several decades, how it occurred, and where it has led us.

I have been working on this text for ten long years. From 2014 to 2021, the Arabic version took seven arduous years. During that time, I found myself pondering the course of events in the Syrian scene in particular and the Arab states in general amidst the repercussions of the Arab Spring. Like many of my generation, I was in a state of disappointment and confusion as we were witnessing for the first time a real people's revolution erupting simultaneously in more than seven Arab states in what came to be called the Arab Spring of 2011. In less than three years of its spark, some of these states fell into chaos and war, whereas others experienced a stronger return to old dictatorships. The results were so shocking that they affected our belief in the justice of the causes behind the Arab Spring and made us question our inner perception of ourselves as Arab nations and peoples. This shock did not only annihilate any opportunity to change similar to that of any other Arab state but also collaborated in killing any political, economic, or intellectual reformation in such states.

The events of the Arab Spring came as no surprise to many observers with knowledge and experience. The authoritarian repression, economic hardship, and significant disparities, along with no salvation looming on the horizon, provided a suitable environment for the escalation of the popular protests. Nevertheless, the origin and timing of events posed hard questions and a point of contention among various parties. Were these events a result of exceptional courage on the part of a youth-driven popular movement or some foreign-schemed conspiracy? Despite our convictions and strong beliefs in our just cause and the dismay of the disastrous outcomes these popular uprisings ended in, nothing and none could change the opinion of either side. Still, regardless of our view of the spark, these popular movements succeeded in massing hundreds of thousands of people in the squares, facing death with high heads, only to demand freedom and dignity—a fact that is hard to dispute. Heedless of poverty, hunger, or the systematic looting of their riches, the persistent base of their struggle was to acquire high values, bringing pride to whoever participated in this movement.

Despite the slowing of military and political events on the Syrian and regional scene, the humanitarian catastrophes and social calamities resulting from this war still bring something new almost daily. Especially after the eruption of the Syrian estrangement, unforeseen by many, and the reaching of the Syrian individual to the outskirts of this earth as a refugee or a migrant.

The largest challenge I encountered while writing this book was my concern that, in writing such a challenging book, my words would fall short of my intended meaning, especially because its title might offend many Syrians. The word Nawāri in our society is an insult and an offense, met with counter-swearing at times and beating at some others. In our collective consciousness, the Nawāri has an extremely negative image, charged with all traits counter to all that might be ascribed to us: the "respectable "people.

Not once did I hear the Nawāri word positively describing anything that would please us to be attributed. Far from it, an image of a dark, slim, barefooted, and disheveled individual jumps into our minds, gazing with yellow eyes, sneering with crooked and worn-out teeth, sulking, and speaking only profanity. In our mind's eyes, the "Nawãri" is nameless, featureless, voiceless, and lacks everything denoting a human form. That "Nawãri" is the opposite of which, meaning the non-Nawãri should distance themselves from anything similar to them. Nawrãna (savagery) is the deplorable outcome that all fear. It is the root cause of why one pushes their children to go to school every morning if they do not follow instructions for being well dressed or keeping their shoes clean. They would be chided, saying, "Don't be a savage! It is of low caste and less of a human! Even a total lack of it! There is no place for "Nawãr" amongst us, the civilized society! All forms of Nawrãna must be fought.

I find myself obliged to assert that this book is not about the tribes or ethnic groups referred to in this description. Any projections I make are not intended for them as individuals or groups. I apologize to all such groups for centuries of oppression and belittling practiced unjustly towards them. All I do is borrow this unfair stereotype projected on them in a generalizing and unjust manner and project it back to us as individuals of the Syrian community. Henceforward, every "Nawãri" word can be exchanged with the clause "the Syrian living under authoritarian and totalitarian oppression for the past sixty years." This community has found in its understanding matters that it tried to evade by blaming the other and to rid itself of it by adhering to a group against which it would be easier to distinguish. Thus, the "Nawãr" description in our community is an easier choice of word to describe the other, whom we can outstrip and try our best not to be. All of this is done without us getting to know one Nawãr well enough to objectively examine their life from a different perspective and without conceit.

This understanding—that of differentiation from the other—carries within its layers one of the biggest issues of the collective consciousness in Syrian society, with all its different categories and backgrounds. On the other hand, such loose, pre-made, and existing forms of projecting probably facilitated Syrian society's plummeting into the quicksand of disintegration after the break of the Arab Spring in 2011. The total disintegration was demonstrated all through the lines of differentiation of age, class, education, economy, region, race, and sect. With the variations of disintegration lines that rapidly emerged and the divergence in the Syrian community, the individuals ceaselessly distanced themselves from the other. Arabic has no word to denote the concept I am trying to outline here. Even other languages resort to using the verb form of the word "other," as in "otherization" and "othering." Thus, keeping the other as being othered with total and complete differentiation. It is a mechanism to create a barrier to isolate the targeted individual from the public. This chapter starts with the purpose of creating two groups. It is no longer just "we" and "them," but the "all" and the "adversary," for the "all" to be protected from the vicious "adversary" and confront their evils.

With time, the exclusive circle of that "all" grew narrower and more homogenous. The communities in Syria fell into degeneracy, taking them back to the circles of narrow alleys and from there on to the community of big families and the nucleus family. Subsequently, many familial connections were lost, even among siblings. This degeneracy does not only represent a moral failure but also an indication of the lack of perspective for the existence of a mutual identity among the individuals of Syrian society. As time goes by, the "Nawāri" expand their definition of the other—the enemy—facilitating dissociation from that other and taking a defensive position.

This process of differentiation starts in our minds—between what is acceptable and unacceptable. It is projected on our reality to identify who those are that are "not us." And this accompanies our almost total lack of understanding of what "us" means. We find ourselves falling into social disintegration. It does not only destroy the existing social foundations but also hinders the building of any substitute or alternative ones. This disintegration that makes us Nawār in each other's eyes is the state desired by the authoritative regimes oppressing us. Totalitarian regimes are the very ones that strenuously strive to keep individuals entirely disconnected from their communities.

The Nawār utilizes any grievance, whether personal or part of its focus circle, which might sometimes broaden. All of this is unacknowledged by the Nawāri to justify their detachment from their community, neighborhood, reality, and even responsibilities. In Syrian society, everyone is isolated and entrenched in a mold they hand-shaped to be distinguished from and avoid the "adversary." This mold, with a mission to build a homogenous and bonded human grouping, grew into a barrel to be worn by an individual, and whoever is outside is the "other," threatening their very existence. No wonder bumper stickers reading "People's betrayal made me love traveling" and "Always in tears" became viral for decades in Syria. Besides, volumes of radio songs lament betrayal and disloyalty. And saying, "The walls have ears" is a hollow excuse for not being candid, even among siblings and cousins, and fearing nothing but that the next blow would be dealt at the hands of your own flesh and blood. It is society's utter failure, embodied in the withering of an individual behind imagined walls, isolating them from the world. Behind these walls, everyone is equal in their animosity, insignificance, and inhumanity. The more we consider ourselves Nawār, the more convinced we get of our Nawrāna. But wait! I am not a Nawār. It is they who are the Nawār. They are the cause of our misery, backwardness, and downfall. Consequently, I do my part carefully, reminding myself persistently of the dangers of Nawrāna and incessantly abhorring it.

However, that individual is abruptly taken over by the strong waves of Nawrāna, leaving them powerless to escape, despite their best efforts. Millions of individuals, who are diligent in their Nawrāna, eagerly struggle to keep afloat on the surface of defeat or surrender and delve deep into the predestined role of Nawrāna. No matter how disintegrated communities can be, they remain whole and affected by each other. At the moment of truth, we have to live together in our "Nawrāna." The more we consider ourselves "Nawār," the more convinced we are of it." Then we have to play the role, though we hate it. The authoritarian winds have taken over, threshing all fresh heads.

Coping with the Nawrāna state requires rationalizing it, accepting it as a reality, setting excuses, and re-accepting it. Then it becomes a praiseworthy collective identity. Shortly, we integrate it into the historical and civilizational identity that differentiates us from the rest of the world and our eternal bond. It becomes a dream and a part of a glorious history where we once were but no longer are and we most strenuously pursue. Magically, the life of Nawrāna remains a constant nostalgia in the minds of the Nawār, where everyone is longing for a beautiful time that is utterly irrelevant to their reality. Their homes are warm and safe, where simple people live, going about their business peacefully. A hard-working and honest set of people, welcoming to strangers, and having a warm set of customs and traditions. However, the life of the Nawār was part of a historical pathway drifting into the abyss, unbeknownst to us.

It is incumbent upon us to fathom how the Syrians have lost their way and, above all, how the streets of exiles have turned into their homeland. And how they turned from "an educated and amalgamated civilization" and descendants of "the glorious history" to the Nawār caught in a whirlwind. How did they shift from a virtuous society to a suppressed one? How does the Nawār allow the continuation of this oppression and torture? We ended up being peacefully handed from one dictator to another without the least show of opposition. Even though the revolution was a historic opportunity for change, why did the Nawār create another historic opportunity to change their reality, for which they paid its price in dear blood and ended up wasting it as previously?

The Syrian revolution unveiled another facet of our reality. Syria has witnessed a transformation of crime, from the tyranny of a single despot to a succession of atrocities with anonymous murderers. The civil movement for the revolution failed due to the corruption of some of the active groups and their connection to institutions of interest in erasing that very movement. It reached the point where those activists cooperated with the regime and managed to blackmail and then recruit them. Afterward, the civil movement transmuted into an armed one, with army defectors among their lines who refused to kill protestors. This transformation, rather than a push forward for the toppling of the regime, led to nothing but more violence and bloodshed. The armed Islamic factions spearheaded the fighting fronts, paving the way for the rise of ISIS (the Islamic State of Iraq and Syria). All of this is occurring against a backdrop of widespread corruption spreading across the political opposition and several civil society organizations. Consequently, discussing who is responsible for these successive setbacks was postponed.

The fundamental struggle and the core issues were lost. Discussions turned to the purpose, with successive accusations exchanged between all parties about who was responsible for the destruction and devastation. We reached a point where it was essential to examine whether the removal of Bashar al-Assad was the means to solving the struggle. Or the struggle has reached a much deeper and more intricate stage than simply removing the cancerous authoritarian and recovering the patient. We can no longer consider matters in such simple terms after witnessing how the Syrians championed "the Method brothers" (a jihadi Salafist slogan) against brothers of blood, land, and citizenship that collaborated in the establishment of the ISIS state. We have become stuck in a struggle with hazy images of ourselves. Our struggle is no longer as clear-cut as we once thought. The story of the murderer and the victim is lost amidst the ongoing whirlwind of violence. We have allowed the first murderer to get away with his crime. We even participated in creating new killers that walked down the same road and thus deserved to be included with the primary killer on the enemy list. We have become at war with something that is a part of who we are. We are among the masses of the Nawār and oppressed. Try as we might to repent and return to our purity and imagined utopianism, at the end of the day, we look in the mirror at something that somehow resembles an unwanted image. Nevertheless, whether we like it or not, it is ours.

I do not equate the victim with the perpetrator. On the contrary, I strive to end the repetitive loop of the Karpman drama triangle, or the executioner/rescuer/victim syndrome. We have to dig deep into that tunnel connecting our oppression and betrayal. We must rebuild the foundation of the common ground that binds us together. Then, we must learn how to respect the common ground of "us" and what makes "us" as a collective. Only then will we exterminate the primary executioner and whoever followed him. Only then would we commemorate those who have made the ultimate sacrifice for "us."

I hope that by the end of the book, I can present a deeper perspective on some of our ideological and moral crises. In addition to that, what I consider factors into the impediments standing in the way between what we want and what we are. What we want can be either salvation from persecution or catching up with the developed nations and being among the leading civilizations. It might be beneficial to refer to the fact that this book does not aim to outline the differentiations between the Syrians who participated in the revolt against al-Assad's rule and those who decided to rally around him. The book aims to draw on the intellectual traits of the Syrian generations that came to the age of majority before 2011. We are the offspring of the movements of the "Pioneers," the "Revolutionary Youth Union," the one party, and the "Father Commander" (all names of organizations with the one and only leading ruling party in Syria). We share much more than we think as we glare at each other through the crack separating us post-2011. This does not mean that the conclusive moral stand that we took in 2011 is equal at the two ends of the schism. The attitude towards the Syrian revolution is a bigger crack than can be evaluated at the moment.

This book is more of an individual effort to analyze complex political, intellectual, and social problems than a work of satire. This analysis might facilitate portraying a road map and reaching several agenda items that might be crucial to solving problems in our daily reality and our civilizational and existential crises. Moreover, this book is not an attempt at self-flagellation; nevertheless, reading and writing are both painful experiences. This book is an attempt at delving beyond what is beneath the shallow surfaces. It is more like taking up the scalpel to make an incision in the chest. Though it does not reveal the secrets of the mind, it gives us more insight and more details. I do not seek to be another masochistic state due to my Arab cultural experience. My book does not also aim at creating or framing any stereotypes of some societies. There is not one human being on the face of this earth who has all the traits of a Nawāri that are enumerated in the book. Therefore, it is utterly unfair to say that there is a whole group of people who have all of these traits. Especially those who are accused of being "non-civilized" and savage are getting into new phases of their unique journey toward liberation and progress.

This is my first book. I hope more will follow, giving me ample room to build upon the criticism and overview I introduce here, which is to be considered by many as negative, bleak, and heeding nothing but dim surroundings. What this book strives to monitor is several intellectual phenomena and characteristics first detected by the author in himself, his immediate environment, and the community. These characteristics are present in every ancient and modern human community. Nonetheless, such characteristics are considerably and predominantly recurrent in the

"Nawãri" community. That recurrence drove the author to propose a theory about an interrelationship between the prevalence of these characteristics among the individuals of a society and its deterioration. This theory does not venture to foresee whether this interrelation between these two phenomena is causal. And it does not imply the possibility that one is an outcome of the other's existence or exacerbation. This detection and all the accusations made in this book aim at nothing more than describing these phenomena and exploring some of their causes and outcomes as thoroughly as possible. My efforts would not seek to propose any solution for these phenomena, attempt to reconstruct society or impose its intellectual approach.

My choice of the word" probing" reflects a confession on my part about my experience as an individual. This experience is more like a needle biopsy[1], which cannot necessarily outline the complete features, form, or shape of the biopsied organ. It rather reflects the hierarchy and diversity of the layers and foundations composing that body. I do not consider my perspective an external one performed on a sample; I observe through the glass from afar. Rather, I see myself as one of the Nawãr, and I have many of their traits and practices.

No one can deny their origin, which is as permanent as the color of one's skin, despite their best efforts. This is similar to exposed flaws, such as warts on eyelids. Contrarily, the origin and belonging of an individual are not associated with their flaws unless they insist on confirming this association through their beliefs and behavior.

When writing a book, one stands with their bare thoughts under the scrutiny of millions of eyes and history. It is a horrifying stance for me and many in my place. My fear of airing my thoughts to the public eye might have contributed to the delay in completing this book for years. Every time I read an old excerpt of what I wrote, I find myself mocking my own thoughts and

---

[1] When doctors encounter a suspicious lump, they extract a needle biopsy to help them observe and study the tissues that make up that lump and learn more about the disease and its severity. My attempt to understand the soil that yielded our historical events and the intellectual transformations that contributed to outlining this path raised this example in my mind.

their naivety as being unequal to the intricacy of the cause at hand. To enrich my work, I sometimes elaborate on what I seek to convey through academic language, studies, and references. At times, they are successful elaborations, and on others, I write as if my book was in my hands when I was a fifteen-year-old boy. I find myself burdened with foreign terms. I will proceed to explain what I mean in a more comprehensive manner. Or, I would add synonyms to terms I list in both Arabic and English to facilitate further research.

From the very beginning, I tried to keep my book up with the pace of Syrian reality, making it relevant to our problems, the Syrians 'problems. The more delayed I get in finishing it, the more I feel liberated from the prison of the temporal context. For the book to be more closely related to absolute human thoughts and the general masses with no exclusions or limitations, nowadays, the Nawāri can be American, Italian, modern, or futuristic.

Undoubtedly, any expatriate writing about the Syrian reality, especially post-2011, feels as if they are in an out-of-body state. Our engagement in the ideological and political work related to Syrian issues is an inescapable matter and is unaffected by distance. We have grown up under the rule of a totalitarian regime that has forced us to be deeply involved with all issues in all fields. We, the offspring of totalitarian regimes and their survivors, will always be captivated by this universal experience, bearing at its heart the dream of being liberated from it in all contexts: politics, economy, religion, and society.

Authoritarianism is the sort of regime where the ruler demands the people go home and mind their own business while he runs the country. There is nothing political under the rule of autocracy, but rather everything is private, and politics itself vanishes. This is the rule of authoritarianism. Whereas, under the rule of a totalitarian regime, the opposite is true. A totalitarian ruler demands the people be constantly in the public squares, demonstrating their support and satisfaction with his decisions. Under the rule of totalitarianism, there is nothing private, and everything is political. What is private is the only domain that disappears.

This book comprises four chapters. The first chapter starts by discussing what civilization is and what it is not, uncivilization, and what lies between the two concepts. It further elaborates on attempting to explain the lost meaning of civilization, its characteristics, components, and how it can be "supplied." From discussing civilization to leadership. Both are broad concepts that include all of humanity. The second chapter moves on to discuss the starting point of the second level of analysis and how to identify a point or a center for precise inspection of the phenomenon of backwardness and the effects of authoritarianism. Naturally, I chose the starting point to be within the Syrian context and connected to the modern history of Syria, its modern reality, and its interaction in creating our current identity. From external rule to modern occupation, transitioning to internal authoritarian rule, and then totalitarian rule Instead of only discussing the ostensible traits and external conditions, I steered the discussion towards a perspective on the internal sides and the intellectual structure and its traits under the authoritative rule. I focused on further probing how we conceptualize our idea of the "other" that we regard as the "adversary" and later the enemy. Why do the traits of that other remain blurred and unnoticeable? We gradually created an ambiguous image of the other, "the enemy," from which it is possible to project it onto any individual. Hence, we created a nucleus for the self-disintegration of the community, which follows the methodical work the repressive regimes adopted to destroy all social structures in the communities aching from repression.

Afterward, I turned to analyzing the psychological phenomena among the repressed peoples, the Nawăr, and examining how such intellectual principles were built and evolved. In chapter three, I demonstrated five intellectual aspects that distinguish the Nawăr people from the others. In chapter four, I sought to detect the most significant behavioral aspects common among the Nawăr people without being exclusive to them. Yet, the degree of prevalence and acceptance of aspects are crucial in connecting them to the Nawăr people more than any other. In conclusion, I had to make several confessions from the Nawări I have best known.

Lastly, when I wrote the Arabic version of this book, I tried my best to ensure that the Syrian experience and the Syrian narrative were the principal themes. I did not want to project the narrative of Syrians under the totalitarian regime on other regional and international experiences. I have always had regard for the uniqueness of other narratives and their context, and I did not speak about other experiences that I had not seen for myself. Having said that, the ongoing genocide taking place in Gaza at the time of writing these lines against the native Palestinians at the hands of the Zionist state and the unwavering support it is receiving from the Western states reminded me how much the post-colonial states share. They are united not only in the bloody struggle under brutal colonial occupation but also in the continual dehumanization by the Western world and the persistence of their ineligibility to be treated as equal humans and as rational beings capable of determining their own destinies. While our modern struggles vary, we, the Nawãr, are united in our perceived savagery and determined worthlessness in the eyes of many. This demands that work such as mine cut deep into the factors that allow such prejudiced and dehumanizing views to flourish even while daily massacres are broadcast live on our smartphones and TV screens. It also reveals the composition of the racist ideology that many groups project against others, which is manifested again and again in the European/western prejudice against all non-white and non-Europeans and the roots of their presumed superiority. I appreciate how the so called "Western world" is a highly heterogeneous group of countries, each with its uniqueness and character, but this term is broadly used when referring to cultural identity and includes Western Europe and those influenced by its culture. This comprises countries such as the United States, Australia, and North America. Despite constituting a minor fraction of the global population, they control all major institutions and have accumulated the greatest wealth. In the past 500 years, they happen to have been the colonizers of the great bulk of the globe. They dubbed themselves the developed world, leaving all nations to undergo an extremely arduous "developing" journey. They persist in imposing ever-higher levels of hardships and obstacles on these former colonies for them to endure. For us to break the vicious cycle of injustice, patriarchalism in the "developed world," and gaslighting, we must embark on analyzing what makes us prone to this sort of tyrannical abuse and addressing stereotypes forced on us while respecting each developing nation's uniqueness.

My aim for this book is to provide a starting point for a more focused discussion about the repressed communities that are subjected to oppressive regimes and systems. Firstly, for the sake of taking a self-critical view and, secondly, that of the surrounding reality, instead of just disregarding or overlooking it. Also, do not consider that this is an emotional and masochistic book about an unsuccessful individual experience. Nawăr is the first of a trilogy about the intellectual structures of repressed communities. It concludes with a view of how they should be instead of what they are. This duty requires that we have a shared identity and a primary connection that may expand and deepen our understanding of reality and improve our prospects of constructing a better future. And, if our endeavors bear no fruit, they might bring about daydreams of a better future in the minds of those who can build it someday.

Abdullah Chahin
Chicago, United States of America
March 4, 2024

CHAPTER 1

THE MAKING OF SAVAGERY: "THE CONTEXT"

In the beginning, I want to share a word of cautionary advice: this is the trickiest chapter of the book in terms of complexity. It highlights and elaborates on the concept of civilization, its effects, and distinctive features and discusses colonization, its impacts, and how it opened the door for modern dictatorships. The language used is generally that of a theoretical argument, making it closer to an academic editorial that might not be an easy read.

That being said, the book delves straight into detecting the causes and results of the intellectual and behavioral aspects displayed throughout the book. My main focus is to connect their origin to a historical dimension that is necessary to recognize. If the reader chooses, they can read the other chapters and then return to this one. In "The Context", I set the stage for discussing the following chapters entitled: The Caravan, the Roadmap, Belongings, and Litter. This is the structure and the rationale for starting the book this way.

In The Context, I discuss our attempt to break out of the swamps of failure into which we, the Syrian masses, have been deeply sunk for centuries. We have arguably plunged even more profoundly during the last century. I aim to outline the features necessary to escape this doom. They refer to a hazy but coveted and sought-after concept: civilization. To get away from these swamps, we must cross several landmarks to reach the horizons of civilization. There must be a social structure that connects this group's components to have the power needed to cross over and collectively survive.

Chapter 1

Escaping failure

For studying any phenomenon, its subject has to be distinctly identified. Usually, we start by measuring what is measurable to have a quantitative description. The measurements are part and parcel of assessing the impacts and results. For instance, an assumed amount of polluted gas has led to a definite amount of global warming during a specified span of the study. Such studies, even when complex a convoluted, can still be measurable and calculable. Simulation and modeling are possible tools to use in such fields. Studying a social phenomenon, on the other hand, is a very different challenge. Such a phenomenon could not be accurately measured or described would be more challenging, and sometimes unattainable. This applies to most humanities studies because the qualitative aspects exceed the quantitative aspects. A numerical relation can be established between the number of books sold in a country and the degree of its scientific progress. On the other hand, the difference in the number of books does not accurately result in scientific or cultural fruition. The task is more overwhelming if the topic of study is civilization. Even if scores of civilizational aspects can be identified and measured, such measurements do not necessarily lead to an ordinal list of civilized states. These civilizational aspects are not credible proof, as will be made clear later.

Given the lack of a mechanism to study civilization accurately and quantitatively, we are bound to rely on qualitative descriptions indicating whether any state is civilized. To further complicate the matter, it is hard to come up with a definition for civilization and identify who the civilized are. Conversely, failure is identifiable, as are the regimes and societies that have failed to create a civilization or a positive temporal mark on the current world stage. While this approach would cause discord, a degree of consent would be more unanimous to states far from being labeled civilized. For instance, there would be barely any consensus on Afghanistan being an impressive state worth emulating. Hence, it is unanimously described as an uncivilized or failed state.

For a nation striving to escape poverty and underdevelopment entrapment, addressing its social structure—through examining intellectual and ethical aspects—might be the optimal start when discussing civilization and its opposite state, i.e., underdevelopment. To remain motivated toward achieving leadership and acquiring a developed civilizational state or excellence, the starting point has to be getting out of that opposite state. In similar discussions, we occasionally study the opposite, or counter-state, to comprehend what might be an intervention from getting into it. Subsequently, studying failure might be a means of such escape. Yet, there is another junction to be feared. There is a false assumption that to escape the list of failed states implies being a civilized or supreme one.

Civilization and failure are two polar extremes. They fall on a broad spectrum between what is not a total failure and what is not at the height of civilization. Therefore, it may be more feasible to study the clearer and more common case: the vast space between these two polar extremes. For instance, in examining students' performance, instead of studying excellence or failure, which are exceptional statuses, it might be more feasible to examine their thriving and ability to proceed acceptably in the learning process. We will call this status "thriving," given that in any school or university, excellent students are only a few in any group. The reasons for their excellence vary between internal factors such as cleverness and persistence and external ones such as the standard of living, level of education in the parents, having additional help in the house, etc. However, scoring high grades is not guaranteed just by attaining these factors. It is not hard to find clever students from wealthy families who do not excel in school.

Along this space of not achieving excellence, thriving and failure are identified. The majority of students fall within the scope of thriving. But once again, the numerous, varied aspects of thriving or success make it difficult to pinpoint them. Let alone examine them and their effects separately. In the same sense, the elements of failure are comparable to those of thriving or the result of having none or even some of them. Still, failure is detectable, as are its traits on different levels.

Back to the example of students' performance in school: excellence is an exceptional individual case, and thriving, which is not that of excellence, is the general case. In education, failure is the opposite of excellence and is individual as well. Failure has its own set of root causes, similar to the ones leading to excellence; however, addressing these causes does not guarantee to move to the other extreme and achieving excellence. Against that backdrop, addressing these causes undoubtedly offers a way of salvation from this entrapment. Such exerted efforts translate into thriving, which is the neutral and general case, instead of moving from one extreme to the opposite one on the spectrum. The study of individual excellence is not a priority as it has different characteristics and bases. The right course for such a study is to observe the general causes of failure and the means to avoid them.

This spectrum, therefore, comprises three existential states: failure, thriving (success), and excellence. To take a direct leap from failure to instantaneous excellence is beyond achievable, whether regarding a student's educational level or a nation's civilizational status. All nations that achieved world leadership and global hegemony crossed a hierarchical continuum. And on that continuum, either upward or downward changes occur for any nation.

The fact that "thriving" nations are not devoid of conflicts, flaws, or issues is vitally critical to note. And this category includes countries that do not look alike in various ways. For example, Brazil and Turkey are countries that, in my definition, fall under thriving nations. While this is not precisely the word that comes to mind when the names of those nations appear on the news, it is significant to remind ourselves that both have a bare minimum of institutional structures that keep the state running and economies that can continue to run the markets and grow GDPs.

It would be difficult to differentiate between the phenomena causing a specific case—whether excellence or failure—and their results or related phenomena. Hence, no magical plan can ever lead its followers to excellence. Adopting an approach to analyzing and remediating these phenomena, be their excellence or failure, aids in escaping the trap of civilizational failure and joining the procession of thriving/success. Such an approach might set the course for perceiving success factors and failure causes. Whether these phenomena are causal or just characteristics relevant to failure, they are still responsible for adverse outcomes that are not to be ignored.

Upon observing the nations that enjoy "civilizational leadership"[2], regardless of the absence of an accurate definition, all they established was the outcome of accumulating knowledge and civilization of steadily occupying the thriving – the "non-failure" category—and enjoying the privileges of success. Henceforward, any nation that aspires to leadership must exert all efforts to protect itself from falling into the failed states' abyss. Then, it can commit to building a civilizational momentum that allows for a chance to join the leading nations. Without taking such steps, a country or state aiming for a civilizational ascent would be exposing itself to failing miserably. There is more to come on this point later in the book.

My primary concern throughout this section is to describe the civilizational failure and its traits in terms of the psychological, intellectual, and moral standards of the community of which I am a member. The study of failure characteristics, causal or not, is a rectifying approach. This book could be a contribution to my people's salvation from this vicious circle and herald it into the non-failed or thriving category. Yet, I am fully aware that it requires more than such efforts to guide a country to the heights of prosperous civilizations. Looking at the history of the world's superpowers, none acquired their positions without an intellectual revolution. Even if partially or selectively, it transformed their intellectual characteristics towards acceptance, openness, and cooperation among their members.

Progress is unequivocally a journey of several stages, with phases, conditions to be fulfilled, and impediments to be overcome. Aside from that, several factors must be accumulated, sustained, and extended to escape failure entrapment. The tides of change are bound to happen; life cannot be held captive to the status quo. Time and again, change is the sole constant in human life. Its direction is the point with which one is to be involved.

Another clarification about change, it is persistent. Regardless of its consequences, there might be a generic interrelation between the prevalence of these intellectual, moral, and psychological characteristics and the state

---

[2] Civilizational leadership is the ability to exert influence on the rest of the world, with means that are not related to economic or military might. Countries such as South Korea are a good example.

of deterioration experienced in our societies. Addressing failure-related symptoms opens the possibility of advancement for us. No matter how much I wish this theory would be true, I firmly believe it is necessary regardless of whether it bears fruit. Therefore, it is of the utmost importance to address them, apart from the outcomes that might or might not be rendered. This conviction is based on a personal philosophy that is methodological, practical, and process-oriented rather than outcome-oriented. Moral gains do not necessarily lead to materialistic gains; hence, the criterion should be that moral actions must not be fulfilled in exchange for material rewards. Accordingly, the focus should be on acquiring these ethical goals, regardless of their expected positive effects. On the contrary, they must be sought even if they bring about adverse materialistic outcomes or are of no tangible benefit. There is no harm in relinquishing worldly resources to acquire intellectual and moral gains or promote an ethical practice or humane stance. By taking this action, a moral reformation would be initiated, and the faults in utilitarian philosophy and morality produced by the Enlightenment movement in Europe two centuries ago would be overcome.

The mind, conscience, and morals are not solid organs with which we are born and die. They are intellectual faculties developed through action. So are civilization, modernity, justice, and equality. They do not have designated establishments in developed states; they are not assigned ministerial headquarters or constitutional articles. We cannot quote or cite them from a written text. These concepts are the spirit of action. They do not haphazardly emerge in these states. They are also neither eternal nor taken for granted. This spirit is lost if a state ceases to rationalize, self-examine, and pursue lifting injustice from all.

Equally examined in the book, internal and external variables contribute to formulating these aspects. At the outset, I must shed light on some of what we aspire to and what we overlook. I must look into the features of each of these cases, and in the following section, civilization is the main focus. Similar to excellence and failure, there is a polarity between civilization and its opposite. By investigating its formulation and where we fit within its spectrum, we can find a more promising future within our grasp.

Civilization

Before diving deeper into this section, it is essential to produce a clear-cut definition of civilization. Linguistically, it is derived from the Latin origin (civis), which refers to urban dwellers (as opposed to countryside dwellers).

The term civilization in the new sense is relatively new. It might have resulted from the association of the concept with the place where people gather, as in villages and cities. It is also a reference to the people present at those gatherings. The Arabic term for civilization "ḥaḍāra" comes from the root [Hadar], meaning presence. Combining the Latin and Arabic origins, the reference is primarily to individuals who inhabit human settlements, whether a village or a city, and urbanization is one of its pillars. Therefore, nomadic life, which was an earlier stage of human development, is the opposite of civilization. The Arabic equivalent of nomadic is [Badou], derived from [Bada'], meaning the first thing to appear in a matter. Nomadic, in Arabic, means living in the desert[3], which involves mainly moving around and having no permanent home. Thus, civilization can be prominently surmised to mean human gathering and stability.

Within its context, the term civilization radically shifted from the reference to individuals to the outcome of their behavior. Its meaning was expanded to include the physical manifestation of that human congregation, be it the buildings or material products of that settlement, or the other non-material marks this congregation induces. Civilization became a derivative of human achievements and their impact, uniqueness, and grandeur. There are two schools of thought regarding the concept of civilization. One considers the material aspect a measurement of civilization, and another believes that intellectual output is a measure and proof of the achievement and genius of

---

[3] One major misconception about Arabs in general and Bedouins specifically stems from the utilization of the word desert in referring to the place where they live. The confusion stems from its lack of differentiation (in English) between two distinct words: Badia and Sahraa' are both translated to Desert. However, the Arabic word "Badia" where the Bedouins (Badou) live is an area with scanty rainfall and scant green coverage, suitable for grazing cattle. Sahraa' on the other hand is the arid land that is not suitable for human life. Such confusion becomes obvious each time a visual rendering of the Arabs' existence makes it to television and Cinema.

civilization. These human accomplishments undeniably and highly indicate the reality of these communities because their presence at that time proved their significance and excellence. Nevertheless, it must be emphasized that when discussing civilization or comparing two civilizations, there is an unbreakable correlation between the premise, humans, and the manifests and outcomes of the activity and presence of distinguished human beings.

Regardless of the vague scale on which civilizations can be measured and ranked, it is worth noting that civilization has a perceptible long-term effect. It is usually interconnected with an administrative governing structure. For instance, the Roman civilization is connected to the Roman Empire and the Pharaonic civilization is connected to the dynasties of Pharaonic rule in Egypt. Nonetheless, these civilizations' effects extended beyond the direct governing area of these administrative structures, for example, the impact of Roman civilization in the Near East and elsewhere. It is fair to say that genuine civilization influences more than its subjects. This view differs from Karl Marx[4]'s two references to the term cultural hegemony and its description by Italian Marxist philosopher Antonio Gramsci[5]. It highlights the effect of the ruling class on society, whether voluntarily or coercively. However, the impact of civilization spreading outside its direct borders, regardless of assigning it that term, is interconnected with the voluntary integration of people ungoverned by the entity associated with that civilization. This is exemplified by the Islamic influence on worldwide architecture during their golden era between the ninth and twelfth centuries. There could be more than one burgeoning civilization coinciding in the same era, with a booming civilizational effect going beyond their geographical and temporal borders.

Consequently, civilization is defined by its presence and the continuation of its impact outside of its borders and long after it ceases to exist. This long-

---

[4] Karl Marx was a German philosopher, economist, sociologist, historian, journalist, and revolutionary socialist. His name is associated with communist theory, and the eponym Marxism denotes the practices based on his thought.

[5] Antonio Gramsci is an Italian Marxist philosopher and activist. The Gramscian school of thought is the philosophy of Praxis (practical and critical activity—human and concrete practice).

term influential presence has to have other less influential or non-influential presences by which the rise of civilization can be distinguished, differentiated against, and attested to at that time. Subsequently, the substantiated, leading presence marks the outlines of a leading civilization and its disparities from peers, whether neighboring, distant, contemporary, preceding, or succeeding. The existence of differentiation as a unique influence is a primary and definitive condition of civilization.

The different civilizational levels are a fixed fact exhibited throughout human history. The world has never witnessed a united civilizational level at any recorded time; this fact alone sums up what the presence of civilization means in its temporal and geographic context. The world has constantly been divided into developed and underdeveloped nations and others in between. In a world dominated by a frantic race to the top of the global order, ancient countries, and civilizations experienced cycles of development and underdevelopment.

In a race that mostly involved all guns blazing and full military force, the imperial and military might collide in the history of civilizations. They also had to sustain themselves on resources secured by army invasions and occupations of weaker, resource-rich territories. Through this association, there were outlines of temporal (the era of that civilization's dominance) and spatial traits (the map of that civilization or empire). Military power and substantial wealth are two factors that help identify the characteristics of civilization. Waging wars and having the power to seize riches are fundamental aspects of establishing empires that garnered their presence due to what they captured. So far, the discussion has highlighted that civilization is closely associated with military force and material possessions. In addition, ancient and modern civilizations exist in a context that encompasses the strong association between its hegemony and long-lasting impact and administrative structure it builds. All hegemonic civilizations had to develop powerful and well-functioning bureaucratic bodies. This point is not frequently discussed as part of the emergence of civilizations. The human factor, in general, is not visualized as central to establishing civilization. When the human factor is discussed, it typically focuses on a powerful ruler who is the driving force behind armies who can solely vanquish enemies and control their destinies; only thus is the establishment of a civilization determined.

Yet, some ancient empires especially invested in the human factor that affected their civilizational role. The ancient Greek civilization in Athens, for instance, and the Umayyad state in Andalusia, demonstrated such a unique focus. Generally speaking, a minimum level of technological progress and financial capacity was a prerequisite for the states that achieved military supremacy. These are solely attained by having unique human skills that are nurtured by the central authorities and promoted as part of that civilization's strength. And the byproduct of such focus enabled them to embark on quests for expansion and impose hegemony through military power, but also through casting a form of soft power, be that via arts, sciences, or commerce.

Almost all ancient nations that achieved hegemony relied on military conquests in order to increase their financial gains and in return their military power. Through these conquests, we see their way of life and trends were, thus, imposed outside their direct borders. Venturing into foreign seas and crossing plains and mountains were the core elements of reaching the peak of global order for civilizations such as the Phoenicians, the Romans, and many Islamic civilizations. Even if such expansionist movements were economically motivated, they still were pivotal in disseminating and imposing the imprints of that conquering hegemonic civilization within that temporal and geographical context. Nevertheless, military expansion and hegemony do not obligate a civilizational impact on the conquered territories that would cross the boundaries of time. Neither the Mongol invasion of the Near East nor the sequential Crusades from the West left any material or intellectual marks that count as a civilizational presence within their controlled territories. Instead, the Mongols relied on the technology and sciences of the Muslims and the Chinese to complement their empirical quest without adopting, developing, or disseminating them. There is no historical monument of a Mongol civilization worthy of mentioning or visiting today, despite their establishing the largest empire in human history at their age.

Civilizational differences across history

What is the proper approach for comparing civilizations? How can their physical and intellectual achievements be weighed to draw concrete, significant conclusions? Do the intellectual influences of the Greek civilization, witnessed to this day, prove them superior to the Romans? Or are the Romans the Greeks' superiors for defeating them and seizing the leadership and sovereignty? Do not the Romans' grandstands and monuments that once illuminated the ancient world map remain living witnesses?

It remains an equally arduous undertaking to define civilization in the case of relatively modern periods. Was the French Revolution the most pivotal event that announced the earliest outlines of the New World? Does being the first yield of the Enlightenment age, which ignited modern human thought, provide enough evidence for this supposition? Or does the American Revolution best fit that description? Is this an accurate assumption based on the revolution's establishment of a long-lasting federal republic? Given that the United States has the world's largest economy and an enormous influence on modern art, culture, and construction, is this assumption reasonable?

To take it from the beginning, a specific manifestation does not entail joining the procession of human civilizations. The height of a skyscraper in an Arab Gulf state does not denote the existence of civilization. The expansion or presence of urbanization equals sterile material that translates into nothing but the stone from which it was built. Similar to the example of Muhammad al-Maghut's[6] or Ali Shariati's[7] books that do not entitle Syria or Iran to be deemed among the twentieth-century civilizations. Similarly, a civilization does not emerge through the adoption or copying of products. A nation may buy a civilization's product or imitate its management system,

---

[6] Muhammad al-Maghout (1934–2006) was a renowned Syrian writer and poet. He is known for his book "I will betray my homeland", a collection of columns and articles concerned with the dream of freedom.

[7] Ali Shariati Mazinani (1933 –1977) was an Iranian revolutionary and sociologist who focused on the sociology of religion. He is one of the most influential Iranian intellectuals of the 20th century.

arts, and sciences, but this does not make it a civilization. Hence, civilization is an intrinsic value that cannot be simply imported.

Thought, ideals, and values collaborate in making the products of civilization that entirely sustain this state. In this regard, Malik bin Nabi[8] said, "A society that does not create its basic thoughts cannot create the products necessary for its consumption or the products necessary for its creation. And a society during the stage of its establishment will not be constructed by thoughts imported or imposed from abroad." We must develop our own experience, i.e., determine the subject of our thoughts, and reject labeling. We must restore our intellectual authenticity and independence in the arena of ideas to achieve our economic and political independence."[9] Whoever purchases the products of civilization is a consumer, not a producer of civilization. Civilization is an achievement that is not gifted, purchased, or imported. One cannot conjure up a civilization, borrow its components, or clone it from others' experiences.

Despite previously emphasizing the role of weapons and economy in establishing ancient civilizations and empires, there is yet another essential component that ensures the continuity of any empire. It is focused on a broad circle embracing a large spectrum of members of societies where they enjoy a space of freedom, justice, and participation under that empire's flag, created by the bare minimum of justice and law, although mostly selective at that time to those who that law applies to and protects. And this circle expands over time, encompassing more individuals and communities. This space of inclusivity amply provided those empires with suitable conditions for reaping profits outside battlefields. However, it essentially served the purpose of establishing civilization and achieving its hegemony. To elaborate, the Umayyad state in Andalusia differed from medieval Europe in allowing space for justice and law. This space established a society with a clear structure and features, which contributed to scientific progress that galvanized economic, political, and military advancement. This progress

---

[8] Malik Bin Nabi or Malek Bennabi (1905–1973) was an Algerian writer and philosopher, who wrote about human society, particularly Muslim society. He focused on the reasons behind the fall of Muslim civilization in his writings.
[9] Malik bin Nabi, Grand Issues, House of Thought, 2021, P198.

was in part locally made and, in others, imported, adopted, and then further developed and internalized. Nevertheless, some factors narrowed the gaps between ancient kingdoms, such as the limited natural resources and energy and the reliance on human factors in production, which resulted in producing similar outputs to some extent. A few technical aspects marked the differences between the Roman Empire and the Persian Empire in the fifth century AD, for example, but not to the extent that it would take a long time to close that gap. This was due to the slow pace of development, which would have caused civilizational and scientific disparities between those kingdoms. Thus, catching up was not a difficult task. In modern times, civilizational and scientific differences advance at a skyrocketing speed.

The concepts I have presented up to this point have not yet revealed any distinct features of what a civilization is. Tracing a better-defined path, I aim to pinpoint what I perceive to be the fundamental nucleus of civilization and the most crucial components with which it can only be formulated. It is the one identified in the previous excerpt, namely the core and center of the assembling social circle, which happens due to the intellectual nucleus. A human group is centrally positioned, bound by a well-defined agreement that is the foundation for any collective activity. It is inherently a voluntary "social contract" based on a shared vision and interest. Though the authority is not to impose such a contract per se, their efforts may undoubtedly promote or undermine its formation, as we shall see by the end of this book.

The collective consciousness is at the core of the social contract upon which society is founded and driven to the foreground. In his book, Why the West Rules—For Now? British historian and archaeologist Ian Morris[10] presented an analogy that clarifies my point. He said, "Western civilization is essentially an amalgam of intellectual constructs which were designed to further the

---

[10] Ian Morris is a British archaeologist, historian, and academic. He is currently a professor of classical studies at Stanford University. In his book Why the West Rules—For Now (2010), he compares East and West over the past 15,000 years and argues that physical geography—rather than culture, religion, politics, genetics, or prominent figures—is the reason for Western dominance of the world.

interests of their authors."[11] Here, he refers to the participants in policy making; rather than a single, selfish decision-maker. In other words, European intellectual structures formulated collective interests agreed upon by a group of people. This collective achieved these interests by harnessing their collective skills and potential. This is a shift of focus from the masses wasting their efforts serving an absolute ruler or a utopian metaphysical concept to the clearly defined material interests of groups and collectives. He points out that the core difference between Britain and India at the turn of the nineteenth century was that Britain had a human group capable of coordinating, financing, and collaborating. British industrialists manufactured massive iron vessels that surpassed any ship at their time. Its politicians coordinated and executed missions to the other side of the world. Its merchants could enter into agreements and form limited joint stock companies, enabling them to finance large-scale undertakings and secure their financial interests in these complex transactions. Many archaeologists tried to link this phenomenon to the development of the city concept and to prove a positive correlation between the size of the city (in terms of population) and the hegemony of the civilization ruling it. This link, even if logically sound, does not establish Cairo or Mumbai as superior to Vienna or other comparable smaller cities in population.

These historical cities with large populations represent an experience of coexistence and cohesion between multiple individuals who voluntarily co-engage to achieve the group's interests. This does not necessarily mean that this is an act (i.e., the individual's integration with the group) of pure sacrifice and determination for the common good. Instead, it is a relationship for the benefit of all parties involved. This type of relationship between members of a society creates a collective consciousness, enabling them to function, achieve, and prosper, leading to a collective good.

The role of social structure in creating civilization has emerged since the dawn of human life on Earth. Since the times of hunting and gathering societies, humans have been organized into structured groups according to a unique, custom-guaranteed contract. In the BC era, this concept emerged

---

[11] Morris, I.D. (2010). Why the West Rules—for Now: The Patterns of History and What They Reveal About the Future.

with the rise of Athenian civilization, the adoption of democracy, and the rule of the people. Rome was inhabited by a million people in the first century BC. It had street gangs that had the power to stop the government and sometimes paralyze the state's movement. This identity connection (from now on, we will call it collective consciousness) has significantly influenced the formation of human groups.

The establishment of the first Islamic empire in the seventh century similarly illustrated the crucial role of the collective consciousness formed after the nation formation by Prophet Muhammad. The collective consciousness of this emerging state had a new identity. It was based on a unique code of honor that brought about a symbiotic social contract and an internal system of justice that embraced all believers. This broad form of justice crossed tribal borders and affiliations to grant everyone surrounding them their rights.

Another example: during the Renaissance, Europeans realized the significance of the human element in the structure of civilization. Hence, it was brought back to the forefront of European concern, putting human nature in its natural position. While the East was caught in a phase of stagnation in terms of its social development, this realization pushed Italy, Spain, Portugal, and the rest of Europe to the fore. Europe, which had been absent from the global scene for almost a millennium, breathed in the fresh air of enlightenment, which put it on the path to civilizational hegemony. A religious reformation that ushered in the Age of Enlightenment for European thought came after this. Before pushing it to the forefront of world domination, the Renaissance witnessed the emergence of models of collective activities, such as exploring the seas and depths of unknown realms and establishing huge, organized, and reliable trade systems. Florence, a small city in Italy, controlled the trade routes and manufacturing locations along the Silk Road. It differed from other Italian kingdoms for its capability to co-work and the collective identity created through the structure of joint work. Florentines demonstrated tremendous finesse in organizing business, upholding rights, and constructing a trading banking system that exceeded their narrow borders. This did not result from a mere metaphysical belief in a superior human identity that distinguished them but from a unique social contract that brought them together. It produced a collective identity that defined them.

Jean-Jacques Rousseau established an infamous social contract of his, which became part of the building blocks of the social structures in the emerging European nations and gave a new perspective on ruling in Europe and marked the end of the absolute monarchy structure. The advancement of collective consciousness and the subsequent scientific renaissance heralded Europe into the Age of Enlightenment as a global leader. This was contrary to the slow movement of thought witnessed in the Eastern Kingdoms and the weakened collective consciousness experienced in the Far East and Middle East. The indicated collective consciousness is not the identity framework of society, whether ethnic, linguistic, or religious. Instead, this framework may be at its full height when collective consciousness is in its weakest form. Being narrow-minded and hateful of others, the identity framework might hinder the formation of the indicated collective consciousness. It was called "Geist" by the German philosopher Hegel, which means the spirit or human thought. According to Hegel, the Weltgeist, "world spirit," is not actual, transcendent, or divine but a means for the philosophy of history. Yet Hegel thought that historical figures played a much larger part in creating the world's spirit and collective consciousness.

The collective consciousness to which I refer is linked to intellectual structures related to two values: the first is the fundamental value structure of society, such as freedom, dignity, generosity, coexistence, and the preservation of rights. Societies can choose to build their collective consciousness from the opposite types of value structures, such as injustice, racism, individualism, and consumerism. Building a composite from these societal values gives that community its unique "Geist" and exceptional ideological structure.

The second is the structure of knowledge. It is shaped by that nation's cultural and intellectual heritage, its convictions about the concepts of the universe, what it defines as its adversaries and its aspired goals for the future. This structure significantly influences the creation of the nation's consciousness, not only of itself but also of what it can achieve; it formulates its perception of its historical context and the reality it experiences.

Although this collective consciousness is not inextricably bound to a particular and narrow identity— religious, ethnic, or region-based— it is nevertheless constrained by its boundaries. This collective consciousness may have no title or be fully perceived. For instance, the inhabitants of Damascus, Beirut, and Gaziantep under Ottoman rule did not perceive themselves as Ottomans or define themselves as Romans 1500 years ago. Nevertheless, they were linked by a collective consciousness, either as a single block, a population of protectorates, or separately, e.g., a distinct Damascene identity. Yet, under a specific ruling or administration framework, certain realities and circumstances were imposed that influenced a "shared destiny" among them in certain areas, though diversified. Consequently, they were subjects ruled by local administrative systems and taxpayers of the same entity. They shared a single currency unit, commercial ties, weather patterns, and geographical conditions to some extent.

Hence, the collective identity may have self-evident projections that identify it mostly as a narrow group (sectarian, ethnic, region- or class-based), or it could be less obvious and broader in scope. Subsequently, it comprises a larger group that establishes a higher consciousness. This identity may wind up as internationalist or spread across several geographies and ethnicities, as in the aforementioned imperial cases, with which civilizations were linked in the past.

Europe attained its leading position when an elite community nucleus emerged and called for expanding the benefits umbrella across feudal societies. Those elites began to theorize the importance and necessity of the individual's role in their intellectual lives as well as in governance. Additionally, the Enlightenment Age brought about intellectual spaces that randomly emerged far from authority's control. These spaces induced liberation movements from ecclesiastical power and feudalism in Britain and France. It also triggered political changes that internally achieved broader justice in these societies. From the declaration of the Magna Carta in June 1215 to the Bill of Rights in 1689, the concept of shared power and curbing the oppression and abuse of absolute rulers granted more people the right and opportunity to partake in the collective decision-making process. Changes like these paved the road and built the intellectual frame for the first republic in the former British colony and the birth of the United States of America. The United States Constitution, which became the supreme law of the land, resembled how the Magna Carta had come to be regarded as a fundamental law in Britain five centuries before. The framing of a common law that is devoid of the ruler and is appealed to be a historic moment. In addition to the rising equality among the newly formed citizenry (as opposed to the historic subjects of a ruler), the Enlightenment movement's path was flourishingly lit up with a scientific revolution that brought to humanity the driving force of the Industrial Age, driving it forward like never before.

At the heart of these changes in Europe during the Industrial Age, diverse groups had the opportunity to organize and work within a system maintaining minimum rights; in return, people abided by a set of duties and obligations. The dimensions of religious and ethnic identities in Europe ultimately sustained this collective consciousness. However, several class, geography, and political barriers and divisions were removed for this to occur. Consequently, a series of bloody conflicts erupted, some of which were religious based. An example is the Thirty Years War, which was primarily fought as a religious conflict between Catholics and Protestants in France and the Habsburgs but later ended up as a political struggle for control over other countries. Additionally, the Wars of the Three Kingdoms, which took place between the separate kingdoms of England, Scotland, and Ireland, paved the way for the future of Great Britain and Ireland as a constitutional monarchy, with the Parliament as the representative of its political power.

Hence, a central identity nucleus for civilization is required, besides the previously indicated broad circle. This nucleus formulates the collective consciousness and gravitates people within this circle of belonging. While this nuclear identity can come about voluntarily, it is occasionally forged with the fire of war, as seen in these examples in Europe. Subsequently, the formulation of this collective consciousness is conclusive in outlining a medium of influence for this civilization and its ability to expand and annex others into its vessel. It is insufficient to have a public square for people to gather on an equal footing. Instead, a connection binding them and identifying them is indispensable. As a result, this space can be transformed from a mere human gathering in a public square into a civilized society. Still, there is a pressing question: how did this civilization's impact survive to this day?

Civilizational Heritage

The notion of civilizational heritage as the "decisive" factor behind a nation's leadership and hegemony is a point of constant debate within Arab intellectual circles and western alike. At times, it gets a historical tendency embodied in the Arab's past through the examples of Assyrian sovereignty over the heart of the old world and the early Muslims' sovereignty over Asia and North Africa. At others, it is exemplified in the contemporary heritage of the United States, which has earned it unprecedented leadership and hegemony in the world today. Not to mention the attempts to link it to the Roman republic and its pioneering democratic traditions

There is no disputing that none of these human "civilizations" randomly appeared. Far from it, civilization is the outcome of well-invested factors, as widely believed. The amassed build-up of a civilizational momentum earns a nation its global leadership at an appropriate time. According to many experts, civilization is a social system that enables a state to capitalize on its amassed intellectual and material production, which translates into its impact. The more it accumulates in these products, the bigger the impact becomes. And the duration of this cumulative process translates into what we can call "civilizational heritage". Even if this broad definition is to be adopted, coming up with a suitable one for civilizational heritage is challenging, given that all we have is a term with no means of measurement or proof of its existence but only the traces of civilizational impact on the reality of a specific place or nation. In countries like Britain or Japan, an aspect of civilization is too obvious to be disregarded. Egypt, Iran, and Nepal are examples of societies with significant historical civilizational momentum, although they are not as influential today. It would be equally absurd to consider that there is a civilizational impact in the Arab Gulf states despite their well-established forms of urbanization and material infrastructure. Hence, the question: What is the secret of civilization? What is civilizational heritage? Is knowledge heritage a factor in achieving civilization and establishing its heritage? Or is it a result?

In his book The Measure of Civilization: How Social Development Decides the Fate of Nations, British historian Ian Morris tries to provide statistical evidence and methods that measure social development and link it to the progress of nations. Morris constructed a social development index using four parameters: energy capture per capita, organization, information technology, and war-making capacity. His book is predominantly dedicated to the index he constructed. He tries to prove the index's validity by applying it to the experiences of previous nations and civilizations, such as the Chinese civilizations and Western Europe during the Enlightenment Era.

Above all, the book provides an unsound intellectual judgment to prove the accuracy of this index. It traces the past impact instead of predicting the future of current nations and civilizations, making its way from the conclusion to the proposed theory in a retrospective manner that is not devoid of retrofitting. Not only that, but the author also overlooked the subject of the book, which he titled "How to Measure Civilization!", something his book ended up without producing a measurement unit that we can use. Furthermore, it is not feasible to disregard the haziness of these factors and the difficulty of performing a precise quantitative assessment. Thus, we cannot devise any accurate and reproducible measurement that can be validated. Morris's book contains some speculation, and the task is clearly arduous. Indeed, it is exceedingly challenging to pose this question: How do we measure civilization? What are the indicators of its rise and fall?

Several factors make the qualitative approach challenging for researchers, among which is the lack of a quantitative method to measure these phenomena and their impacts, as previously indicated. This type of study is subject to numerous biases, among which we, the observers, commit by deciding on the variables and samples for analysis. It is similarly arduous for many to determine which countries best illustrate civilizational leadership.

Singapore was once a developing country that gained independence, along with the hostility of its neighboring countries. It achieved a massive urban and technical renaissance and took advantage of the cross-pollination of civilization. Thus, it advanced and surpassed the tigers of Asia by following the open market model and creating broad spaces for foreign capital. Consequently, Singapore became a fundamental financial and commercial center and a transportation hub. The annual per capita income is one of the highest in Asia, and its people enjoy high living standards and social welfare. Is it safe to say Singapore is a civilization? Does it possess such a long heritage to protect it from declining again into failure and underdevelopment?

Besides the previously indicated factors, several biases result from our expectations and pre-set agenda for this study. For instance, approach the experiment with the premise that the selected sample has the phenomenon of investigation. The presuppositions of the hypothesis may not be valid in the first place. How can we ascertain that China has an authentic civilizational effect while Niger lacks a civilizational heritage? Hence, upon observing the civilizational impact of a nation, we can detect the features sought in those nations. To elaborate, it is acknowledged that civilized countries have a pluralistic structure and an intellectual open space with open horizons, even if not completely free. If China is widely recognized as a leading civilization, we set out to extract the features demonstrated in this state. Due to our need to confirm the validity of our assumptions and expectations, we may extrapolate them incorrectly.

Another factor that hinders qualitative studies in sociology and anthropology is our inability to accurately extrapolate, describe, and analyze what is an influential factor in the observed phenomena and what is the product of these factors. Is personal hygiene, for example, a factor in the rise of civilization, or is it one of its outcomes? Or is it entirely separate and based on cultural values or local circumstances?

Once we adopt an approach for measuring civilization, we are confronted by contrasting ideas and ambiguous standards. Yet, we—all of humankind—surprisingly possess a natural intuition towards civilization and nations considered to be leading at the civilizational level through the temporal and spatial maps.

This is an attempt to detect some of the outlines of civilization. Measuring the outcomes of civilization at the intellectual, urban, and technical levels may be more attainable than investigating civilization and constructing a quantitative measurement. Also, the civilizational momentum and heritage with which many books and literature pieces are overloaded deserve to be addressed with due research and description. Some aspects of civilization might thus come into focus. These two topics are the focus of the next section.

The byproducts of civilization

In my assessment, civilization denotes a system and a methodology. It is not limited to a set of goals pursued by a nation, even if that objective serves as that nation's main driving force for action and progress. A civilization requires a mechanism for collective action to fulfill a desired goal. This action usually aims to accomplish a benefit for the collective. The adopted system is regulated by exceedingly complex laws based on various economic, political, and social systems. Although it is difficult to illustrate civilization's systems in an algorithmic form and explain how they work, it is possible to trace some of these aspects and discern some of their primary and secondary byproducts.

Similar to many concepts encountered in this book, the byproducts of civilization do not have a clear-cut definition. It usually refers to some of the effects and contributions of a particular civilization that are distinguished from those of its counterparts. Given that numerous social features and civilizational contributions may fall under its purview, some things could be deemed byproducts of civilization, as opposed to the case with civilizational heritage. Some of these features and contributions can be agreed upon as a civilizational byproduct, despite a potential disagreement over which ones they are. It should also be differentiated from the factors that contribute to the development of a civilization. It is the typical dilemma of cause and effect, and which feature or contribution is a factor leading to the development of a civilization and which one is the byproduct of achieving the state of civilization.

The concept of civilization is primarily perceived in its material aspect. As previously indicated, civilization in Arabic is derived from "ḥaḍar", meaning the opposite of nomadic life. It also means the action of presence itself. Hence, civilization has a spatial connotation in addition to the moral one we are exploring. This spatial connotation, urban residence, has developed. That urban residency entails cooperation, synergy, and exchange of ideas and information in various aspects of life, such as the sciences, urbanization, and culture. It is of the utmost importance to make this point clear to distinguish between the essence of civilization and the connotations falling as part of its phenomenon, i.e., the material components.

Ibn Khaldun[12], the medieval Arab sociologist, continuously focused on the material element of civilization, ranging from planning cities and towns to building and reconstructing houses. He believed civilization is only exhibited in cities and villages, and urbanization is the ultimate prosperity. Will Durant[13], on the other hand, thought that civilization is made up of many different elements, with urbanization being just one of them. In his view, civilization is "a social order that promotes cultural creation." He considered that civilization's elements include an economic provision, political organization, moral traditions, and the pursuit of knowledge and the arts. They thrive where turmoil and anxiety end, making stability a prerequisite. Thus, if a person is safe, the motives for striving for creativity and innovation flourish. From that moment on, the natural stimuli incessantly urged people to explore and prosper.

Accordingly, the concept of civilization has a broader meaning than just being an urban phenomenon for a nation. Durant's contribution through the cultural lens indicates the spiritual or intellectual aspect, given that

---

[12] Abd al-Rahman bin Muhammad, Ibn Khaldun Abu Zayd, and Wali al-Din al-Hadrami al-Ishbili. Ibn Khaldun is considered the founder of modern sociology and a scholar in history and economics. He is the author of the book Introduction, which he wrote as a prelude to his "Book of Lessons," and the Muqaddimah of ibn Khaldun, or Ibn Khaldun's Prolegomena, which became a reference in sociology, politics, and history.

[13] William James Durant was an American philosopher, historian, and writer. One of his most famous works is the Encyclopedia "The Story of Civilization," co-authored with his wife, Ariel Durant.

civilization comprises the spiritual and material or intellectual and applied aspects. Therefore, civilization has its material influence manifested in urbanization and its consequences, besides its immaterial impact displayed through ethical traditions and the cultural effects of the sciences and arts. All of these effects constitute a byproduct of civilization.

Civilizational byproducts can be secondary or indirect consequences of an activity demonstrated in that civilization. They are the "byproducts" of the "state" of civilization. Some may be unique and exclusive, whereas others are global and almost absolute, i.e., emanating from and adding to the total values believed in by all of humanity, or can be an undisputable technical matter for their distinction and can be consequently adopted. Some of these byproducts are deliberate or unintentionally inevitable. Some civilizational byproducts may be circumstantial or accidental, not being sought after by civilization in and of themselves. It is even fair to say that they are mostly not the focus or investment of these nations. As evidence suggests, the countries with the most widespread products of civilization are not necessarily those with the best models.

These descriptions seem vague and unintelligible without a few examples. Let us take the political structure of the United States. During its founding phase, the main goal was to remove English control over the eastern coast of North America. Then came the establishment of a country based on the popular representation of the people of the states that joined the newly created political entity. The slogan "No taxation without representation" embodies the American Revolution. The idea of popular representation in an elected assembly was not a novelty. Ironically enough, that itself was a British practice that emerged after the transformation of the government system towards a constitutional monarchy in the United Kingdom.

Besides, for the emerging American United States, democracy was not the principal goal as much as being liberated from the weight of the old world and creating a new entity on a different pillar. The values of freedom are solidly grounded in the Declaration of Independence of the new republic called the United States of America. For example, the founding fathers sought to limit the prerogatives of religious bodies in the country's institutions, though they were not secular in the modern sense. Religious diversity was not an end in itself; it was an inevitable result of the absence of an official state religion that was to be maintained as the dominant. In addition to the open horizons for individual freedoms, religious diversity, in this case, is an unintended by-product. There were persistent efforts to eradicate alternative religious identities, such as Islam among slaves, indigenous peoples' natural faiths, and other beliefs among non-white non-Europeans.

For over a hundred years, the United States has taken pride in being the land of opportunities. These opportunities afforded by the natural wealth of the new world were this country's code to open its doors to immigrants, which gave it ethnic diversity. This unintentional ethnic and cultural diversity created a novel cultural identity that granted the United States civilizational uniqueness on the one hand and the ability to communicate and have common ground with several cultures around the world on the other. Hence, ethnic, and therefore cultural, diversity are some of the byproducts of this hegemonic civilization that was not sought. It is also not historically unique to it. Given the fact that this feature was one of the products of preceding cultures, such as the civilization of the Carthage Kingdom, the Roman empire, and some of the Islamic caliphates, and many others. Considering this, the founding fathers did not prioritize the development of Silicon Valley [14]. However, it would not have occurred if American civilization had not developed the ideal conditions on its soil to attract the best brains from around the globe.

Let us look into the issue of individual freedom and freedom of belief as an effect closely related to the equation of failure/success in civilization. Zooming in on the reality of a group of nations through this variable's lens, a high level of personal freedom is demonstrated in numerous countries of civilizational leadership. In contrast, all underdeveloped nations, with no exception, suppress personal freedoms and deny intellectual and religious

---

[14] Silicon Valley is the southern region of the San Francisco Bay Area, California, in the United States. This area has become famous due to the multiple developers and producers of silicon chips used for computers. It presently encompasses all high-tech projects in the area, and the phrase "high-tech" has come to be associated with it.

pluralism. Consequently, reproducing this experience—creating a free space for a society's members—can pave the road to civilizational advancement. Having said that, there is no guarantee that this situational possibility guarantees civilizational advancement. It is merely a condition that must be met. A mandatory prerequisite, in other words. There is an even stronger argument for observing the adverse effects of denying individual and collective freedoms, whose harm cannot be hidden or justified. Aside from the utilitarian mindset and a moral standpoint, providing this open and free space for expanded individual and collective freedoms is the right moral choice, regardless of its effects (negative or positive). The moral act has a high material, and sometimes political, cost that adversely affects its material aspects. Because of that reason, some choose to avoid it. Challenges such as receiving refugees or spending money on homeless people is an ethical issue that hugely impacts how the world's capitals govern, from New Delhi to Washington.

The ascent to the pinnacles of civilizational leadership requires rigorous moral balancing. Several civilizations' outcomes significantly affected many nations' current realities and prospects. Subsequently, the desired civilizational outcomes must be balanced with the possible repercussions resulting from the byproduct being examined. Achieving such an illustrious goal is sought-after at any cost, but that does not mean that limits should be removed. Our present-day technological progress has a high and accumulated environmental price that future generations will pay for centuries. Another example is the modern European Renaissance, which came at a dear price as it transferred injustice and enslavement from its inner territories to its colonies worldwide. During the colonial era, these adversely affected countries fell into an abyss. Even after closing this dark chapter in human history, the technical revolution—besides its unjustly stolen material goods and financial profits—increasingly widened that gap in a manner never witnessed before by the occupied and colonial empires. This further indicates the uniqueness of this outcome, where the civilizational gap is increasingly growing wider. The historical legacy of traditional tyranny ravaged the rest of the ancient world during a time when Europe's civilizational and cultural institutions were vigorously expanding. The time it took to build this widening gap gave Europe the advantage of settling its scores of internal conflicts and figuring out how to reformulate the relationship between religion and the state. The European kingdoms created a new "international" contract among themselves based on settling internal disputes and maintaining boundaries and neighborhoods after centuries of internal warfare and the reformulation of the framework of religion and state.

In this time and age, the world witnesses another colonial era where a globalized economy has taken over natural and human resources. The colonizer no longer needs to be a nation-state or a geographical region but could be a transcontinental corporation that imposes its will on the entire world, a model that has been proven very effective in the past, as exemplified by the East India companies of the Dutch and British. Most nations in the world—advanced or developing—have governments tied to the interests of these corporations to varying degrees. But they still cannot necessarily control these commercial global entities. This is beyond the scope of this book. Nevertheless, it is necessary to confirm that civilizational outcomes may be adverse for other nations' present or future (of that nation and all of humanity). To illustrate, it is inconceivable to expect a positive effect from nuclear arsenals. Claiming that these weapons have contributed to creating world peace nowadays does not eliminate their future devastating effects. These weapons are manufactured to be used, and to justify that they are only meant to deter others is naive and absurd.

The intellectual and material output—and especially the bestowal of some of that output among the collective—and civilizational hegemony have an organic, reciprocal relationship; there is also an interrelationship between the cessation of those outputs and the deterioration of political, economic, and social conditions and the resulting civilizational decline. Contributing to the world and the state of hegemony have both causes and consequences. This connection between the contributions and continuity in the hegemonic leadership can be traced throughout all past civilizations. Whether the reference is to the collapse of the ancient Greek empire, historical Islamic kingdoms, or the diminishing civilizational impact of some Western European countries and the United States, this interrelationship is unmistakable in these worlds. It is worth noting that civilizations are likely to be declining themselves. The last signs of this decline in contributions can internally manifest, as in a nation's loss of ability or interest to nurture its constituents and provide them with services and welfare. No matter how much money is spent abroad, any nation that denies its citizens fundamental rights in their homeland and prioritizes their welfare, lacks civilized leadership.

Civilizational contribution differs from financial spending for securing geopolitical interests or maintaining loyalty. Giving in the name of civilization is primarily free of material rewards in some instances. For instance, the polio vaccine was developed by American scientist John Salk, who offered it to the world without charging for it or selling his intellectual property; neither the United States nor any other country claims any ownership of it. This form of giving helped the world rid itself of polio almost entirely. An artistic example is how hip-hop swept the world without being forced. Nonetheless, it has a strong presence in nearly all languages for no direct financial interest to the nation of its origin. Hence, it is necessary to distinguish between pure civilizational giving for the benefit of humanity and financial giving driven by and bound by interests.

Given all that has been mentioned above, another feature arises, which also merits attention. Burhan Ghalioun[15] best sums it up as the condition of being "civic"; it is between civilization as an external phenomenon witnessed by a nation and its longing for what might be called "civilized". Ghalioun compares civilization and the state of being civic, saying: "Suppose civilization was considered to be the steady growth in the material, mental, and spiritual systems, transforming society from being primitive to being civilized and pushing it beyond the production of needs to that of luxuries or the development of the quality of needs satisfaction, as Ibn Khaldun elaborated. In that case, the state of being civic is founded on the principles underpinning or constituting the first nucleus of these systems. And suppose civilization is connected to regulating humans' relationship with nature, the degree of their control, and the patterns of material and spiritual production. In that case, the state of being civic is connected to regulating human social

---

[15] Burhan Ghalioun (1945—) is a Syrian-French professor of sociology at the Université de Paris III Sorbonne University in Paris. He also rose to fame as a leading opposition figure during the Syrian popular uprising in March of 2011.

relationships and the degree to which they are transformed into relationships based on peaceful communication, not violence or coercion, and vice versa." [16]

Intellectual contribution is therefore embodied as civilizational bestowal, having the utmost and most lasting impact. Following Burhan Ghalioun's proposition, we will refer to it as "the state of being civic" for now. Nations in this state are built on statutory and moral pillars like justice, equality, and other principles that have broad implications[17]. It is possible to witness urban forms devoid of civilization. Without its concomitant universal impact, the intellectual byproduct does not signify civilization. This contribution can also take a material form. Eventually, the sensed or perceived impact becomes a new norm in everybody's life. Whether it is the smartphone, we carry around artificial intelligence or the rule of law in a country like Sweden. These factors are recognized by everyone. Rarely would these civilizational contributions be denied or refuted as a sign of civilization.

As the urban, cultural, economic, and social achievement of a nation at a specific moment, a state of civilization differs from the individual's state of being civilized (or civic) as that state of mind that governs human behavior. The first is limited to a narrow temporal and spatial context and related to a collective state. As for the other, it seeks personal or group intellectual advancement based on a human propensity, making this "civic" state a goal in itself. Civilization is a manifestation in the form of materiality, mentality, and intellectuality. The state of being "civic" is a set of principles upon which civilization can be established, and human social relations are regulated. Subsequently, this state is a fruit of civilization, a product, and not an automatic result.

---

[16] Burhan Ghalioun, Assassination of the Mind: The Ordeal of Arab Culture Between Salafism and Dependency, Fourth Edition, 2006.
[17] This expression differentiates between the practical ethics that impact others, such as the examples mentioned or generosity. Those are necessary ethics for individuals whose direct impact is limited to themselves alone, such as piousness or stinginess.

Is Civilization a means or an end?

Do people think of civilization as an end or a means to happiness and a sense of achievement? This question, in this manner, is misleading, holding us captive in a whirlwind of dichotomies and false choices. It presents two unequivocal answers (civilization is an end or a means to another goal), presupposing that civilization is a self-evident and unanimously defined concept. I don't think this matter has been fully thought through. Whichever one chooses, the answer proposes a difference in the practical approach of those who adopt either. This is yet another hotly debated issue. The methods of action differ in execution when considering whether civilization is an end or a means. A nation's strategy for developing varies in these vast and extensive realms of application depending on its various goals for significant concerns such as economic development, political reform, establishing civic institutions, obtaining financial success, and many others.

Being a human-made achievement, civilization cannot be a sought after objective for anyone. Besides, it is not a means to another end, as those ends vary according to humans. Happiness, well-being, prosperity, justice, and dominance are only a few of these objectives. Throughout history, the achievement of civilization for the sake of civilization has not occurred. A group or a nation seeking to join civilized nations for the sake of a title is unheard of. Similarly, civilization cannot be considered a mere stage of the development of the human tendency for self-preservation relying on gathering, survival, and safety. It is acceptable to assume that human beings are motivated to achieve leadership and civilization by deeper, and frequently grander, motivations.

In his Story of Civilization, Will Durant explains humans' pursuit of civilization by clarifying how life is perceived. According to Durant, life is to be perceived in light of two facts: its limited span and its sanctity. This understanding is more like the soul's resurrection in the afterlife, too theoretical and abstract. The exam hour, in itself, is trivial in terms of the restricted period. Yet, offering an exceptional opportunity that might make or break someone's life is crucial, especially when taken advantage of. At all events, human beings in any civilization venture into life wholeheartedly and confidently. Without a word of complaint or groan, they are not elated and do not chase life's pleasures. According to this understanding of life, they know when to put on their guard and when to consider an unreserved lifestyle.

The establishment of civilization requires specific conditions to be met. Among these are material prerequisites such as suitable geography, determining climate attributes, proximity to trade outlets or distance from enemies, and certain key natural resources such as water and arable land. Civilization also requires administrative and organizational factors, such as political and social structures. And lastly, it requires security. The intellectual components are also crucial to civilization, including culture, its products of the arts and sciences, and the prevailing ethics.

Several of these "intrinsic" prerequisites might be the goals of a nation or a group, particularly the organizational and administrative objectives, which are controllable. This is unlike the "external" factors (such as geography, climate, and natural resources) that are out of human control, excluding invasion, occupation, and wars of expansion to capture these factors. For ancient empires to grow, that is the path to take. Pursuing these intellectual factors may be a goal in and of itself, irrelevant to its expansive intentions or global dominance. Factors such as achieving democracy or increasing per-capita income are a goal in themselves. These factors can also be means to other objectives, such as hegemony and dominance, be they military, economic, or others. Hence, we understand how the prerequisites for achieving civilization (as opposed to civilization itself) are a path that may lead to a desired goal without a guarantee. This might be a source of confusion between the conditions for achieving civilization and the concept of civilization. The fulfillment of specific prerequisites to build a civilization does not necessarily lead to its establishment in a given nation. The fact that India and Indonesia are democracies does not guarantee they are considered part of the league of advanced civilizations of our time. Following the same logic, if a large portion of the Arab Gulf population is wealthy, that does not mean these countries have a direct pass to civilization.

Therefore, the prerequisites for achieving civilization, in contrast to civilization, can be pursued as a goal. We observe these endeavors highlighted in many core plans undertaken by various governments of developing countries in the twentieth century and the current one. Setting up many of these prerequisites for achieving civilization as a goal is no more than merely imitating the civilized and does not fit to becoming a peer. High income does not ensure a pioneering intellectual movement, groundbreaking scientific advancement, or competitive military capability. Hence, nations' approach to creating the conditions necessary to achieving civilization is decisive in distinguishing between parrot nations mimicking and others whose goals are higher than a mere superficial similarity with the leading nations of civilization.

The transition from leadership to domination

Over the past five centuries, there has been an enormous and unprecedented civilizational divide between an advanced world that has taken the lead and an underdeveloped world. This tremendous chasm has never been witnessed in history, neither in the level of "civilizational" differences nor its persistence over time and its exclusivity to certain parts of the world. This stage emerged with the European Renaissance in Italy and gradually, in an indiscernible manner, across Europe. By the eighteenth century, world cultural differences had become more prominent. It was beyond possible to bridge the chasm between these two worlds in terms of physical and organizational differences with the onset of the nineteenth century.

The early phases of the Enlightenment Age underlined an elite humanist intellectual movement that called for the realization of reason, freedom from political and religious authorities, and the pursuit of freedom and justice. This age's philosophers and historians laid the foundations for connecting this movement with Greek philosophy and, thus, restoring it along with European glory. However, more pronounced characteristics are not to be disregarded. First, it was a movement voiced by the British and the French contexts. Second, it was a product of the development of the bourgeois classes in France during the reign of King Louis XIV and in Britain during the English Civil War (1642–1651) between Parliamentarians and royalists over the rule of England. Through a royal aliment, the bourgeoisie grew partly as an attempt to restrain the increasing power of the feudal lords in the countryside and create economic and political leverage in the cities close to the royal palaces. This newly formed class enjoyed privileges backed by royal despotism based on marking the distinction between the elites and the commoners. However, what made the Enlightenment era stand out from preceding epochs of prosperity and leadership was its concurrence with the scientific advancement that led to the Industrial Revolution and, later, the modern technological Revolution.

Before the Industrial Revolution, nations' wealth did not demonstrate huge differences since their economies were agriculture-dependent and manually labored. Sooner, these wealth gaps quickly widened due to the rapid industrialization of the West. Though various industrial technologies were of Far Eastern origin[18], this revolution and its profits were exclusively the prerogatives of a few Western European countries. Thereby, their hegemony surged to an unmatchable level. In the post-first industrial revolution, a few European and American countries created wealth that, at that time, made them possess more than 63% of the world's wealth while representing only less than 20% of the world's population. Contrastingly, India, which began as the largest economy in the world) and accounted for one fifth of the global population, owned only 3% of global financial wealth on its independence[19]. For over 200 years now, this discrepancy has not changed much for several reasons.

This confiscated wealth was partially invested in increasing the living standards of the Western population. Furthermore, technical and social revolutions followed the industrial revolution, which widened the civilizational and economic gap between the developed and developing worlds.

Yet, the hard truth remains that the Industrial Revolution was not the sole determinant of this remarkable achievement and vast disparity. Indeed, a more crucial factor was key to accelerating the growth and progression of certain parts of the world while halting them in others. The European colonial movement preceded and later accompanied the Industrial Revolution, significantly affecting civilizational, urban, and economic disparities. The

---

[18] The Chinese used hydropower in the paper industry for centuries. They invented and utilized gunpowder before anyone else, but it was not widely used in manufacturing or power production.

[19] A great source to learn more would be the book by historian and diplomat Shashi Tharoor (released March 2017) Inglorious Empire: What the British Did to India.

European colonial movement preceded the Enlightenment era by centuries, and its usurpation of the world was not this age's invention. Far from being the case, this movement might have contributed to the Enlightenment Age by blending European thought with global thought and weaving in beneficial ideas. In addition, the Enlightenment, which brought forward a justice and equality revolution, was also a tool for launching a worldwide colonial movement. The Renaissance yielded an advantage that was exploited by the European continent to metamorphose into an extensive global invasion unprecedented in all of human history. The colonial expansion and accompanying pursuits of international trade and financial accumulation are among the most significant sources of the Enlightenment movement's cradle, specifically France and Britain.

The Enlightenment movement did not appear in vacuum or was dissociated from its political, economic, scientific, and social contexts. These factors immensely contributed to formulating Enlightenment thought and outlined its features. Despite their global resonance and historical mark, the enlightenment's perspectives were the byproduct of their circumstances. The creators of that era's intellectual production were bound by their realities based on their intellectual principles and personal interests as members of a newly emerging Western society.

Enlightenment thinking managed to peacefully coexist with the slave trade, colonialism, and other moral crises that had to be addressed and would have needed to clash with if these values were absolute, universal, or free from private interests and self-motivations. This point is not intended to refute Enlightenment thought so much as to point out that human thought is generally captive to its motives and bound to its space-time[20] dimensions. The civilizational impact is fundamentally a historical mark of civilization. These marks may denote the horrendous crimes of those civilizations, as in the case of the atrocities committed in Africa and India under colonial rule. Millions of lives were lost, and hundreds of millions were exploited for nothing but personal glory. Similar to this case is the discovery of North America and the so-called new world annexation to the long list of European colonies. Conversely, the historical mark may indicate a shining moment in

---

[20] Space-time continuum: a modern term in physics.

some nations' history, such as the discovery of electricity or the birth of the Universal Declaration of Human Rights. However, most often, people pick the adverse outcomes of civilization in terms of present-day standards, regardless of how progressive these were at their time.

In all the previously mentioned cases, the historical context of previous civilizational differences had notably dissolved post-era. For instance, there is no trace of a living example of the lasting impact of the Pharaonic civilization in Egypt in the fifth century AD[21]. Also, presumably, the civilizational superiority and dominance that resulted from either the Enlightenment Age or the colonial era should have ended with their ending. However, the reality is that only a few nations have maintained uninterrupted world leadership to this day. After two centuries of the failure of the French Revolution and the Napoleonic campaigns throughout the globe and losing the vast majority of its colonies, France remains a leading country with regional and international dominance. The same can be said about Great Britain. Though the star of the empire upon which the sun never sets has now been eclipsed, the riches hoarded in previous eras did not completely vanish. The colonialism era, which made its mark on both the colonizer and the colonized, is primarily responsible for this chasm and long-term hegemony of the west. Others believe that the constant, systematic looting of these previous colonies' wealth was in the interest of the former imperialists. Others attribute this to the fact that the Enlightenment philosophy fostered modernity, besides the persistence of the values of equality and liberty in those nations. Though these viewpoints have a valid rationale, some misinterpret the whole picture. Among the things lacking in these theories is a pivotal point about how these differences continue after the causes cease to exist. Despite the globalization movement that tries to propagate many of these modern values worldwide, and with the globalization of industrial processes and the liberation of the vast majority

---

[21] The last of the Pharaonic kingdoms was the thirty-first dynasty, which included the final kings of Egypt in the era of the Persian occupation (343 BC–332 BC) before the entry of Alexander the Great and the beginning of the rule of the Ptolemy's. However, the Pharaonic civilization's leadership ended with the end of the Bronze Age in 1177 BC. By the fifth century AD, this civilization's impact almost entirely vanished.

of former colonies and being handed to local regimes, essential differences between the former colonizer and the colonized remain. Moreover, they do not fade away over time and continue to broaden and grow starker in some cases.

In the age of globalization, the developing world has benefited from technology, which is a decisive outcome of the industrial age and a substantial pillar of the second industrial revolution[22]. Reasonable economic development has been achieved in a few countries. Yet, the developed countries have benefited far more from the conditions provided by economic globalization than the developing countries. Richard B. Freeman, an economist at Harvard University, summed up the impact of globalization: "The triumph of globalization and market capitalism has improved living standards for billions while concentrating billions among the few. It has lowered inequality worldwide but raised inequality within most countries."[23] This issue culminates in several crucial questions. Is globalization directly responsible for depriving the world of the means of prosperity and development while hoarding them at the feet of the former colonial states? Can we turn a blind eye to all its developmental effects demonstrated worldwide, convinced that the underdeveloped countries chose to continue to be dependent on those former colonizers, whether voluntarily or forcibly? By adopting such theories, do we adequately address this dilemma? Have we successfully diagnosed it to affect change and restore this lost world equilibrium?

To do ourselves and history justice, the definitive intellectual foundations of the features of a civilization must be separated from the outcomes of that era's practices. Despite all the valid criticism of it and its founders, Enlightenment thought had a human tendency based on virtuous moral pillars as a means to justice, freedom, and equality. To properly discuss any civilization, one must address its intellectual effects, those responsible for

---

[22] The second industrial revolution, also known as the technological revolution, was a phase of the Great Industrial Revolution, which lasted from the second half of the nineteenth century until the First World War.

[23] Richard B. Freeman, Harvard, and NBER, LSE CEPI "Drivers and consequences of growing inequalities," OECD Policy Forum, Paris, 2 May 2011.

them, and their paramount role in establishing and perpetuating civilization. According to Muhammad Abduh's[24] viewpoint, for a nation to be civilized, it has to be founded on moral laws since actions are the interpretation of morals, at the top of which come justice, equality, and consultation. It is pointless to proceed with this rationale without going through the practices of that civilization and its material effects, which leave their imprints on the history of this planet (and frequently its geography).

So far, it is yet to be known what civilization, its standards, its essence, and what makes its irrefutable impact on history are. What triggers the ways and mechanisms undertaken by civilization to achieve its goals? At this stage of the book, there is no attempt to address the civilizational aspects of a nation; it is a contentious issue worthy of independent books to entirely discuss what is known and what is yet to be known.

This book is neither a summary of the story of civilization nor a critique of its history. Nevertheless, it is an attempt to identify some of the features of civilizations, not only in an endeavor to break the code of civilization but also to understand why a group that came into contact with civilization did not acquire or get affected by it. Now is the time to bring forth the Nawrāna's concept of civilization to which the book is entitled. In this context, that concept denotes a state that peculiarly "immunized" societies against modernity, progress, and maturity. Thereby, they were taken on a ride to regression and disintegration, losing all track of time, neither moving nor keeping pace with it, but only walking backward against the current of time. I decided to embark on a journey to analyze this state that is contrary to civilization. Hence, this is a probe into all its dimensions. On the banks of civilization, we need to thoroughly investigate the opposite side, i.e., un-civilization.

The Un-civilization

The term "un-civilization" emerged in the early 16th century and was widely used at the turn of the 18th century. It commonly described

---

[24] Muhammad Abduh (1849–11 July 1905) was an Egyptian Islamic scholar, journalist, teacher, author, editor, judge, and Grand Mufti of Egypt.

colonized nations deemed brutal and barbaric by the Western colonizer; at the same time, the term "civilization" started to denote its contemporary concept. Simultaneously, the colonization movement spurred its spread. The European explorers and orientalists were the first to use the word "uncivilized" in describing the peoples of the East, as they lacked the customs and traditions accepted in the colonizing Western community. The European explorers and orientalists were the first to use the term "uncivilized" in describing the peoples of the East, primarily because they lacked the customs and traditions accepted in the colonizing Western community. This view was pivotal for the European colonizing thought that differed from preceding colonization and occupation movements that blatantly identified themselves as nothing but a military occupation seeking materialistic exploitation. Contrastingly, European colonization came under the guise of the world's savior, who, by ruling these barbaric nations, would bring them into line with the civilized world and rid them of ignorance and darkness. In return, they would benefit from the riches "neglected" by what they dubbed the uncivilized. Thereby, the colonizer had but to see the total lack of civilization and manners in the customs of the individuals of these colonies according to what appealed to that comer from the "civilized" world.

From the sixteenth to the early nineteenth centuries, the civilized/uncivilized dichotomy defined and categorized peoples, nations, countries, and continents. It became the key to European imperialist jargon. During the sixteenth and seventeenth centuries, the all-Christian perspective of law and morals was to grant the right for European expansion when the indigenous Americans came under European ruling. In the eighteenth century, the Enlightenment school of thought conceptualized the man (which has historically referred to white, protestant males above 30 years of age who are property owners) and the other (ideally, other men in other parts of the world). It facilitated the replacement of the old Christian/non-Christian dichotomy with the European/un-European vision for the world overview. In the late nineteenth century, the European civilization's language shifted to use official imperialistic terms. Such practices played an essential role in dubbing un-European languages and cultures as lower class. Among these were the linguistic and cultural forms that emerged due to European colonial expansion. Hence, the superiority of the colonizer's language and culture came to be supported by international law.

The nineteenth century witnessed the emergence of international law following an obsession with categorizing nations as civilized or uncivilized in terms of their boundaries with regard to geography, the law, and humanity. Endowed with civilization, the civilized were recognized as "proper" subjects of international law. While those lacking "true civilization" are uncivilized and were expelled from the umbrella of international law. The binary division between civilized and reactionary nations nullified the possibility of equal comparison or mutual recognition. This division created a contradiction ingrained in the principle of the universal application of international law and equality between nations by dividing peoples in this manner. These descriptions include unsolvable and unrelated claims based on the heterogeneity of the ascribed content in different regions and times.

Europeans' perspectives on the colonial territories did not recognize the local behaviors and customs common among those regions' inhabitants. Whether marriage, worship, commerce, or any local tradition, everything had to be measured against the newly forged "Western" standard. Therefore, these customs had to be classified according to customs and behaviors accepted in European society. Subsequently, whatever is outside that society becomes naturally uncivilized and unacceptable. This exceeds heinous and immoral acts, which might be more prevalent in some societies than others, to include all behavior inconsistent with what the West considers a moral standard.

The conceptualization of this Western supremacist perspective accompanied all its colonial movements. On one side of the earth, Europe was building its enlightening human values in their reality. On the other side, these same European countries were rigorously striving to abort any attempt by the original inhabitants of their colonies to adopt these values or demand the rights equally sought by the Europeans from their authorities. During the French Revolution outbreak in 1791, the enslaved Africans in Saint-Domingue, currently known as the island of Haiti, revolted against the French colonists, demanding autonomy and freedom from slavery and the unjust economic system. Although their demands were those of the protesters in France who stormed the Bastille and fought to overthrow the absolute monarchy in France, the French did not perceive the "uncivilized" mob in Santo Domingo as a people worthy of these privileges. The privileges they claimed to be uncompromising rights proved only valid for civilized white Europeans. Hence, this new classification determined who was entitled to freedom and self-determination. The label of civilized people, given exclusively by white European colonizers, was a prerequisite to deciding who deserved freedom and equality. Meanwhile, the uncivilized were unworthy of the prerogatives of the civilized.

Countries with recent colonial history proficiently utilized the divisions of "indigenous" and "non-indigenous" people, or "settlers," among others, in colonial societies. They distinguish in an overly manner between Europeans and people of non-white origin. Even in Europe, racial politics existed among the whites themselves. These racial distinctions were used against many nationalities and races, such as Poles, Slavs, Greeks, Italians, and Jews. European literature was marked by outrageous racist expressions against other European nations, perceived as less civilized. Ethnicity was not the only factor in formulating this difference between Western Europe and the other.

Unlike race, ethnicity refers to cultural traits that can be used to differentiate between human groups. Racial and cultural distinctions were utilized as social exclusion tools throughout contemporary European history. Although the less civilized nations of Europe were not subject to the same practices of colonialism and looting to which African, Asian, and South American countries were subject, they undoubtedly remained second-class nations and unworthy of the prerogatives of civilized people. These countries' citizens were victims of forms of dominance in their territory and as migrants to the countries of colonial Europe.

Under the authoritative colonial lens, the other is and will always be inferior, whomever that other is. This view produced two intellectual signs in the colonial West. The first is their distinction from all of humanity in terms of their characteristics, whether these are inherent characteristics with which they are born, such as race, or acquired, such as language and religion. These distinctions are interpreted as discrimination. The second is their eligibility to dominate the world and possess everything that falls into their hands because of the distinction with which they are endowed. As for the undistinguished, they have no right for the self-evident reason of lacking sufficient civilization. Therefore, they would not make good use of what they own; the European colonialists should take whatever pleases them and reap its fruits.

In Australia, the "Terra Nullius" myth[25] in Australia, based on the idea that lands sought and colonized by the British were uninhabited or primitively used by less-developed aboriginals, was the central intellectual foundation of the colonists. Thereby, colonial possession through occupation and settlement was justifiable. From their perspective, these inhabitants did not benefit from the natural resources in those lands, which entitles anyone to exploit them. Israel established itself on the same "land without people for a people without land" myth a couple of centuries later.

Renaissance philosophy created a utilitarian-based doctrine, and Enlightenment thought further established and preserved this materialistic principle. This principle expands the circle of beneficiaries among the offspring of the nation or civilization while denying such communal existence in other nations and civilizations, besides the right to have such a collective. This perspective is demonstrated throughout the European wars—the Thirty Years' War and the Wars of the Three Kingdoms in the seventeenth century, the colonial movement, the First World War, and beyond. Even when there is no declared state of war, vision-centered approaches such as Orientalism and others have contributed to building the broad international identity of all Europeans as one nation after centuries of civil and external wars. It further establishes a practical basis for how to treat other nations and civilizations. As the Western perspective started to study the East to grasp the distinctions between its various components and hierarchically classify them, colonial European remained the standard compared to none. Furthermore, when European thought finally came to recognize the right of "indigenous people" to "determine their destiny" in the name of benevolent

---

[25] Terra Nullius in Latin means "nobody's land". This term was used by many settler-colonial powers to justify their occupation of many parts of the world.

liberalism, it was inconceivable to perceive this without the white European being the viceroy over them.

The undebatable acknowledgment of the civilized white's entitlement to dominate others preceded the justification attempts, which came at a later stage. The justifications for their right to dominance changed over time. Religiously based justifications were a way out in the beginning, as they "the god-fearing believers" were facing the "godless" barbaric societies. Later, this was replaced by pseudoscientific-based reasoning in several eras; among the most important scientific theories utilized to justify this differentiation were those of phenologic and then biologic foundations. The reasoning for white supremacy was described based on its external distinctness from all other races. Therefore, the same exterior that created this distinction must have also played a role in creating the roots of the white Europeans' intellectual and cultural superiority. The development achieved in the nineteenth century in the study of eugenics was exceedingly convenient in presenting this theory, deemed scientific at the time. Henceforward, eugenics theories were formulated to preserve the purity of species, and their counterparts in the dysgenics theory justified how underdeveloped nations came to be what they were. Furthermore, a continuous phase of forming new biologic flaws might be in progress that will be passed down to most underdeveloped countries.

The intellectual effects of this theory —despite its eventual debunking and reclassification as a pseudoscience—persisted and resurfaced on more than one occasion. Among these occasions are the Nazi movement in Germany, the rise of extreme nationalism in Europe today, the racial discrimination movements against blacks such as Jim Crow in the US, the apartheid in South Africa, and the apartheid in Israel today. Discrimination reveals its true colors whenever civilized whites deal with the other, even when playing their benevolent part in the "white" charitable projects in the "colored" developing world.

Regardless of the collapse of supremacist theory based on biology, racial, or ethnic grounds, this difference persists in contemporary Western consciousness. In this day and age, this differentiation is attributed to internal, cultural, or behavioral factors displayed in the civilized individual that might not exist or be as developed as in the civilized. Hence, as the references change, the outcome remains the same. Civilized individuals have been competently elevated to a rank above all other races, and there are solid singular factors that validate this theory. Considering another viewpoint of this issue, similar to its opposite state, uncivilization is attributed to inherent factors related to uncivilized nations that justify the competence and entitlement of this classification.

This expulsion from under the umbrella of civilization was instrumental in consolidating European prerogatives in the colonies and confronting any liberation attempt and any demands for equality between the civilized Europeans and all others. A civilizational difference, primarily attributed to the nature of people in those societies and their culture, substantially perpetuated the colonial movement and further justified depriving entire parts of the world of what were settled to be the rights of the Europeans. Other justifications were used to prove and confirm this civilizational difference, including those quoted from their religious rhetoric attributing it to misguidance and the absence of true faith. And as previously mentioned, at one stage, evolutionary biology was accepted as a "scientific" justification. It linked the European white race to civilization on the one hand and all other races to the lack of it on the other. These justifications varied in their extremity and persuasiveness, but their reasoning was one: Europeans come first and on top of all!

Colonialism had to be founded on this expulsion of the others from under the umbrella of civilization. Moreover, this view of other nations came before the European colonial phase and certainly did not end with it. It is present in the current civilized world's treatment of the issues of what is currently known as the Global South. Multiple changes had to be made, to mask the racist nature of this perspective. The word "development" replaced the word "civilization", and the concept of economy took the place of culture. Economic development is the measurement of civilization, and its absence is the absence of civilization. Contrary to the term civilization, development has its clear standards; the level of income, education, and child mortality rate are objective, measurable, and indisputable criteria. There are naturally vast developmental differences between the developed and developing worlds. This new consolidation of concepts and terms was no more than a subtle linguistic substitution. Nevertheless, the developed continued to rule supreme while the developing remained subservient. Within this same context, several forms of disqualification exist for those stuck in their journey to development.

Escaping the uncivilization state is almost impossible from developed and developing countries' perspectives. In addition to the inevitable internal variables like skin color, indigenous culture, language, and race, there must be external factors that are causing un-civilization. Moreover, the uncivilized individual may pursue cultural assimilation in pursuit of the anti-uncivilized status, meaning to join the civilized. Hoping that the double negation is canceled, the assimilation is an essential way in proving the uncivilized flawed and the civilized superior. However, this quest for integration into the civilized nations does not remove their stigma of belonging, themselves or one of their grandfathers, to the inescapable un-civilization.

This idea of assimilation is palpable in our societies. Unless one belongs to a well-known feudal family in Syria, one is not among the civilized, at least implicitly, in the residential sense and civic origin as the son of the city, with the layers of meanings that come with such terms. Even if an individual, who does not come from the city nor is part of a known feudal family, acquires what would have entitled them to an equal or superior level among the civilized group, they still do not stand a chance of total equality. Moreover, in other contexts of this coveted full equality, a two-century ancestry is not to be condoned, as in the coming of a Fallah/ peasants' and a Nawăr s' ancestry.

This example reveals a racist phenomenon often found among undeveloped societies, though not restricted to them. It directly reflects the civilized nations' perspective on the undeveloped. For example, in the United States, I saw the conditions of immigrants of Arab origin whose ancestors immigrated over 100 years ago. Large communities from the Levant migrated to the East Coast of the United States at the end of the nineteenth and early twentieth centuries. The only homeland they know is the United States; Christianity is their religion; they fully adopt mainstream American culture; and are ethnically white, according to the census bureau. To this day, they are considered an "immigrant" community that does not fully belong to the "true" American identity. Acquiring full admission into the American identity takes more than belonging to a white Christian group. It took nearly two centuries for some descendants of immigrants to be fully integrated into American identity. Until recently, Italian or Jewish surnames signified a lower social class. And to this very day, some Americans of Polish, Croatian, and Ukrainian ancestry, regardless of their racial origin and religious affiliation, are considered lesser Americans simply because of their surnames. Naturally, this is even more pronounced among Americans from Asian or Hispanic backgrounds.

This oddity in dealing with Americans from "immigrant" backgrounds is not necessarily embodied in racist behavior. It is precisely what we observe in an undeveloped society. It suffices to perceive a difference between the original group and the other striving for assimilation. In addition, this differentiation results in discrimination that seems almost irreconcilable between groups. This study examines a cross-cultural intellectual component in conclusion. While my goal is not to justify the underdeveloped state of colonized nations or summarize the history of people over hundreds of years in one or a few aspects, it is very significant to explore the concept of civilizational differentiation between nations and its implications on the conception of the other.

Global leadership and hegemony, as phenomena, cannot be understood separately from the exertion of force and power. The rise of civilization is associated with a type of leadership that the nation fostering this civilization can never attain by adopting a consensual approach with other countries. Violence and force are indispensable instruments to prove civilizational supremacy. There has never been a civilization that did not exercise military power to attain hegemony. Additionally, the members of a leading civilization must demonstrate a sense of reigning supreme over all nations through their views. Accordingly, the designation of the un-civilization state for the underdeveloped world is expected. Those who considered themselves the only "civilized" took on a self-initiated missionary project. It was responsible for the enslavement, conquest, administration, or subordination of the "uncivilized" under the pretext of legal, economic, social, and/or hierarchical relationships derived from the doctrinal values of the civilized.

Hence, projecting the "Nawrāna" or savagery accusation on a particular person or group simulates the European colonizer action that already expelled the Nawāri outside the so-called civilized framework as an introduction to their stripping their eligibility. This book explores the effect of such actions within the Syrian society context under the totalitarian regime.

The Ineligibility of the Uncivilized

The expulsion of the other from the realm of belonging, regardless of what this belonging is, translates into inconsistent, implied assumptions, claiming that they are unresolved and eternal differences. This civilizational gap cannot be bridged or changed. Therefore, the colonial movement did not perceive its role as temporary or phased out in the overpowered countries. Its permanence was deemed inevitable and indispensable to achieving the common good for both parties: the invading colonists and the oppressed colonized.

Hence, the idea of civilized and uncivilized nations was originally inherent in the colonial movement that erupted out of Europe and swept the world. The colonial movement peaked with the rise of a world order based on laws established by "civilized" nations to preserve rights. This new law aimed at controlling relations between the colonial nations and preserving their rights in the colonies and over the oceans. Putting it differently, the perspective of the occupied countries did not incorporate their residents, interests, or priorities when establishing these laws. The civilized colonial nations exercised guardianship over their colonies and their inhabitants equally. They did not deem those uncivilized nations adequately capable of managing their affairs or assessing their interests. Other than that, the colonizers neglected the colonized nations' interests all along the time. This patriarchal guardianship and purposeful exclusion from participating in establishing international law were artfully played, knowing that these laws would not be for the benefit of the nations strained under colonialism. Dismissed as savages, these nations might have had some customs and traditions but no regulatory-based or accepted legislative structure. How can they be part of their own development or be considered in the drafting of international law? Why would international law incorporate or acknowledge these countries?

By dismissing the competence and political and social eligibility of the "uncivilized" nations, the "civilized" states had the exclusive right to set the draft of international law. In this sense, the resistance or political action of the "uncivilized" makes them outlaws, subversive, brutal, or no more than marginal source of disturbance. By way of illustration, the Spanish colonists argued that the indigenous peoples of the newly discovered America were still barbaric because they did not have "messages, books, arts and crafts, organized agriculture, manufacture, and other things which are indispensable to human use." Still, according to them, they were "not utterly stupid," as they had "accurate notions of things" and organized forms of marriage rituals, family life, laws, and the judiciary.

The interrelationship between the civilized/uncivilized dichotomy and international law was witnessed during the nineteenth and early twentieth centuries. It was particularly noticeable with the principle of recognition and the promotion of an implicit norm of Europe's civilization mission and its guardianship of the uncivilized, ineligible world. Carlos Calvo[26] concentrated on Europe's perspective of the uncivilized states. In his book, A Dictionary of Public and Private International Law[27], he states that civilized nations are endowed with civilization because they have developed morals, customs, and uses that denote an identified moral, political, and economic education. He adds these morals are organized according to a fixed and rational basis and the principles of order and human justice. Moreover, in this confrontation with the uncivilized states, the colonial states acted as promoters of education and guidance with a mission to transform the

---

[26] Argentinian diplomat, historian, and lawyer (1824–1906). His book "Theoretical and Practical International Law of Europe and America" (Derecho internacional teórico y práctico de Europa y Americ) was published in 1863. The book focused on the essence of what became known as the Calvo Doctrine. It was in opposition to the historical rules governing foreign investment.

[27] It states that foreign investors can appeal the decision of expropriation by a foreign government in their home country. It advocated a return to the local courts of that country. Nonetheless, the book reinforces the common supra-European, patriarchal view.

peoples into become civilized. Besides, they were expanding the land of civilized countries and establishing civilized authorities under a name that surpassed the barbarian areas. Colonialism steadfastly "humanized" its mission of colonizing the world, misleadingly evading that it was no more than an exploitative economic process backed by the systematic destruction of those nations and usurping their right to their fortunes and self-determination. Denying the eligibility of these people was an introduction to solidifying this fixed belief. Eventually, their ineligibility became synonymous with being less than humans. They were banished from what the colonizer considered relevant to humans and humanity itself. In their minds, they mutated them into wild beasts and dealt with them accordingly.

The Non-humans

In several ancient Chinese, Egyptian, and Mesopotamian inscriptions, enemies are frequently described as "subhuman" creatures. We can also observe the Nazis' description of the Jews as "Untermenschen" or sub-humans. This was not passed around in a figurative sense but in a literal sense. When people are deprived of their humanity, they are reduced to animals, stripped of their rights, and exist only to serve the actual human being.

Dehumanizing people was detrimental in one of the most destructive events in human history: World War II, in which more than seventy million people died, mostly civilians. Millions were firebombed, and more fell victim to nuclear weapons and systematic genocide. Dehumanization was the instrument of these massacres.

It would be a mistake to put the ancients' description of their enemies as animals on an equal footing with the Nazis' belief in the inhumanity of the Jews. It is our collective failure to trace the fundamental moral flaw that led humanity to moments of extreme cruelty, such as dropping atomic bombs on hundreds of thousands of people in cold blood, leaving sick migrants to die at the borders, or being responsible for incarcerating them in these conditions where they then die of heat or illnesses.

Dehumanization is a phenomenon as old as humanity itself. The view of uncivilization held by the dominating states is not so different from this one. However, this concept was rarely intellectually examined throughout history. War was rarely absent from the human experience. In Europe, the Renaissance and Enlightenment ages perpetuated this perspective of dehumanization, unlike wars that are only momentary confrontations.

The humanity of the Enlightenment era was no less condescending towards underdeveloped nations. Immanuel Kant[28] argued in his essay "To Perpetual Peace" that "peoples or nations which do not form states" can be regarded "as individuals" who are either "savages or civilized." This is because civilized nations have constitutions, choosing "rational freedom" and establishing "legal constraints." The constitutions requested that each other avoid "mutual harm," favoring their security. On the other hand, the savage countries refused to establish their constitutions and remained committed to "their wild outlawed freedom... and being involved in a continuous conflict with one another."

Civilized nations "profoundly disdained" uncivilized nations, describing their condition as "savagery", brutality, and an untamed deterioration of humanity." Immanuel Kant described a quote by Anton Amo[29] as irrational. His grounds for this rejection were that "this fellow was completely black from head to toe," meaning, for Kant, being a black African is sufficient confirmation of stupidity.

As for David Hume[30], in a footnote in his essay "Of National Characters", he formulated his thoughts as follows: "I am apt to suspect the Negroes to be naturally inferior to the Whites. There never was a civilized nation of any

---

[28] Immanuel Kant was an eighteenth-century German philosopher (1724–1844), one of the most notable philosophers who wrote in classical epistemology, and the last philosopher of the Enlightenment age.

[29] Anton Wilhelm Amo is an African philosopher and writer from Ghana and the first African in history to teach at European universities.

[30] David Hume (1711–1776) was a Scottish philosopher, economist, and historian and an important figure in Western philosophy and the history of the Scottish Enlightenment. This article was received as part of his Essays, Moral, Political, and Literary, published in 1774 in two volumes.

other complexion than white, nor even any individual eminent either in action or speculation... Not to mention our colonies, there are Negro slaves dispersed all over Europe, of whom none ever discovered any symptoms of ingenuity; though low people, without education, will start up amongst us and distinguish themselves in every profession. In Jamaica, indeed, they talk of one Negro as a man of parts and learning; but it is likely he is admired for slender accomplishments, like a parrot who speaks a few words plainly."[31]

That was a part of Hume's moral, political, and literary works. Hume explicitly wrote that there are multiple human races, adding that non-whites are inferior to whites. Although the footnote was considered merely an offhand commentary, it reflects his profound views on the methodology of anthropology. This can be linked to excerpts in Hume's other works and the broader Scottish and European intellectual and historical framework.

Hume persistently affirmed the blacks' "natural" inferiority as a distinction from other races. He generally regarded all the non-whites as inferior to the white race, and the difference between Europeans and American Indians was as close as that between humans and animals. He declared his rejection of slavery in his works, rendering his ideology of white supremacy ambiguous; his refusal of geographical or climatic reasoning meant he could not provide a convincing causal account of what he considered racial difference.

In a review of ancient Roman history with the Jews, Voltaire[32] wrote his book "Mimosa Treatise on Cicero." He noted, "They are, all of them, born with raging fanaticism in their hearts, just as the Bretons and the Germans are born with blond hair; I would not be in the least bit surprised if these people would not someday become deadly to the human race." The following year, he wrote an essay titled "One Must Take a Side," which was introduced as "The Last Word in Metaphysics." In this essay, he ridiculed

---

[31] David Hume, "Of National Characters," 1777 (revised version of an essay first published in 1748).

[32] François-Marie Arouet, better known by his pen name Voltaire (1694–1778), was a French writer and philosopher who lived during the Age of Enlightenment and human dignity.

each major religion. He was particularly mean to the Jews, saying, "You [Jews] have surpassed all nations in impertinent fables, bad conduct, and barbarism. You deserve to be punished, for this is your destiny." This is not the speech of a man who thinks the Jews are just people waiting to become enlightened.

Voltaire was hostile to Islam, particularly in his play Fanaticism, or Mahomet the Prophet. He portrays Muhammad, the prophet of Islam, as a fraudulent and lecherous villain lacking remorse and repentance. He is far from the traits of classic tragedies heroes and seems to be a tyrannical, oppressive, ambitious, vicious, and lust-driven con artist. Voltaire pinpointed similarities between the Arabs and the ancient Jews, who pursued fighting in the name of God and shared their passion for the spoils of war. Furthermore, Voltaire was a downright racist towards blacks in his works, most peculiarly in his book "Treatise on Metaphysics."

The colonial stage further solidified the concept of dehumanization worldwide at gunpoint. While the Enlightenment era produced theoretical theories, European colonialism implemented these radical and eclectic ideas in its understanding of "humanity." In contrast to the dehumanization of ancient times, the Western colonial era had an unfailing perspective toward others. This state was previously directed at individuals with whom they had no direct relations other than a temporary state of war or at one group of people in a given circumstance. In contrast, European colonial dehumanization was unceasingly directed at entire nations. Europeans saw entire groups as non-humans, collectively stripping them of their humanity. This was at a time when Europeans played God with the destiny and fates of others, legalizing and perpetuating this discrimination.

Recognizing self-determination as a prelude to civilization

After gaining their independence from the British Empire, the new American colonies sought recognition of that independence and incorporation into the civilized nations' community at the end of the eighteenth century. As for the previous colonies that could not acquire their recognition and were deemed wild entities, they were incorporated among the civilized nations. Thus, the European countries' recognition, especially by the mother country, Britain, serves two purposes. Firstly, to avoid costly military recolonization, and secondly, to allow the settlement of trade agreements with the largest market in the world.

The first United States constitution was written in 1787, Haiti in 1805, and the former Spanish American colonies after 1811 to demonstrate that they were not in "untamed anarchy" and organize their governments. The founders of the United States Constitution incorporated the language of the law of nations into the text as a civilized practice. France recognized the United States in 1777, Britain and the Netherlands in 1782, and Spain, Sweden, and Denmark soon followed.

However, the United States' recognition of its American neighbors—as in the case of its civilized counterparts—was complicated due to the problems of slavery and the prevalent ethnic composition of the new states. When half a million slaves revolted in the French colony of Saint-Domingue, Haiti, in 1791, declaring themselves free and starting a struggle for independence, this struggle continued for over a decade. The Haitians fought the Spanish, British, and French armies without the help of any of the liberated colonies. Shortly after the defeat of Napoleon Bonaparte's largest military campaign sent to restore the colony and re-establish slavery in 1802, former slaves declared their independence and the territories they controlled as "Haiti." At that moment, they became the second independent country in the Americas after the United States. Although, the process of their recognition was delayed for an extended period due to the sweeping opposition of states under the pretext that effective recognition would be granted as a peer country. They believed that it would direly impact their trade and administration of the colonies of the Americas, the Far East, and Africa. European countries and the newly liberated United States believed that "the manner of recognizing a state... is solely a civilized nation's prerogative" and that the Haitian revolution "incites a catastrophic racial revolution throughout the continent." US representatives were against recognizing Haitian independence because slavery and the slave trade were still instrumental to the American economy.

Eventually, France recognized Haiti in 1834, after 32 years of constant war and the destruction of this small colony. The French recognized Haiti in exchange for an agreement in 1826 in which Haiti paid 150 million francs as reparation to French farmers and slave owners. The US recognition of Haiti, a fellow in the liberation movement, did not come until 1862, after the outbreak of the American Civil War.

Consequently, it was illogical for Europe to see the two American colonies from the same perspective; hence, it is impossible to accept the independence of the black, savage human beings. Despite the fierce war between the colonists and the inhabitants of the eastern coast of North America that ended with their defeat (1775–1783 AD), the recognition of their independence was not delayed, even by the British Empire. Britain officially recognized the independence of America by signing the Treaty of Paris in 1783. Several factors were crucial in creating the European perspective of discriminating between the two American colonies and treating them differently due to their proximity to European civilization. The United States and its inhabitants of European immigrants were considered an extension of that civilization. Unlike the slaves of Haiti, who could not be an extension of that civilization, even if they remained suffering from occupation for long centuries. It was determined by several factors that this difference was sufficient to prevent them from ever being treated equally. Denying Haiti's independence implied that its inhabitants were ineligible and incompetent to manage their affairs, thus, disregarding their autonomy. This outlined the European position in considering them a different and underdeveloped nation unworthy of joining the civilization process, which could only be in the European style. Even if they mastered French, believed in Catholic doctrine, and created poetry and literature!

The nineteenth century witnessed powerful waves of colonial seizures and liberation that took the world by storm. In South America, several former European colonies gained their freedom. And Latin American nations spent most of the nineteenth century struggling for independence. Despite the tireless attempts exerted by Spain and other European powers to keep their grip over Mexico, Chile, and other Latin American countries, most Central and South American countries had independent republican governments by the end of that century. With the increasing intolerance of European powers in Latin America, France, England, and Germany shifted their colonial interests to West and Southern Africa and East Asia.

Napoleon Bonaparte[33] took control of France in 1799. In the early nineteenth century, he embarked on conquests comparable to Alexander the Great, whom he dearly admired. At the same time, Britain was overwhelmed by an industrial revolution that changed its economic and social structure and heralded the beginning of the Victorian era. The era witnessed the inception of a vast international empire to the extent that "the sun never sets" on it. At the end of the nineteenth century, the expansionist policies of ambitious European rulers began to gain momentum, such as Kaiser Wilhelm II (1888–1918) of Germany and Emperor Franz Joseph (1848–1916) of Austria. They proclaimed the beginning of their colonial movement across the world.

Africa became a mixture of European colonies. Yet, a colony such as Liberia was founded by Americans who advocated the abolition of slavery as a homeland for freed slaves to be returned to whence, they were sent back. Sierra Leone, similarly, was founded in 1787, when several waves of freed black settlers from England, Nova Scotia, and Jamaica arrived in the area. Colonies were primarily established to exploit the natural resources of the African continent. This movement included the entirety of the African continent except for Ethiopia, which remained the only African country far from direct colonial control.

The close of the nineteenth century witnessed the General Act of the Conference in Berlin on West Africa (Berlin Act) of 1885. It highlighted the colonial discourse of the late nineteenth century that solidified the relationship between "civilized" and "uncivilized" nations. Although there is no coherent standard for defining the concept of civilization, these nations dared to classify and define "uncivilized" nations. The parties to the Berlin Document agreed to "regulate the most favorable conditions for the development of trade and civilization in certain regions of Africa," a continent of uncivilized and barbaric nations.

---

[33] Napoléon Bonaparte was a French military and political leader of Italian origin who rose to prominence during the French Revolution. He led several successful military campaigns against France's enemies during the Revolutionary Wars. He ruled France in the late eighteenth century as Consul General and then as Emperor in the first decade of the nineteenth century.

The un-civilization resulting in the negation of existence

The 1886 Treaty of Berlin Convention[34] considered several areas of Africa as free spaces available for occupation due to their status as uncivilized or "empty" land that could not be stated. Subsequently, by legitimizing occupation as an instrument of civilized mission, the Berlin Act promoted European private interests as public in "rushing" to colonize Africa. The Europeans refrained from recognizing the African colonies as inhabited states, which alleviated the burden of the entire official administration of those colonies. The lack of territorial entitlement to these colonies eliminated the possibility of violating any laws of those countries. Despite being seized by the colonizing states; their laws were not applicable in these lands. The French laws were not in effect in their African colonies. Directorates weren't associated with the French ministries to run matters, following the example of the French territories. At that time, the absence of laws and official administration structures in those colonies invalidated any claims by the indigenous peoples of sovereignty over their land or even belonging to it. Since they were not its subjects, they did not exist in the first place! In another similar context, the lie of "a land without people", was not an Israeli concoction but a traditional European ploy for legitimizing the occupation and depriving the indigenous population of their full rights. Therefore, the Zionist Jews' occupation of Palestine was no more than Europeans artfully practicing "civilization" in the form of colonization.

In the Berlin Conference and the Australian Colonial Act, words such as "occupation" and "acquisition" were used to refer to the African territories as similar to terra nullius. The intended meaning was either "empty" or "ownerless," where there was a possibility to establish European sovereignty over the unoccupied territories.

There was no recognition of human beings inhabiting these lands, let alone their rights to them or their right to self-determination. The label un-

---

[34] The Berlin Conference of 1884–1885, also known as the Congo Conference or West Africa Conference, regulated European colonization and trade in Africa during the New Imperialism period and coincided with Germany's sudden emergence as an imperial power. Its outcome, the General Act of the Berlin Conference, was seen as the formalization of the partition of Africa.

civilization paved the way to deny their existence entirely. This was the accumulation of dehumanization practices according to the rationale of European colonial civilization. They started by dividing human beings into two distinct classes: we, the civilized, and they, the savages. This would be followed by denying the eligibility of the savage and uncivilized and ended by utterly denying their existence.

The assimilation of un-civilization into post-colonial systems

The nineteenth century witnessed the emancipation movement from the grip of European occupation sweep across the American colonies and later in Asia and Africa in the twentieth century. Unlike the quasi-genocide of the new world's indigenous peoples and the resettlement of colonial citizens' influxes into the Americas and Australia, the European colonial movement of the old world failed to exterminate the indigenous peoples of Asia and Africa. This is because the European colonists in these regions were few compared to the settlement movement in the new world in Australia and the Americas. In addition, the absence of development and infrastructure building in the European colonies in the old world compared to that in the new world reflected the consumeristic policies applied in those regions. Hence, they were not considered an extension of their civilization and lands. That was military sovereignty to protect the looting of these countries' natural resources and strategically exploit their locations.

By the end of World War II and between 1945 and 1960, 36 new countries in Asia and Africa had gained autonomy or complete independence from their European colonial rulers. The decolonization process did not follow a specific pattern. Some areas had peaceful and orderly decolonization, and some European governments welcomed a new relationship with their former colonies. Whereas in others, there were military confrontations.

Most of these countries gained independence by going through protracted revolutions and struggles. Several of these colonies ended up with moderately stable governments, while dictators or military councils ruled some for decades, and others saw protracted civil conflicts. None of the colonial countries left without leaving behind adverse impacts on their colonies. Among these was the continued monopoly of natural resources, as in Iraq, Iran, and several African countries. Also, the borders of these regions, divided amongst colonizers, were arbitrarily drawn; thus, they were altered culturally, geographically, politically, and socially.

Whether in academia or Global Solutions Summits, the conditions of the African continent and the global south, the Third World, are limited. The scope of discussion is limited to relief, conflict studies, epidemics, development, and nothing beyond. This is a possible consequence of the failed repressive regimes that ruled these countries after their independence. It is widely unacceptable to allude to colonialism's role in setting the stage for these countries to become what they are. Reverting these problems to colonialism is highly opposed, though this feature is particularly shared among newly independent countries. The argument is that since colonialism is over, it would be inaccurate to attribute any of these problems to long-gone issues. During a trip to Nigeria in July 2018, French President Macron tweeted, "60% of the Nigerian population is aged under 25. That's 60% of the population, which, like me, did not witness colonization. We are the new generation. We are going to dispel prejudice by rebuilding a new future through culture." Many Western decision-makers believe that a half-century of independence is sufficient to eliminate the dire impacts of colonialism.

Colonialism was more than an economic system. The colonial powers completely disrupted the societal structures, economically exploited these regions, and neglected or destroyed the local communities. The French replaced the local culture with their own, and the British made sure to distance their culture from the indigenous culture. In all cases, the governmental structures, if any, of the local authority were entirely replaced. They were not associated with the institutions supervised by the colonial state that was the "guardian."

As previously explained, the colonial power implanted enslavement from the beginning. African societies were only for these powers to use in all aspects of life. They destroyed their several thousand-year-old identities and cultural structures. Colonialism also replaced the local food crops of these communities with those of exclusive use to them, called cash crops. Several African nations still stick to growing cocoa, coffee, or cotton almost exclusively, despite their inability to meet their food demands. The colonial powers positioned themselves as slave owners who kept them alive for their exclusive exploitation.

After the end of colonial occupation, the newly independent countries suffered from the total destruction of government structures and power. Agriculture could not meet the people's needs, and the infrastructure was unsustainable. The colonial powers left a legacy of corrupt bureaucracies. Though, in theory, their time ended, their existence took different forms and further created unreasonable trade agreements that persist to this day without the prospect of being terminated.

Colonialism created several challenges. Among these are road systems disconnected from neighboring countries, impeding travel and trade. Also, it forcedly ingrained a mentality of dependency, which, unfortunately, continued throughout many aspects at the hands of powerful local elites. During the occupation, the colonizer held close ties with these elites. Multiple foreign companies and governments promoted and sustained corruption as part of the legacy of these newly independent nations. Besides, the colonizers perpetuated poverty, neglect, and the fragmentation of social structures for decades. Hence, the toxic legacy of colonialism survives and thrives on land and in people.

Neo-colonialism is the term widely used to describe their current political scene. Though politically independent, they still use the same colonial administrative structure, where Western countries drain the resources and peoples of Africa. For this reason, Kwame Nkrumah[35] wrote, Neo-colonialism is the worst form of imperialism; it translates into power without responsibility for those who practice it, but exploitation without recompense for those who suffer from it. In the old days of colonialism, the imperialist power had to justify their actions on foreign lands for their internal frontiers. The people who served the ruling imperialist power expected some protection against their opponents' aggression, as the colonizers enforced a monopoly of violence and control. In the age of neo-

---

[35] Kwame Nkrumah (1909–1972) was one of the first African anti-colonial activists, the first president of independent Ghana, and the first prime minister. He was the most prominent advocate of the African Union and one of its founders.

colonialism, the situation changed, and the new power structures that stemmed from the colonizer's structural and administrative bodies emulated the bygone colonizers and started a struggle for domination and a monopoly of absolute violence. Neo-colonialism was manifested through the armies that fought hard to gain control over those newly independent states, following the same model as their former colonizers. This explains why Africa's struggle against dictatorships and misrule is one of the last traces of colonial rule. Many had fought and died for political independence, but this new, or neo-struggle, is incomplete as long as neo-colonialism remains in power in Africa and several states of the Arab region.

The post-colonial concept has a hazy definition. By way of a tentative description, it is the consequence of colonialism in an occupied territory where political control of empires, European or otherwise, has ended. The newly independent states are eventually part of a global order of economic and cultural hegemony established by their former colonists.

Post-colonialism is widely viewed as part of a global dialectical that focuses on oppression and resistance, mainstreamed in all fields. Thus, it developed topics such as gender, sexuality, religion, and linguistic identities. This era can also be defined as an oppositional stance against the legacy of colonial dominance by discerning strategies of resistance to new colonial powers and disrupting preconceptions. Among these preconceived notions is addressing the original struggle that eliminated colonialism and contributed to its end. It stands ever-defiant in this struggle being mainstreamed at all levels, caught in the web of colonialism as it was before independence. Another one traces holding on to aspects of the past and reliving them currently. These perspectives overlook past and current incidents between the moment of autonomy and the present time, to the extent of refusing to evaluate reality unbiasedly. Many post-colonial thinkers lean towards blaming either bygone colonialism or the people or nations that were exclusively subject to colonialism in the old days. This is because they currently enjoy "full autonomy" and should take full responsibility for their destiny. This book attempts to go beyond these two emotional approaches. Nor colonialism is to blame for current affairs or events, nor are the newly-liberated peoples are at fault and solely responsible for their fate. This section addresses the first notion, and the rest of the book covers the other at length. The adopted approach does not seek to point fingers but to deeply understand and analyze more consciously how to fully realize these people's liberation.

Examining the post-colonial era as an era completely separate from colonialism would undeniably be incomplete. This would produce an inaccurate perception of the current state and its root causes in those countries. Among the most crucial effects of colonialism are its intellectual and social impact on the occupied peoples and the perpetuation of oppressive ruling structures. As a result, the civilized/uncivilized rift was internalized[36] within the components of those peoples. This assimilation requires partial identification of society with the bygone occupier. Later, the identifiable part would replace that occupier and continue to rupture the social foundations. This assimilated part would persistently emphasize its difference from the public to prove its supremacy and entitlement to rule or run the resources. Moreover, it tenaciously sticks to its association with that former occupier, intellectually and culturally.

Post-colonial states had to act as long-term sovereign states in front of their European audience. This façade obliterated the effects of centuries-long destruction and exploitation by colonialism. These seemingly independent countries had to adopt a sovereign approach in line with the expectations of their audience. Anyone who rules must act in a civilized manner acceptable to the European perspective. This expectation applies whether the government is installed through elections or a coup. However, this façade may coincide with brutality in governing and a continuation of the corruption and exploitation institutionalized[37] during their occupation. This state of affairs might ever be more favorable and further endow those newly created regimes with legitimacy.

Terms like "independent" and "sovereign" notably underline the formal ability to pass and enforce the laws of a national government. More importantly, these concepts indicate a complex set of responses, values, and assumptions about the world associated with a shared awareness of the

---

[36] In psychology and sociology, assimilation involves incorporating the attitudes, values, norms, and opinions of others into one's identity or sense of self.

[37] Institutionalize: from institutionalization. It is the creation of an institutional system. It is derived from the linguistic root "to establish" in Arabic.

naturally evolving cultural realities of its people, traditions, language, and environment. Hence, it is paramount to create—organically or compulsorily— a unified social image that aligns with European definitions of state-based entities. Eventually, these entities will be the foundational modules upon which modern Europe is based. This attempt to create a homogeneous society by force caused a deeper rift among the post-independence peoples, who were already fragmented.

Who represents the Syrian persona is a much-debated issue. Are they the characters of the famous television series Bab Al Hara/Ally's Gate[38] or Hammam Al Quishani/Al-Quishani Spa[39]? Was the general public an illiterate group with conservative and narrow-minded communities dominated and exploited by patriarchy? Or were they graduates of European universities who are all political and social activists?

I believe both can depict part of the Syrian society during and after independence, which may explain much of the underlying problem. This is because the natural outcome of these conflicting and divergent factors within the same geographical and social space is a dispute over the right to represent and lead society, and one of them eventually prevails.

No insult is intended at the founding fathers in the newly independent Arab countries, their counterparts in Africa and elsewhere, especially those who did not get into power by force. The hard fact is that their education and social status are essential to being chosen for their positions. Most of these figures in power graduated from the universities of colonial countries, and some worked in their institutions. There is nothing wrong with that. Still, it must be pointed out that the citizens of post-colonial countries were not on an equal footing regarding status, prowess, and education. The majority of the population of those nations had inadequate education, and some were

---

[38] A Syrian TV series that takes place in a popular Syrian neighborhood during the French colonial period. It was widely criticized because it celebrated the narrowmindedness and masculinity of Syrian society and its disregard for the diverse community at the time.

[39] The work presented historical facts in the Syrian neighborhood of "Hammam Al-Quishani" / (Al-Quishani Spa) during Syrian independence from France and the subsequent coups and political transformations.

graduates of folk education systems such as Quran classes and religious schools. Prominent political figures were almost entirely from Sunni feudal families, and some Christians were from wealthy and educated families, as in Syria and Lebanon. Even after decades of independence, this reality did not change much. Regardless, it took long decades until individuals from rural areas and minorities started to rise and take over cultural circles. Especially those who came into the limelight for their brilliance and creativity, such as Mohammad Al-Maghout[40], Hanna Mina[41], and others. The issue herein is not historical judgment or responsibility but rather an attempt to delve into our modern history and discern the social fissures and intellectual flaws that may have contributed to what "we" collectively are today.

What follows is a discussion of the factors that led post-colonial societies to a point where discrimination spread among their various components. Moreover, some formerly colonized populations debase each other, similar to the behavior of the European occupier. In this manner, this new tyrant is the successor to the bygone colonizer.

External colonialism left an internal colonial system in their formerly occupied countries. Consequently, the people remained aching under regimes of robbery and looting guarded by their leader and founding father of these newly liberated countries. Liberation from European colonialism was not achieved for all classes of society. In many cases, a group of people were free and colonized the rest of that society. Hence, a single nation was differentiated. Its fabric was torn into a domineering form comparable to the bygone colonizer and occupied people that remain the target of exploitation and oppression. The following section is a journey through some traits of this newly developed social differentiation.

---

[40] Muhammad al-Maghout (1934–2006) is a Syrian writer and poet from Salamiyah City in the Hama governorate. He is also one of the most prominent poets of the prose poem, or free poem.
[41] Hanna Mina (1924–2018) is a Syrian novelist from Latakia. His works became famous after he produced his novel "The End of a Brave Man" as a TV series in Ramadan 1424 AH/1994.

Successors of colonialism

Many post-colonial countries transformed into absolute dictatorships in Africa, the Middle East, or East Asia. They came to power through civil wars, assassinations, and military coups. Only a few countries escaped that fate. These modern dictatorships often differed from what preceded the colonial era. The forms of post-colonial dictatorships in Africa do not resemble their pre-colonial institutions.

The foundations of democracy and the rulers' limited powers are neither new nor alien to the political traditions of Africa. In his book "Gold Coast Native Institutions: With Thoughts Upon a Healthy Imperial Policy for the Gold Coast and Ashanti[42]," Joseph Casely Hayford[43] describes some of the political tradition for that region, currently Ghana, and the election of rulers by a council. This council had the power to dismiss the governor and charge them if a valid reason was found. The governor was entitled to appeal. Yet, they would be removed if found guilty. In the Oyo Empire in present-day Nigeria, the ruling monarch was forced to commit suicide if the Consultative Council "Oyo Mesi" disapproved of them. The Oyo Mesi was a privy council of elders that served the purpose of controlling and monitoring the power of the ruling king. In the West African kingdom of Futaglon[44], Chiefs were elected by consensus among traditional community leaders. They ruled for a limited time and could be removed by the Senate before the end of the designated term.

In The Destruction of Black Civilization, Chansler Williams[45] tells the story of some European explorers who got infuriated by the King of

---

[42] The Gold Coast is the name of the English colony that is today the territory of Ghana in West Africa. It was known as the "Ashanti Empire" before British colonization.
[43] Joseph Ephraim Casely Hayford was an African lawyer, author, and journalist from the Gold Coast colony.
[44] Fouta Djallon is a mountainous region in West Africa, extending from eastern Guinea and Senegal to the south.
[45] An American sociologist, historian, and writer. He is famous for his studies of African civilizations before their encounter with Europeans. His most important work was the book (The Destruction of the Black Civilization), published in 1976.

Votaglon, who made them wait two weeks to meet him. What triggered this problem was that this particular African chief had to be granted the Senate's permission to meet foreigners. This underlines that African kings only had access to restricted power.

Colonized African kingdoms and nations remain an obscure subject matter in literature. If it exists, it is almost always authored by African writers. This indicates that the European mindset acknowledges neither signs of civilization nor culture in their former colonies, as doing so would refute the European perspective, propagating their proclaimed mission of developing the uncivilized world and savage nations.

Colonialism replaced the consensus ruling systems preceding its oppressive system, which often used violence to suppress the African people. Their voices—those who had the courage—were brutally suppressed. In some cases, the colonizers massacred the protesters. For instance, in 1929, a Nigerian women-led protest[46] was met with the British colonizers firing at the unarmed protestors, killing about 50 women. Occasions where the military still shoots unarmed protestors, such as in Togo[47], nonetheless display the same reaction. These numbers amassed to millions of Africans who were murdered en masse, with their entire families at times, because of the protests that erupted against the brutal colonizer way until the 1960s. The shameful history of the European colonization is a topic that is too huge to be covered here and to massive for a few examples to summarize it.

In post-colonial countries, new armies emerged comprising remnants of the colonial forces to serve the colonial powers' geostrategic and political interests in suppressing local resistance. They consisted of the labor force reserve recruited by colonialism to facilitate mobilization in times of war. These armed forces later led coups against the regimes established in the

---

[46] The Women's War, or Aba (Igbo women) riots, was when British Nigeria witnessed turmoil in November 1929. The protests erupted when thousands of Igbo women demonstrated against the orders of officers, who were accused of restricting women's role in government.

[47] Togo is a tropical country in sub-Saharan Africa. Faure Gnassingbe, who succeeded his father as president in a military coup in 1967, is currently in charge. Togo ranks as one of the oldest African dictatorships.

occupied states, like the Free Officers[48] in Egypt and Idi Amin[49] in Uganda. Many emerging leaders were military officers who served in armies under the command of the British, French, or even Ottomans and were graduates of their military schools. Throughout the Arab world, various internal security institutions were established, instructed, and trained by British colonial forces, notably Saddam Hussein's secret police. They designed these bodies to control people from a distance. In plain language, they were intended to protect the state from its citizens rather than from foreign armies. It is widely argued that these bodies continued to function after the fall of the colonial empires.

The absence of democratic political institutions has been one of Africa's challenges since it gained independence due to its acceptance of colonial-era institutions. In this regard, Julius Nyerere[50], the first president of Tanzania, noted, "In reality, colonialism—along with its traces of racial supremacy—was replaced by a mixture of neo-colonialism and the rule of local elites. They often loathed and despised themselves, African traditions, and the people who work the land." The unconditional support of the West for African and Arab dictatorships is another issue that these nations have experienced and continuously confronted. In Togo, for example, General Gnassingbé Eyadema came to power through a military coup and led a repressive regime. Yet he had France's support. French President Jacques Chirac described Eyadema as "a close friend of mine and France." His son, Faure Gnassingbé, continued his father's repressive legacy and received the

---

[48] Several Egyptian army forces founded the Egyptian Free Officers Movement, which staged a coup against King Farouk in Egypt at midnight on July 23, 1952 AD. Among its members were Muhammad Naguib, Gamal Abdel Nasser, and Anwar Sadat, who took over the presidency of Egypt.

[49] Idi Amin Dada (1925–2003) was the third president of Uganda from 1971 to 1979. He is always described as a military dictator who joined the British colonial military forces. He staged a military coup in January 1971, deposing President Milton Obote. His rule was known for human rights violations, political repression, racial discrimination, and extrajudicial executions.

[50] Julius Kambarage Nyerere was a Tanzanian anti-colonial activist, politician, and political theorist.

same French support. Mobutu Sese Seko[51], Idriss Déby[52], Blaise Compaoré[53], and Jean-Bédel Bokassa[54] were among the numerous African dictators who received French support.

These former colonial countries' positions towards the dictatorships of Africa were not unfamiliar. Middle Eastern dictatorships equally enjoyed their share of support and respect. Jacques Chirac[55] saw Hafez al-Assad[56] as the only Arab leader capable of uniting the region. Henry Kissinger compared him to Otto Bismarck[57] and called him "the Bismarck of the Arabs." In another neighboring state, American intelligence supported the Baath Party and Saddam Hussein, who seized power in 1963. The United States and Britain backed Saddam in his war against Iran, providing

---

[51] Mobutu Sese Seko came to power after a coup against President Yusuf Kassa Fobu, the country's first post-independence president, in 1965. He established an authoritarian regime under the rule of only one party, the People's Revolution Party.

[52] Idriss Deby Itno has been president of Chad since 1990. He came to power after the ousting of the former president, Hissein Habré. He amended the constitution to remove the limited terms for running for office. He was a graduate of the Muammar Gaddafi International Centre for the Revolution.

[53] Blaise Compaore was President of Burkina Faso from 1987 to October 31, 2014. He came to power in a bloody coup in October 1987, and violent protests erupted at the end of October 2014 against his intention to run for a fifth term after 27 years. Subsequently, he was forced to resign and flee to the Ivory Coast.

[54] Bokassa was an army officer and head of state in the Central African Republic and later under the name of the Central African Empire. In January 1966, he led a coup until being overthrown by a French-backed military coup after losing control of his frenzy following the declaration of the empire.

[55] Jacques René Chirac (1932 – 2019) was a French politician who served in various positions, eventually was as President of France from 1995 to 2007.

[56] Hafez al-Assad (1930–2000) was a military officer and the Syrian president who came after a military coup. He served as the 18th president of Syria from 1971 until his death in 2000. Hafez was also a key participant in the 1963 Syrian coup d'état, which brought the Syrian regional branch of the Ba'ath Party to power in the country.

[57] Otto Eduard Leopold von Bismarck (Otto von Bismarck) was a Prussian and later German statesman and diplomat. From 1862 to 1890, he was Minister-President and Foreign Minister of Prussia. He masterminded the unification of Germany and served as the first chancellor of the German Empire or the so-called "Second German Reich."

weapons, money, space intelligence, chemical precursors, and biological weapons. Around 90 American military advisers helped Iraqi forces select targets for air and missile attacks. The monarchies of the Arab Gulf are always lavished with total admiration and support from the West, which reluctantly criticizes some of their human rights practices, though occasionally.

The colonial states ruled their colonies with iron and blood. They deliberately established regimes that primarily ensured their strategic and economic interests, which were not in line with those of the local population. Therefore, it was necessary to seek the support of military institutions and militias to seize power and annihilate any attempt to stop their interests' progress. Hence, post-colonial rule continuously relied on a centralized system and decision mechanism from top to bottom that was imposed during colonialism and remained dominant after the colonists' departure. Arguably, it is no surprise that numerous post-colonial states were undemocratic. The establishment and continuation of post-independence states relied on their status as colonies, which sustained economic, political, and cultural servitude.

The environment created by colonial policies best served political peace and stability in the former colonies, placing them at the mercy of their previous armed forces. Furthermore, the former colonizers welcomed re-normalization with those emerging dictatorial regimes, besides politically and militarily supporting them, as in the case of most African dictators.

The newly independent countries had a legacy of oppressive military regimes and bureaucratic systems set up by colonialism to serve their goals of exploiting those countries' riches and natural resources. The colonial commissioners and those in power methodically educated these national systems to harness and take advantage of all their capabilities and natural resources. Under this arrangement, the colonizers had amply provided a driving force for their economies. Their colonial-era-ingrained education and training systems substantially shaped their future, which was eventually stolen from them. The formerly established systems of governance and administration followed suit with the colonizers to the extent of continuing to be suppressive and destructive tools of the popular will and the social structures of those countries, which I will expand on in the next section.

Education for indoctrination

During their colonial days, the French deliberately utilized education to indoctrinate the African people, into the idea of the inferiority of their culture, as with all the nations they colonized. In addition, they formed a group of educated civil servants to serve their interests. Henri Simon, a minister of colonies, designed a secondary education program to transform the best into perfect French. In Africa, former colonies were governed by Africans indoctrinated into French culture. They served the interests of their French masters at the expense of their people. Post-independence rulers did not deny this dependency. Léon M'ba, Gabon's first president, classified these leaders—he was one of them—as the indoctrinated French. M'ba once declared that every Gabonese has two homelands: Gabon and France.

The British followed that methodology in their colonies. Education equally instilled contempt for the local culture and the denial of any historical dimensions or cultural depths of the colonial nations. During this phase, the British colonizers focused on teaching English cultural and civilizational values. They exclusively taught British history and English literature.

Post-colonial countries kept many of the colonial-era curricula in their education. In Syria[58], the Franciscan schools, the Laïque Institutes, and others were considered historical and cultural urban landmarks even after the Baath party came to power. Their historical symbolism continued to be indicative of their noble and superior civilizational perspective, despite signifying nothing but an ultimately colonial stigma. Currently, graduates of these schools and institutes boast of their superior education over other schools. Yet none of them studied the French curriculum, which was official until the late sixties.

Colonial countries widened this gap between the education medium and language away from the local cultures and local languages, adopting their

---

[58] Same case in Egypt and Jordan, which did not fall under the French occupation.

languages. While certain factors did the job of distancing the occupied nations from their cultural origins, changing the language guaranteed the continuation of this rupture.

Moreover, the colonial-era education systems focused on cementing the regional and religious identities of the diverse groups of the occupied peoples, using them to categorize groups within historically mixed societies. On the other hand, the post-colonial era forcefully imposed the identity of the modern international state, which was often foreign to those areas of newly liberated peoples. This sufficiently motivated the adoption of the languages and curricula of the colonial era since they partially stand at an equal distance from the diversified linguistic and cultural fabric of society.

A particular example worth noting here is when Kemal Atatürk[59] changed the letters of the Turkish language after the declaration of the end of the Ottoman Empire. Despite the survival of the Turkish language, this decision alienated Turkish citizens from their cultural heritage, whether it was inglorious or priceless. The Turks had to completely rewrite their historical literature treasures in the new alphabet to be able to read them.

Internal repressive regimes and neo-colonial economic hegemony were only a few issues that plagued the post-colonial-era world. More critically, the entrenched dependency theory dictated that the world system should orbit around the rich nations, leaving the poor ones at the margin. Thus, neo-colonialism exploited vulnerable countries' human and natural resources to fuel the economies of rich countries. This theory concludes that the countries at the margins of this world system suffering poverty are the outcome of their integration into the global economic system. In this integrated system, one group is the source of raw materials for another to exploit, which is the source of industry and technology. Accordingly, this group is fully entitled to reap the fruits of this system. The dependency theory is derived from the Marxist analysis of economic disparity. Under

---

[59] Mustafa Kemal Atatürk, (c. 1881 – 1938), a field marshal and statesman, is considered the founding father of the Republic of Turkey, serving as its first president from 1923 until his death in 1938.

this global system, the underdevelopment of some nations on the periphery is caused by the development of the countries at the center.

Wealthy nations imposed this dependency, which covered more than just the political and economic spheres. Their culture and lifestyle, ranging from clothing to food, music, and the arts, had the upper hand in galvanizing the supremacy of the countries occupying the nucleus of it all. Though they were "economic" exports, they were substantially intellectual and cultural. The cultural hegemony of industrialized and economically influential countries sets the boundaries and values of general culture and unified forms of civilization for global consumption. They leaned towards de-linguicization[60] and de-valuing ontologies—the theories of existence—which were far from individualistic. They set Western culture as the only form of science, excluding non-Western approaches to sciences, arts, and indigenous culture from being forms of knowledge. Dr. Ali Al-Abedy[61] noted that imperialism "involves large-scale interactive systems, heavy contexts of identity distortion, misperception, loss of self-esteem, and individual and social skepticism about self-efficacy."

The varied impact of the colonial-era education process was of a complexity that further deepened the societal chasm. Since that impact was not balanced or homogeneous, urban areas and well-off families' children were the targets, leaving rural areas off the radar and out of the sphere. There were two realities. City schools relied on Western scientific-based curricula and foreign languages; in contrast, Quranic schools in villages and remote areas had access to limited traditional forms of education. This difference in the language and content of education developed several contradictory intellectual and cultural systems, always contesting legitimacy and eligibility. On the one hand, the local culture continued to be related to the limited traditional education, endowing it with "legitimacy" for preserving the indigenous languages, values, and social norms. On the other hand, modern schools with their imported curricula won eligibility for being more scientific, closer

---

[60] European languages replaced indigenous African ones.
[61] A Somali-Canadian sociologist. He has prolific productions on education in Africa.

to the spirit of modernity, and more efficient in engaging science and management.

Western countries relentlessly undermined local cultures through education, economy, and politics. They did not burn their libraries or kill their scholars but expelled them from the "cultural and/or civilized inheritance" arena to the dark terrain of a "backward" past. As a result, the pre-independence mother culture was associated with colonialism, which in turn was viewed as directly causative for their backwardness and colonization in the minds of the very offspring of former colonies. This explains the rise of a compelling need for a modernization movement as per their former colonizers' paradigm. Thereby, eligibility went to urban Western curricula institutes in urban areas. The administrative, political, and educational colonial systems might have contributed to following this path.

This system divided society into two "populaces," each following a different culture. They shared no common ground but have been continuously engaged in an ideological confrontation ever since, regardless of unifying the curricula applied on both fronts. One thing is almost certain: this gap continues to deepen due to increasing polarization. This is witnessed in the monopoly of some intellectual aspects. To elaborate, the traditional culture became synonymous with religiosity and conservatism, while the newly created culture became representative of science and openness. Today, these dichotomies have developed into the ultimate undisputable presumptions that, if not abided by, would carry a stigma in the eyes of both cultures' believers. A highly educated individual can never be simultaneously connected to the ancient heritage, just as a religious individual cannot be "open-minded" and "progressive!" This Montagues and Capulets rivalry is the foundation for two social classes in these states: the true citizens and the mob.

The intersection of colonial education and economic systems created an elite representative of an intellectual and social minority. On the other side of the scale, others are from different cultures, environments, and orientations. The irony is that they are superficially united under the umbrella of mobs, having barely anything in common. As an illustration, Syria, which has diverse ethnicities, cultures, and religions, has no unified identity to form the nucleus of a national identity. Eventually, what only united this mob class was their exclusion from the elite's circle, and whatever lies outside it sufficiently justifies differentiation and alienation among them. The mob continued to identify itself as the Nawãria (savagery) popular class that must be rehabilitated and civilized.

In our Arab societies, what is described as "folkish" is relative to all that is tacky or foul. A folkish restaurant has to be dirty, a folkish shoe signifies cheap and poor quality, and the folk culture is tarnished with patriarchy, masculinity, and seclusion. I could not pinpoint anything described as folkish as good or positive connotation. In contrast, everything identified as "modern" is lavishly applauded as civilizational. Folk music only fits "truck drivers." While cultured individuals listen to Beethoven or at to any imported "unpopular" music, even if this is American country music[62] or Swiss yodeling[63], themselves forms of folk music of other nations!

One of these forms had to prevail in this intellectual rivalry. I concur that one ideology's dominance over the other was decisive in this intellectual conflict. It was predictable that the state and ruling institutions would be bequeathed to those of foreign education who worked in colonial-era government bodies. Accordingly, those loyal to the colonial countries in positions of power had to guard this hefty heirloom. Colonialism favored the most bureaucratic regimes, even if they were the most brutal and dictatorial. Who would beat the military organizations that operated under the supervision of the colonial powers to this prize? Subsequently, the post-colonial era had to be cloaked in camouflage military uniforms.

This phenomenon is no longer raging within the Arab arena or only in the underdeveloped world. In contemporary American society, a high-and-low ideological civil war is waged between two highly disparate camps. On one frontier, the conservatives stand as representatives of Christian religiosity,

---

[62] An American folk music genre with roots in ancient musical genres and many Western cowboy music styles, its folk roots originated in the southern United States in the early 1920s.

[63] Yodeling is a form of singing that involves repeated and rapid voice pitch changes. Alpine yodeling was a longtime rural tradition in Switzerland, Austria, and southern Germany.

white supremacy, low education, hawkish-style patriotism, government mistrust, anti-vaccination, hatred of elites, and the Republican Party. On the other frontier, liberals embody non-religiousness, advanced education, cosmopolitanism, individual freedom, the protection of minorities, big government and the Democratic Party. In this confrontation, no one would dare publicly declare themselves a conservative Democrat or non-religious Republican. This extreme polarization and repulsion created one homeland holding two peoples sharing a continually eroding ground.

Education is inseparable from this equation, which comprises social status, geographical location, and general economic and scientific family status. Yet, I chose the education system as a surrogate for all of them due to its role in shaping individual and collective identity, granting legitimacy, and establishing the reality of belonging to the elite or the folkish. Consequently, the elite has identifiable, ethnic, and geographical dimensions, distancing it from the vulgar mob. The intellectual elite is now more than just "intellectual" but also a component of a set of social conditions required to attain that rank. Even Ph.D. holders from rural areas force themselves to be detached from their popular culture and deny their regional affiliation before their "conditional" and partial transfer to the elite.

In this context, it was imperative for whoever rises to power in the third-world countries to hoard as much elitism as possible and ascertain that whoever is underneath is ascribed to populism. As a result, the tendency of African and Middle Eastern dictators to over-Frenchification and Anglicization is all but subtle. The purposes of alienating the communal feeling were to develop closer relations with the West, acquire the eligibility to rule and own this elitist's wealth and win a privileged social status in their native societies.

These elite groups transformed into another form of domination and ruling colonialism, hindering their people's progress. In this manner, they enjoyed the privileges of science, culture, and, as might be expected, ruling. Hence, only the newly invented form of elitism (which lacked all traditional attributes of elitism) attained these exclusive prerogatives. In these societies' realities, elitism became inherited, as it did during feudalism and monarchies.

At this juncture, several groups gravitate toward extravagant religiosity and get rooted in the local customs and culture, utilizing "populism" in their fight against elitist oppression. This exaggerated attachment does not necessarily reflect a true belief but a means of superficial differentiation to express a rejection of the new colonial elites and their absolute totalitarian rule.

Along the path of post-independence, there came to be a state of identification[64] between a part of the independent nation and its former colonizer, in which they continued to crush and enslave their people. On the other hand, there came forth a similar state of identification among the non-elite masses, the mob, and the Nawāri approach, giving away the rule to their ever-rising ruling elites. From then on, we started to see each other through the dichotomy of the civilized and the Nawār. It brought about more tragedies in our contemporary history. Later, it contributed to creating populist dictatorships (such as the new Ba'ath under Salah Jadid[65] and Hafez Al Assad), which in turn will be an alternative elitist of new bases or an escalation of populist trends in various parts of the world.

---

[64] Identification in psychology is a mental process that involves a person growing into resembling someone else. It can be a defensive or developmental process.

[65] Salah Jadid (1926-1993) was a Syrian military officer and politician who was the leader of the Ba'ath Party, and the country's de facto leader from 1966 until 1970, until he was ousted by Hafez al-Assad's coupe that he named the "Corrective Movement" on November 13, 1970.

Chapter 2

The Caravan

The ugly Nawãri and high society!

Among the readings that inspired me to write this book was a brief book entitled "The Ugly Chinaman and the Crisis of Chinese Culture"[66] by Bo Yang[67]. His own inspiration for this resonant book was a speech he gave to the Chinese community in the United States in 1985. He sarcastically criticized many shortcomings of Chinese society. In his view, those shortcomings were directly responsible for its backwardness, the deterioration of Chinese culture's civilizational component, and its inability to enter the modern era and achieve the civilizational primacy to which it aspires. That hour-long speech induced laughter and applause, but its reverberation proved it was no passing happy hour or a mere joke. It became a topic of frequent debate with his acquaintances and friends.

Published that same year, his book followed the speech's main points. It discussed the narrow-mindedness of the Chinese individual and the lack of openness to whatever contradicts their convictions. He highlighted that vanity, neuroticism, and megalomania characterize the typical Chinese individual. In his opinion, the traditional cultural heritage produces nothing for China in the modern age but physical filth, negligence, and unproductivity. According to his viewpoint, the Confucian heritage undermines free thinking, instigates fear of power, and stifles urban development and equal human rights. Yang's book does not provide a rationale to substantiate these superficial impressions. He reiterates that

---

[66] Bo Yang: The Ugly Chinaman and the Crisis of Chinese Culture.
[67] The nom de guerre of a Taiwanese writer is Gou Yidong (1920–2008). He was a Taiwanese historian, poet, and opponent of the Chinese government. He was imprisoned by the Chinese government several times for his intellectual activities.

these are purely personal observations and not to be considered reliable academic work but more of small talk over dinner.#

The "Ugly Chinaman" was widely denounced for being inaccurate, belligerent, and blatantly expressing a fascination with the West, particularly the United States. It was an attempt to make the Chinese feel ashamed of their identity and traditions. Despite being a source of historical pride, Yang claimed that the Chinese people's backwardness was due to their traditional heritage. The glaringly oversimplified approach, in my opinion, is his book's worst flaw. I cannot help but think of the common tendency and similar approach adopted by many intellectuals in the Arab and Islamic worlds and post-colonial nations in general toward people's cultural heritage. That same approach is widely adopted among intellectual and academic circles worldwide.

The Chinese government banned the book under the pretext of insulting China. Regardless of its repeated harsh criticism of the Chinese government, the dictatorship of its regime, and hostility to Western democratic practices, the book, in a sense, actually promoted modern communist propaganda in China. That propaganda is based on a total severance from the ancient and long legacy of China and the enforcement of the new revolutionary phase of communism, which revives the Chinese glory. The cultural revolution call was and still is the most crucial discourse championed by a wide range of leftist movements across different nations.

The "Ugly Chinaman" stirred interest among vigilant circles within the Chinese authority. As a probable result of Yang's observations about personal hygiene, the Chinese government became more focused on forcing the Chinese to take care of their external appearance in front of the world, particularly the West. Moreover, the Chinese government focused on curbing Chinese business' presumptuous behavior towards the countries whose markets are targets for their products. The use of soft power[68] was mainstreamed in addressing international issues and leveraging China's

---

[68] A term that refers to dialogue and persuasion as the means to create shared options and develop the ability to attract without using force for dominance.

political weight outside its borders. Since the 1990s, Western-based urbanization features have been ostentatiously adopted throughout China.

On the other hand, the Chinese readers had split opinions, varying from welcoming to rejecting its offensive and harsh attack on Chinese culture. The majority of intellectual society could not deny the book's criticism of issues such as personal hygiene, vanity, and other individual qualities that were commonplace features of the Chinese character at the time. Yang's book might have contributed to prioritizing such policies for the Chinese government, although they could have been in motion. The extent of this book's influence on current Chinese reality cannot be fully measured. Chinese individuals are nowadays models of active workers; they have cleaner hygiene habits, are less arrogant and boastful of their historical achievements, and are more open to others. They demonstrate growth in their societal sense and community relations and are more developed in popular and governmental relations with the world. These individual changes coincided with the rise of China as the largest manufacturer and the second-largest economy in human history[69]. The interrelationship between the transformation in the collective consciousness of the Chinese individual and China's emergence as an economic power does not necessarily imply the causation of the first to the second. Yet, upon reviewing the rise and fall of civilizations, the human component has most markedly created civilizational differences in the leadership and backwardness of nations.

Another "ugly" reading I came across was The Ugly American, an American book by Eugene Burdick[70] and William Lederer[71], published in 1958. Initially non-fiction, it was a true story based on Burdick's and Lederer's encounters with its characters during a visit to Vietnam. To avoid confrontation, the publisher chose to turn it into fiction, which further facilitated the exaggeration and generalization of some traits to heighten interaction with the novel. These efforts successfully placed the book on the

---

[69] World Economic Outlook Database, October 2023 Edition. (China)". IMF.org. International Monetary Fund. 10 October 2023.
[70] An American political scientist, novelist, writer, and co-author of The Ugly American.
[71] An American naval officer, writer, and author.

New York bestseller list for 76 weeks. Lederer was a high-ranking naval officer, and Burdick was a political scientist. Both were appalled at the American arrogance and incompetence in dealing with local communities and cultures in Vietnam during the Vietnam War (1955-1975).

The term ugly American was widely used to indicate the self-assuming and selfish American policy towards the world. At that time, the American approach was based on buying loyalty anywhere to serve its mega-enterprises' interests and launch attacks on the Soviet Union and global communism. In the Far East, American policy revealed the incompetence and ineptitude of American diplomats in their management methods, interactions with people, and how they chose their agents in those regions. Their motives were not humanitarian and even neglected the interests of the local population. To further their personal goals, they unfairly used their positions of power.

The Ugly American caused a change in the diplomatic policies of the US government towards their use of soft power. It was also a major catalyst for establishing the Peace Corps[72] program under the Kennedy government in 1961[73], which aimed at disseminating American culture and increasing Americans' knowledge of the world's diverse cultures.

This specific change was publicly and directly connected to the Ugly American. Later, numerous US military and diplomatic mission members endorsed the book's content and reinforced its credibility. These might have been skin-deep reconsiderations without substantial change in the core and objectives of their mechanisms, which is reasonable enough. The fact remains that this is the wildest dream of any author: that their book does create change. The Ugly American authors were as lucky as they could be in this regard! Yet, how does the difference in the mechanism and approach

---

[72] The Peace Corps is an independent agency and program of the United States government that trains and deploys volunteers to provide international development assistance.

[73] [Source] https://peacecorpsworldwide.org/establishing-the-peace-corps-the-ugly-american-part-5/

of American diplomatic procedures fit into this quest to outline the collective consciousness of the Nawāri society?

European and international societies were utterly oblivious to the existence of a country named Syria. It was misheard as "cereal", the crunchy breakfast staple, a situation I frequently encountered in the US. Out of these unknown quarters of the earth, the Syrian citizen was thrown into the limelight and turned into a global figure overnight. Syria's map, regions, and economic and social problems became more widespread and well-known than ever dreamed of! Syrians went up and down over hundreds of thousands of miles of seas, oceans, and lands and drowned and floated to reach safe shores in any corner of the globe. They were forced to be diplomatic envoys shipped to the world via death barrels bombarding their towns and cities by the Syrian regime. Media screens zoomed in on every action of this disheveled, dark-skinned individual with deep scars on their humanity. Under these lenses, Syrians were dissected, criticized, studied, and questioned globally. Their food, their daughters' costumes, their integration into their refuge, or lack thereof, and their attachment to or disinterest in their authenticity. This Nafar[74]/individual is currently the Orient's disreputable envoy to the world in the name of Syria and the Arab and Islamic nations. Whatever the verdict is, this nafar/refugee is always to blame for the downfall of their country, the rise of ISIS and its brutality, the satanically lavish lifestyle of Dubai Bling, and the extreme poverty in Mali. That ever-blamed Nafar/individual is responsible for everything except their dignity, individuality, feelings, dreams, and identity as human beings, which are to be determined for them by those who are in charge of casting judgment on him or her. This term frequently refers to an outsider with no identity, this person is but a mere number and only exists as a numerical statement. One, two, or eleven Nafars/individuals killed or drowned, and so on! This will always refer to a "Syrian refugee" swimming across the La Manche channel, a Syrian refugee girl scoring top marks in the SweSAT, and another male Syrian refugee beating a citizen in Belgium. Their blurred and featureless faces will never gain any features as they spread all around the globe. They were the

---

[74] A term commonly used by Syrians and smugglers referring to refugees trying to cross to Europe. Nafar in Arabic means an individual of men or a small group of three to ten men. The verb form of this word indicates hatred and repulsion.

offspring of a horrific reality to which they bore aversion yet remained its ever-embodiment, besides being accountable for it. It is survival the Syrian way. Before their aversion to dying in their homeland, they were featureless and had no individual existence but were mere Nawãr among the masses on a movie screen. The Nafar state is a singular case of solitude and isolation. It is more like grains of rice or bulgur that are separately identified but measurable as a whole! This quantitative approach to the Nafar/individual is not only adopted by Western spectators. The Nawãr similarly eyes their fellow migrant, following the Al-Nawãri's doctrine. Subsequently, this state becomes simultaneously a cause and an effect.

The Ugly Japanese is the third ugly I have tried to contrast with as much as I can in content and perspective. Authored by German author Friedmann Bartu, it provoked a backlash, as this 1992-published book was harshly criticized and utterly rejected. It highlighted the economic hegemony of Japan at a time when it was the second largest economy in the world and the way Japanese companies dealt with the Far Eastern countries in particular and the world in general. Bartu projected his observations of how Japanese companies acted upon individual Japanese and Japanese civilization as the source of this "economic arrogance," according to his viewpoint.

Received as a racist work, it viewed Japanese society condescendingly and unfairly, representing the opinion of a Western European author utterly ignorant of Japanese society's composition and cultural attributes. Japan, which has never been colonized, refused this biased critique by a person with generalizing impressions. This is my concern, which I persistently strive to avoid as a writer holding a single perspective illustrating the big picture of a society profusely filled with highly diverse and unique traits. As a Syrian author, and naturally a Nawãri, I seek to generally highlight some aspects of Syrian culture that I perceive as standing in the way of a real Syrian societal advancement. Creating patterns or stereotypes is not my target; I aspire to mimic an outline of the scene in front of me through my lens. The reader may agree with some of my observations and will inevitably disagree with many of them. These efforts at examination remain useful and even urgently necessary, at least from my point of view.

These "Ugly" books mentioned earlier used crude language and hyper-exaggerated what they deemed shortcomings in their nation's collective consciousness. From their authors' views, these defects were either core shortcomings in their cultural fabric or the product of false beliefs adhered to by those nations. At any rate, their criticism of the societies aimed mainly at pointing out and correcting defects, advancing society, and reaching a better future. In this book, the aim is not self-chastisement or renunciation of cultural and societal heritage. It takes a self-critical stance toward experienced facts and the intellectual and cultural responses that shape many practices in the society to which I belong.

However, this book in your hands does not summarize my observations from abroad or try to project some of these strange observations onto our societies. On the contrary, as an inside observer, my imagination was lit up with these observations as I was examining the human interactions surrounding me and what was written about them.

Reading such a social critique of societal psychological traits was not what motivated me to write this book. The real motivation was what I experienced firsthand through interactions with various groups in Syrian society and the direct adverse impact of our mutual dealings. Besides, psychological and intellectual traits stifled any interaction that had a positive and constructive impact among the members of our groups. Some of these are societal, while others are organizational. Apart from the broad affiliation with a group of people destined to inhabit a state of queerly outlined borders, the common factor is their almost identical interaction patterns. On one side stand the masters and elites, and on the other stand the rest, the Nawār. This palpable disparity on an existential level illustrates an ugly relationship between the members of one group, presuming the unity of conditions and destination.

The Nawāri and the legend

Many tales, stories, and legends were woven about the Roma, their origins, and their upbringing. Some believe they came from the lost continent "Atlantis" before its disappearance and stayed in the area of the Strait of

Gibraltar[75], where they learned all the magic arts. Moving in groups, they set out to all parts of the world to treat people and heal the wounded using therapeutic, religious rituals.

One hypothesis suggests they are a "Persian" sect bearing the Greek name Athinganoi, meaning the untouchables. They are magicians, charlatans, and fortune-tellers who came to Greek Hellas in the eighth century CE. Others claim these were the Egyptians who pursued the Jews and lost their way back. Contrary to this theory, some believe they are the Jews who fled from Egypt and roamed. Another hypothesis says they are the descendants of Jasas bin Murrah Al-Bakri[76], the killer of King Kulaib, who caused the Al-Basous war[77]. Among the wildest stories about the Roma and their origins comes one about a group of "thieves and vagabonds who dyed their skin using fruit juice for its chestnut hue and created a language of their own to protect their secrets."

This excerpt is from an unattributed online article about the Roma in Aleppo. Although it deemed these a collection of stories and legends, it indicated that their origin and history might probably be that of Indian tribes that fled from the brutality of ethnic genocide at the hands of Buddhists for converting to Islam. Hence, there are no accurate details on the history of a minority of approximately one million Syrians, according to some estimates (i.e., one out of every 25 Syrians), and nearly 20 million people currently among us in this world. There are few critical studies on the Roma and their origins, which might be attributed to the fact that they had no written form

---

[75] The Strait of Gibraltar is a narrow strait that connects the Atlantic Ocean to the Mediterranean Sea and separates Europe from Africa.

[76] Jasas bin Murrah Al-Shaibani Al-Bakri (464-534) is a brave poet of the Arab princes in the pre-Islamic era. He was called the protector, the savior, and the defender of Al-Dhamar for killing Kulaib bin Rabi'ah because of the she-camel of Al-Basous, the daughter of Al-Munqith bin Salman Al-Munqiqi.

[77] The Al-Basous is a war that took place between the Taghlib bin Wael tribe and its allies against Bani Shayban and its allies from the Bakr bin Wael tribe after the killing of Jasas bin Murrah Al-Shaibani Al-Bakri of Kulaib bin Rabia Al-Taghlabi in retaliation for his aunt Al-Basous bint Munqith, who was from the Bani Tamim tribe after he killed Kulaib, a she-camel that belonged to her neighbor Saad bin Shams Al-Jermi.

of their language but only an oral form through which they preserved their legacy in songs, music, and tales.

The Roma, Gypsies, "Zut,"[78] or "Nawăr" in the Levant date back as early as 1199 AD, when a large group of them, numbering around twenty-seven thousand, were captured during al-Mu'tasim's reign. Historical references mention that Ali bin Abi Talib[79] was the first to recruit the zat or sabja in the state as guards of the Basra treasury. The Roma of Syria were dispersed all across its governorates and regions, and mainly around big cities. Like all other ethnic minorities, they were not officially recognized or accurately accounted for in terms of their population and their living, educational, and employment conditions. The Nawăr of Syria mostly live in poor conditions, are cast off, and are disdained by all the communities in cities and metropolises, who regard them as no more than rogue gangs. People speak of their witchcraft, religion, and practices in theft, kidnapping, and selling of children, with no proven cases of such serious allegations. Yet, none is told of their folk and alternative medicine and dental implants, for which they have been famous for centuries.

Nawări, gypsy, Domari[80], Gurbati[81], and shawi[82] are among the many interchangeable and inaccurate names used to refer to a group highly

---

[78] Zut is an Arabized name for an ancient Indian people whose color tends to be black or dark copper tan. Al-Zat lived in Persia.

[79] Ali ibn Abi Talib (c. 600–661) was the cousin and son-in-law of the Islamic prophet Muhammad and was the fourth caliph who ruled from 656 to 661 until he was assassinated.

[80] Al-Domari is the worker who lighted and turned off kerosene lamps in public places in the old days.

[81] Gurbat in Urdu means poverty, lack of means of livelihood or deficiency of money. And is used to refer to the Gypsie groups seen around villages.

[82] Shawaya, or rural tribes, clans of sheepherders, or semi-nomadic Bedouins, are Bedouins who own more sheep than camels. It has been commonly used since the mid-nineteenth century AD to refer to all the Bedouin Arab tribes residing throughout Iraq, Euphrates Island, the middle and upper Euphrates Valley, the Levant desert, and the Syrian desert due to their partial migration from the desert and their displacement towards the countryside. By limiting their camel ownership for grazing, they managed to transform their nomadic lifestyle into a semi-nomadic

differentiated from the rest of humanity. In the collective consciousness of many, it is a group that best symbolizes the other and the opposite in an absolute sense. That other, who must be cut off, cast off, denied any similarity; this psychological relationship gradually developed into a rejection of existence that went as far as preceding hostility—even innate hostility.

For any "non-Nawãri" individual to feel absolute hostility and existential rejection toward the Nawãr, they must go through intellectual phases to take such a seemingly radical stance, which is semi-rationally taken based on some incomplete and fragmented logical judgments. These barely known names denote those who lack morals and humanity, of which they are ignorant, anyway. Attempting to probe the depths of the collective consciousness of Syrians, who resent the Nawrãna, might facilitate grasping our problems. I will provide brief and simplified definitions of these names. In my pursuit to support the book with well-cited and documented references, I collected and read everything written about the Roma in Arabic and English. I found no books by members of the Roma tribes representing their perspective in their original language or translated. They had no written language to chronicle their suffering and voice their opinions. The words "reading and writing" did not exist in most of their spoken languages, so they used those of other languages in the regions they inhabited when possible or if required[83]. The Roma's ignorance of writing and lack of records led to the loss of the original meanings of their customs and laws. Subsequently, all my impressions are those of an outsider. Here I am writing

---

one. They tended to own and graze livestock (such as sheep, goats, and horses). This consequently distinguished them from the Bedouins, who at that time only relied on camel grazing in Najd, Hijaz, and their outskirts.

[83] Jamal Haidar, The Roma: A Memory of Travels and Biography of Torment, Arab Cultural Center, 1, 2008, p. 11.

about the Nawār, as Pushkin[84] and Lorca[85] did before me, not knowing who I am writing about that well.

The Roma, a group of Indo-European tribes, previously lived in the northern regions of the Indian subcontinent near the Indus Delta. They migrated westward to the Middle East and Eastern Europe almost a thousand years ago. Some migrated to the east and settled in China and Burma (Myanmar today[86]). They were dispersed in small groups favoring the Bedouin life in closed communities.

During their Westward journey, the Roma were divided into two groups: one group headed north and became the European Roma, known as Roam and gypsies[87], and the second group went south and became known as "Domer", which means un-known tribes.

The Roma peoples are primarily divided into the Romani and Bohème of Europe, the Kawliya in Iraq, the Nawār in Palestine, Syria, Jordan, and Lebanon, the Salib[88] in the Arabian Peninsula, the Çingene Khorakhan[89] in Turkey, and the Kailash in Pakistan. In the Persian historian Hamza al-Isfahani's book "The History of the Kings of the Earth", the Roma have many names implying insults, such as Tatars, infidels, Arabs, Greeks, Turks, Jews, Pharaoh's people, Athenians, and fools. These insults are an

---

[84] Alexander Sergeyevich Pushkin (1799–1837) was a Russian poet, playwright, and novelist of the Romantic era. Many consider him the greatest Russian poet and the founder of modern Russian literature.
[85] Federico García Lorca (1898–1936) was a Spanish poet, playwright, painter, pianist, and composer. The Nationalist Revolutionaries executed him at 38 in the early days of the Spanish Civil War.
[86] Rohingya Muslims are one of the Roma tribes who have inhabited Myanmar since the eighth century CE. They are one of the most persecuted minorities in the world, according to the United Nations.
[87] It goes back to the Egyptians in English because the British believed that the Roma were of Egyptian origins.
[88] The Al-Saleeb or Al-Salib tribe is an Arab tribe whose lineage goes back to Luay bin Ghaleb. They were isolated in the Northern Arabian Peninsula until they began mingling with the other tribes by the mid-twentieth century.
[89] Çingene means gypsies in Turkish. Khorakhan is an umbrella term for Muslim Roma in the Balkans, Southern Europe. and West Asia.

attempt on the part of the urban area residents to exaggeratedly discriminate against the Roma for being nomadic loners or having a lineage to an enemy tribe or human group.

The Roma's language diversified as they dispersed in multiple areas; the diverse regional tongues of these regions influenced their varied languages. Each had its dialect. Domar[90] is an Indo-Aryan language spoken by several Roma tribes in the Middle East, especially in Turkey, Iran, Egypt, parts of the Caucasus region, North Africa, and India. Some of them share similar cultures and traditions. Until the late twentieth century, the Roma people continued to move around, leading a nomadic life. They are among the most persecuted peoples, having been victimized by settled peoples throughout history. They were exposed to aggressive practices such as forced deportation, deprivation of citizenship in the countries in which they resided, and deportation from various regions in Europe. In 1725 CE, King Frederick William I of Prussia decreed that every Roma person over eighteen should be killed. In Germany, all matters relevant to the Roma were the object of public hostility and were the Nazis' target during World War II.

The "most neglected people"[91] and "most oppressed minorities"[92] are a few of the nicknames for the Rohingya tribes, who are the most well-known Roma tribes in the world today. Despite their decades-long tragedy and the ethnic cleansing carried out by their country's army under the leadership of Aung San Suu Kyi[93], a Nobel Peace Prize laureate, no recorded testimony

---

[90] A distinction should be made between the Domrian language and the term "Domri", which refers to a municipal worker whose profession was to light lanterns in mosques, streets, and alleys until the introduction of electricity to cities and villages in the twentieth century. No city other than Beirut and Damascus was lit by electricity before World War I.

[91] Mark Dummett, February 18, 2010, "Bangladesh accused of crackdown' on Rohingya refugees," BBC.

[92] Myanmar, Bangladesh leaders 'to discuss Rohingya'". AFP, June 25, 2012.

[93] Aung San Suu Kyi is a Burmese politician, diplomat, author, and a 1991 Nobel Peace Prize laureate who served as State Counsellor of Myanmar and Minister of Foreign Affairs from 2016 to 2021. In 2017, many critics called for Aung San Suu Kyi's Nobel prize to be revoked, citing her silence over the genocide of Rohingya

has ever been heard from a member of these tribes about the facts of these events. Intergovernmental organizations and foreign experts took the lead in reporting on this tragedy. The international community, however, chose to look the other way, leaving them out in the dark without media coverage and being unresponsive to these unknown victims. The perfect victim to benefit from their suffering with no ado or inclination to rush to their rescue. The "nameless victim" concept is the "unknown soldier" who mocks our intellectual battles. A victim who got stripped of their humanity, facial features, and acknowledgment of their suffering. What a perfect point of argument for any political debate or intellectual agenda! The Rohingya tragedy and the persecution of the Muslims of Myanmar, formerly Burma, have been recurring since 1978, decades-long tragic realities without any self-narrative or trace to their side of the story.

For nearly a thousand years, the Rohingya were Roma tribes that inhabited what is known today as Myanmar. However, the government of Myanmar denied them citizenship and gave the go-ahead for mass killings against them to drive them out of their villages. In 2012, the Rohingya suffered violent acts and an ethnic genocide following an uprising that erupted in response to extrajudicial executions by Burmese army forces. An attack on buses carrying Muslims caused 11 casualties. Following the months-long crisis, the government promised the international community it would protect ethnic and religious minorities in Myanmar. However, the Burmese grievance narrative continued in the Muslim community for years, chiefly based on fabricated stories that cast enough doubt on their credibility. Many tried to alleviate the doubts and get the facts right, but the Myanmar government continuously committed systematic ethnic cleansing. Consequently, the number of Muslim Rohingya dropped from 3.9% of the total population in Myanmar in 1983 to 2.3% by 2014, according to a report issued by the Burmese government in 2016. Disregarding all evidence of crimes against humanity, the international community did not respond or express its concern, while the media dedicated no coverage to these crimes.

---

people in Myanmar. On 1 February 2021, she was deposed by the Myanmar's military and arrested and remains in Prison by the time of writing this book.

Finally, by 2017, the United Nations[94] and Amnesty International[95] had issued reports condemning the ethnic cleansing. Throughout these years, the Muslim Rohingya people's voice was not heard even once to tell their side of the story to the world. To this day, no international media outlet has ever given them that opportunity. Nonetheless, their tragedy is a reality that occasionally comes up in the news bulletin to remind the world that the Rohingya affliction still exists. But then, let us move on to the following news item!

Suffering that same calamity, the Syrian Nawãri became a hot commodity for the television of Barrel's government[96], besides a CNN program promotional poster that can later be recycled as a brochure cover for a charity. Yet, ever voiceless and without a cause, another victim the world needs to put down as a John Doe crime. Their narrative has to tell the story of a poor victim who complains to no one and accuses no one. It is not for them to use this right because this is the sole prerogative of whoever pays for their image as a commodity advertisement.

That Nawãri has been transformed into an icon for whatever ideology fancying its disfiguration. In Syria, Sharif Shehadeh[97] uses the victims of barrel bombs in the same exploitative manner that Moaz al-Khatib[98] would concoct whatever story would serve his purposes. The Nawãri alienation inspires all stories worldwide, true and fictitious. Only the Syrians are denied telling their story or dispute whatever is said about them. Usurping the Syrian self-narrative, the only medium where a victim can voice their pain serves none but those reporting this grievance. Serving as a means to an end, it achieves their interests while being utterly oblivious to the

---

[94] "UN condemns Myanmar over plight of Rohingya," BBC, December 16, 2016.

[95] "Rohingya abuse may be crimes against humanity: Amnesty," Al Jazeera. December 19, 2016.

[96] This is a metaphor for the Syrian government, which regularly used barrel bombs (plastic or metal barrels filled with TNT and schranples) during its military campaigns on civilian areas in Syria.

[97] A Syrian journalist best known for his defense of the Bashar al-Assad regime on satellite channels during the 2011 Syrian revolution.

[98] A Syrian Muslim preacher who presided over the Syrian National Coalition for Opposition and Revolution Forces for four months before resigning in March 2013.

victim's interests and needs, besides ignoring the negative or positive impacts of such a deed on the victim's welfare and future.

It is a sound argument that any party should be allowed to tell its own narrative, especially in these times of social media and open horizons. Nonetheless, it is arduous to establish a narrative. It does not exclusively orbit around the circumstances and story of the narrator, events, or temporal and spatial contexts. It takes finesse to structure its external perspective. External factors must be considered with due diligence, such as the recipient's culture, reality, and general knowledge of their surroundings. The key to turning an ordinary tale into a gripping narrative is to rewrite its structure in terms of its outward layout. Architecting such a well-tailored narrative requires a deep knowledge of all these details, which may shift the focus away from the cause and conditions of the victim. Therefore, the aching stories of victims boil down to sheer passing accidents and statistics, further pushing them into an abyss of injustice and denying them their voice and right to scream out their pain. For such an engaging structure, the author has to see through the eyes of the recipient and use their language. The victim has to present an audience-amusing show and not one of affliction. What a harsh plight millions and millions of Syrians have had to bear and put up with during the past ten years!

Hadol[99]: The others out there

Through tales, music, plays, and other expressions of folklore, people preserve chronicles of exceptional bravery, cowardice, self-sacrifice, and meanness. Even if official history overlooked or obliterated such moments, they contributed to what these human groups are today. Folklorists are known to have led historians and anthropologists to folk traditions that epitomize shared memory of centuries-long historical events, especially those that profoundly affected their lives. However, the colonial era and the emergence of nation-states in the former colonies necessitated the destruction of their peoples' authentic identities and the construction of a new identity more consistent with the administration and control systems'

---

[99] "Hadol" is colloquially used to refer to others. It is synonymous with the noun "these".

objectives. A newly created identity had to be formulated to have ample space to hold diverse groups lacking any sense of belonging. Though externally identified as a whole, any individual or sub-group within this seemingly unified body can distinctly detach themselves from this newly fabricated collective identity. Against this backdrop, a flaw is tolerable in the Syrian identity structure. This newly formulated state holds citizens older than its recent fabrication. While that individual or sub-group has no defined identity, differentiation strikes at the heart. Why not! After all, they are no more than the hadol/those out there.

In light of this discussion, the redefinition of where the Nawãrs' concept fits in Syrian culture reveals the negative connotations of this labeling. This term denotes an individual or a group denying others their right to belong. The past decade has increasingly witnessed discourse about classifying all others into one big category with a single identity different from what we are. This is the otherization phase. This is an act by which a group or an incongruous individual is ostracized or discredited. Thus, that other, who becomes the enemy, is dehumanized by highlighting their differences from us. Hence, the other's conversion and inclusion under the hadol/those-out-there categories are the early signs of that process. Consequently, the other becomes the antithesis of what the self is in its simplest and most abstract form. Simply put, everyone who is not me is the other.

The victim's affliction may easily be forgotten if they lack the jargon to formulate a narrative suitable for the recipient and appropriate for the outsider's perspective. In this case, more flexible narratives arise that best fit the goals and tastes of the narrator and the recipient. Even when a BBC journalist covers the crisis in Myanmar and interviews the persecuted Rohingya, the focus immediately shifts to the general perspective of the story. The journalist would formulate the narrative consistent with their initial impression, regardless of what the victim taxingly communicates.

Therefore, the disturbing noise made by the Nawãr's is an annoying clamor, muffled within their circles and received by none outside. This might not be their fault, the Nawãri, but rather due to the intellectual and moral deficiency of the recipient. This deficiency exacerbates and worsens their calamity, keeping the Nawãri people ever featureless and voiceless. In this state, they remain deprived of their individuality and soul; just a number in a pre-defined group heaped with preconceived judgments. Hence, they are Sunnis from a sectarian perspective, Arab Muslims from an international perspective, and third-world humans from a geopolitical perspective. They ever exist within a pre-limited group and are only perceived within a fixed context.

The Nawār legend is not a historical fable based on made-up events; it tells the story of a living, breathing person. The only issue here is that this mythical being has its features shrouded in mystery to the extent that they befit any proposed narrative. This narrative of grievances is a white label ready for any branding. Accordingly, the mythical being has no voice to tell their story. With a muted presence, the legend serves the narrator's dictation of the story rather than necessarily being theirs. The resulting version is formulated to indicate the credibility and validity of the external perspective that hijacks their narrative. Regardless of this outsider's motives for fabricating this new narrative, the result is either dehumanizing that Nawāri victim or producing a more accessible and encompassing stereotype to facilitate addressing their cause and being disposed of its complexities. By way of illustration, the Syrian issue gets turned into a Sunni-Shiite dispute, an axis of evil, against the regional forces seeking normalization with the enemy (Israel), or a civil war with economic or climate-related origins.

Turning the page to the closest neighboring country to Syria, it is not that safe to say that the Iraqi question during Saddam's rule was devoid of sectarian implications. For the West, sectarianism, especially the Sunni-Shiite dispute, was fundamental on the Iraqi scene. It gravely spiraled down and became the main focus shortly after the fall of Iraq's regime and the American occupation. It is worth noting that, despite its rootedness, the sectarian dispute was not a crucial issue in this dilemma until after the American occupation and the establishment of the sectarian- and regional-based quota system in government. The Iraqi society deemed the sectarian perspective central, influenced by the Western vision of Iraq. It was initially a concoction of the occupier's division of this colony to facilitate ruling and classifying its population. Despite the long-standing sectarian division, sectarian-based violence erupted in 2006, only after three years of US occupation and their fostering of sectarian identity. On the one hand, the media intensively highlighted the sectarian issue, finding ample justification in the regional geopolitical struggle with Iran. On the other hand, a great grievance befell the Sunni leaders in Iraqi society under the pretext of "de-Baathification" in an attempt to cut off ties with Iran and support Shiite forces in reaching positions of power. With these elements at play, the Iraqis were nudged into a stereotypical perspective that became their reality.

I do not deny the rooted and decades-long sectarian issue between the Sunni and Shiite components in Iraq, which further worsened during Saddam's rule. Nonetheless, larger and more complex divisions within Iraqi society are undeniably persistent. Some are regional and class-based, while others are ethnic, such as Arabs, Chaldeans[100], and Kurds[101]. All these lines of division were also fueled and escalated during Saddam Hussein's reign. These were not random actions and cannot be included in Iraqi grievances based on an American-Western conspiracy. This is not the focus of my book, anyhow. I only highlight the tendency towards adopting external perspectives of the internal identity in Nawăr society, besides self-redefining.

The essence of the other

The European mindset has abided by Essentialism[102] since the Greek philosopher Plato[103]. This perspective played a significant role in outlining

---

[100] Chaldeans are Aramaic-speaking, Eastern Rite Catholics. Most of them live in modern day Iraq and Syria.

[101] Kurds are an ethnic group native to the mountainous region of Kurdistan in Western Asia, which spans southeastern Turkey, northwestern Iran, northern Iraq, and northern Syria.

[102] Essentialism is a philosophical perspective based on the principle that all things have an "essence," i.e., an "idea" or "image" associated with a set of attributes. These attributes are essential to its identity and function. There is a form to the cow, e.g., its skin color, its face shape, and its udders. And the essence is associated with a cow's body, namely, giving milk, grazing, and cultivation. Through this essence, a cow's image is associated with milk, grass, a farm, and the countryside.

[103] Plato (428-347 BCE), is ancient Greek philosopher, student of Socrates (c. 470–399 BCE), teacher of Aristotle (c. 384–322 BCE), and founder of the Academy, a famous college of philosophy in the northwestern outskirts of Athens.

their concepts and ours about the world. It is based on believing in an invisible essence that determines visual identity and behavioral patterns. In modern times, these identities or phases are frequently assigned a direct relationship to genetic factors. We associate various features or stages, such as race, civilization, and sexual orientation, with an inescapable and irreplaceable genetic idea, bearing in mind that the genetic concept is more complex and dynamic. This concept does not only encompass somatic (corporal) traits such as race and skin color. It is also fundamentally connected to characteristics outside of the genetic makeup, such as underdevelopment, brutality, or laziness. In that sense, the essentialism of the black race is laziness and regression, and that of the Nawāri is un-civilization and non-humanity.

Developed to comprehend everything and everyone around us, essentialism is immutable. This means that the Nawāri lives on in this state, and the lazy are ever unchangeably lazy. It indicated their traits are also homogeneous, meaning that all Nawāris are brutish and underdeveloped. Essentialism entails discreetness in that blacks or Nawāris differ from other beings or humans. Eventually, it will be inheritable. The Nawāri's destiny has been sealed since birth, just as blacks, in the contemporary American stereotype, are sluggish and regressive from their earliest moments.

The British divided the Indian population into groups based on religious affiliation, which resulted in an essentialism-based differentiation between the two largest groups: Hindus and Muslims. This essentialism-based differentiation led to the destruction of the unity of the Indian subcontinent. The geographical distribution of these groups exceeded that of two rival states founded on religious essentialism. In addition, the subcontinent was split into four separate countries, along with other still-disputed territories. It is worth noting that the Hindu group, known today as a pan-religion, has never been a monotheistic religion and is not espoused by a specific ethnic or class group. During the British Mandate, as nowadays, Hinduism was just an umbrella term[104] with no clear definition other than referring to those brown pagans.

The word "Hindu" with a religious connotation was not extensively used until the late eighteenth century, whereas it is still figuratively used to describe indigenous traditions. Hindu nationalist ideologies and political languages are linguistically and socially highly diverse because Hinduism does not represent a specific religious group.

Consequently, the use of terms like "Hindu nationalism" and "Hinduism" in religious and nationalist discourse was controversial. At least for the British colonists, Hindus could be externally recognized as a uniform community. Thus, the colonial bureaucracy of Great Britain succeeded in creating meaningful "Hindu" symbolism within the general position of secular nationalism of the emerging "Hindu" Indian national movement.

The colonial era was not the only era that displayed Hindu differentiation from the rest. The Vijayanagara Empire[105] had the same tendency when the non-Muslim components of the Indian subcontinent's population united to confront the Islamic expansion from the West. Yet, this moment of differentiation and consolidation was short-lived. Besides, the groups gave this self-identity its label; it was negative in the sense of being formed to oppose the emerging Islamic identity. It was not an independent or well-defined identity.

During the eighteenth century, monotheism and the exclusivity of Christianity were the main influences on the British colonists in India. Consequently, when exposed to the various Indian religions, they were drawn to spot the similarities, though superficially, with what they were accustomed to in the Christian environment and adopt an over-simplistic approach. They mistook the different religious practices for one overarching tradition. Coming from a relatively highly literate society, they similarly

---

[104] Similar to the medical term "wastebasket diagnosis," it refers to any combination of symptoms without a clear diagnosis.
[105] The Portuguese of India established the Kingdom of Bisnaga in the Deccan region of southern India in 1336. Its rise staved off Islamic expansion in this region of India in the late thirteenth century.

believed that the Indian religion should contain legal texts, just as Christianity did. Their local intermediaries were mostly Brahmans, the only ones that knew the languages, primarily Sanskrit, due to the importance of studying ancient Indian scriptures like the Vedas[106] and the Bhagavad Gita[107]. Both the British scientists and their Brahmans translators produced a new law which was mostly from Brahmanical literature and ideology. They dubbed its origin to be is a single Hindu religion.

Despite having the third-largest Muslim population in the world, India is mostly considered a "Hindu" country. From a Western perspective, it is recognized as a Hindu civilization. Regardless of the fact that the British colonials brought Hinduism into existence in the nineteenth century. The word itself is of non-Hindu origin; the ancient Persians used it for the first time to refer to those who lived near the Indus River. Then, the Indian rulers used it as a suitable acronym for identifying non-Muslims and Christians. After that, it developed into a third division encompassing numerous religious practices, languages, cultures, and other groups. Not to mention, the Euro-Christian conception of religion is inapplicable to any of the several natural religions under the "Hindu" group.

It is inexcusable that such labels are still being used in the West, except for ignorance or a state of persistent "Christian fear of pagans". Assigning a single identity to richly diverse societies might be a natural tendency for highly organized and united Western societies. Nowadays, cultural diversity in many Western societies means exclusively politically appropriate identities. Therefore, there are specific stereotypes that individuals are free to follow. The issue is that this diversity takes a rigid stance toward true cultural pluralism, choosing to recognize some and ignore others. Neither the individual nor the group has the right to form an identity. Surprisingly, these adopted identities from an external perspective overtook and transcended deeper and more influential lines of essentialism in different

---

[106] A Veda is a collection of poems or hymns composed in archaic Sanskrit by Indo-European-speaking peoples who lived in northwest India during the 2nd millennium BCE.
[107] The Bhagavad Gita is a 700-verse Hindu scripture, which is part of the epic Mahabharata.

Indian societies, such as the caste system. Moreover, they canceled dozens of other languages and cultures for no other reason than being denied Western recognition.

To make matters worse, Nawãri society submissively falls for these external stereotypes of essentialism. In some cases, this destructive effect is exacerbated by adopting alternative categories of essentialism concocted to differentiate them from the outside world and their immediate surroundings. An ethnicity-based identity would be chosen only because it is detached from its culture, though initially, this was not a differentiating factor; some selected religious-based divisions in a more specialized manner. Others adopted Sufism[108] or Shafi'i[109] doctrine as an alternative identity. In other cases, a historical-based identity was invented by which to abide, as in Egypt with the Pharaonic[110] identity and Lebanon with the Phoenician[111] identity. These historical identities resemble a reliance on a myth rather than exerting due efforts to construct a new one that respects reason and is subsequently supported by its history and culture. Do present-day Egyptians eat Ancient Egyptian cuisine recipes and use hieroglyphic writing because

---

[108] Sufism is a mystic body of religious practice found within Islam which is characterized by a focus on Islamic purification, spirituality, ritualism, asceticism, and esotericism.

[109] The Shafi'i school or Shafi'ism is one of the four major schools of Islamic jurisprudence within Sunni Islam. It was founded by the Muslim scholar, jurist, and traditionist Mohamme bin Idrees al-Shafi'i (767–820) in the early 9th century.

[110] Pharaonism was an ideology that rose to prominence in Egypt in the 1920s and 1930s. A version of Egyptian nationalism, it argued for the existence of an Egyptian national continuity from ancient times to the modern era.

[111] Similar to Pharonism, Phoenicianism is a political viewpoint and identity in Lebanon that sees the ancient Phoenician civilization as the primary ethnic and cultural foundation of the modern Lebanese people, as opposed to later Arab immigration.

it is not a spoken language? Do Lebanese visit Attarte[112] and Eshmun[113] temples, reciting their poems about the Aqhat epic[114] written on papyrus?

Some Nawār tend to explore essentialism classification for differentiation; for example, by adopting a narrow-minded, intolerant religious identity, another one is created following similar bases. These foundations serve the purpose of denouncing everyone who is not us. This happened when the pro-revolution Syrians nicknamed all Syrian regime supporters shabiha[115], and the Syrian media outlets slandered the Syrian refugees in Turkey, calling them "Sourkies" or "Erdogan's Syrian mercenaries!". This differentiation of essentialism is comparable to the version crafted from delusions and the totalitarian simplification of the external perspective of those societies. In all events, the true identity of those societies gets lost. These fragmented societies will not be able to establish a cohesive and inclusive nation if they miss the chance to develop a contemporary and realistic identity,

Differentiation of essentialism is not limited to group versus group. There is another dimension between members of the Nawāri group, adding another layer to the differentiation produced by the projections of others' perspectives on us. To illustrate, we are recognized as sects and tribes, social classes, or separate regions. The differentiating dimension between individuals is crucial in formulating the Nawāri identity that views all others as their antithesis and enemy until proven otherwise. I've heard it many times: "I didn't know him or her, but he or she turned out to be quite decent!" In plain English, there is a presupposition that a stranger is not so decent, even if they are. Yet, there is no reason to refute this rule that whoever is a stranger remains, in theory, a not-so-decent person until conclusively proven otherwise. And because we lack the audacity to declare

---

[112] Attart was the Northwest Semitic equivalent of the East Semitic goddess Ishtar.
[113] Eshmun was a Phoenician god of healing and the tutelary god of Sidon. Eshmun. God of healing.
[114] Aqhat is a Canaanite myth from Ugarit, an ancient city in what is now Syria.
[115] Shabiha or Shabeeha is a term for state sponsored militias of the Syrian government loyal to Assad family. They became death squads upon the demonstrators in the 2011 civil uprising in Syria.

our selfishness, we constantly search for a name to call all who are not "us", bearing in mind that it has to be strange and contrasting, or at least different from how we perceive ourselves. Consequently, the necessity to create the Nawãr group. Those wicked Gypsies! Eventually, we are all one in being Nawãr and Gypsy thieves in the eye of the world.

Those Qurbat[116]!

Outrageously enough, the Nawãri may adopt the stranger's and oppressor's approach previously directed towards themselves, projecting that same perspective within their group. Through this exercise, the Nawãri deprives their fellows of the right to be different and the ability to break out of the intellectual and social mold to which they have unthinkingly surrendered. In addition, they deprive them of the right to own a narrative that does not follow another one or a grievance thrown at the entire group. The Nawãrs become the relentless guards, preserving and overseeing this myth's establishment, implementation, and preservation in theory and practice. Out of laziness or a lack of resourcefulness or knowledge, the Nawãr performs this act at some point because establishing an identity requires tireless efforts and thinking. No less work is a prerequisite for an identity to be defined, disseminated, and accurately reciprocated to the outside recipient. Given this, the Nawãri resorts to the myth as a quick fix to identify their "exclusivity" and the others' "otherness" for total differentiation from their surroundings, as previously indicated.

Yet, it is beyond belief how extensively this practice is spread among the Nawãr themselves, besides the mechanisms developed to guarantee its perpetual implementation. It detrimentally affects the Nawãr because these myths furnish a false sense of unity or occasional deep rifts, as previously elaborated. Surprisingly enough, the Nawãri embraces all these myths woven about them and adheres to the context and perspective most appealing to outsiders, validating their view and assessment.

How absurdly the Nawãri abides by these myths! To illustrate, it is queer how Arab community restaurants in the West mostly hang desert scenery

---

[116] Another slang word for Nawar used as a derogatory term in Syria.

paintings with Camels all over them, even though the majority have never lived in such places or ever seen, let alone rode a camel! How they willingly go for costumes that endorse Western stereotypes, for example, at Halloween or any multicultural gathering! How shocking that the Nawāri meticulously and wholeheartedly confirms and conforms to such false stereotypes! Even at moments of provocation and differentiation, the nawāri believes these myths to be their optimal models.

The inferiority and sense of otherization directed at the Nawāri in our societies are among the few shared factors between the Syrian opponents and regime cronies. Harun al-Assad[117] chose "Qurbat" to describe the American neighborhood residents in Latakia who dared to honk their cars' horns at him when he blocked off the street for a chat with his cousin Jackson al-Assad. Another instance was when the veteran Syrian dissident and journalist Fouad Abdel Aziz dedicated an article entitled The Revolution's Qurbat[118], expressing his disgust at a debate between Samira Masalmeh[119] and the Syrian opposition coalition. "I bet if the Qurbat carried out a revolution, their leaders would not have committed what you are doing nowadays to yourselves and against the martyrs!" he carelessly said. Imagine what our revolution would have been like if taken over by the Qurbat. And what makes a specific act "qurbati"? But before all this: who is that Qurbati?

"Qurbat, Roma, or Nawāri are all the same, swaying slender bodies clad in beautiful brocade dresses to please the beholder." This is just another example of constructing a negative counter-identity to be forcibly imposed on a particular group. This description of the Qurbat was not used against an opponent, envisaging them with their tattooed chins and foreheads and living in their kharabeesh (nylon or burlap tent). Instead, any human being who performs wrongdoing displays a trait of the Qurbat and Nawār. Thus,

---

[117] One of the cousins of the Syrian dictator and is linked to illegal drug and weapon smuggling
[118] Article was published in Zaman al-Wasl on January 9, 2017.
[119] A Syrian opposition figure and former editor-in-chief of the government newspaper Tishreen.

people dehumanize the Qurbat and include their opponents with this group to be mercilessly expelled from society.

The new identity imposed on this Qurbati group is subject to a new dynamic similar to external violence to which they are exposed. Through this new creation, external injustice and violence are embedded and turned into internalized oppression. This concept indicates the oppressed group's use of the oppressing group's methods against themselves! It occurs when one group realizes the inequality it suffers compared to another and desires to mimic the more privileged one. Marginalized group members may have an oppressive view of their group or assert negative self-stereotypes. Internal oppression may occur at the individual or group level or lead to conflict or discrimination within the group.

Apart from blaming the victim and justifying the violations committed against them, there are factors at play for understanding the dehumanization of the Nawãri and stereotyping them, which in turn facilitate the systematic and unapologetic racism practiced within the Nawãri society. On one hand, some of these factors pertain to the mentality and thinking of the Nawãri society that generates this racism. On the other hand, isolation and detachment on the Nawãr's part allow for the continuous and unchallenged aggravation of inferiority and otherization. Their discourse on the level of thinking and practice does not seek to justify their suffering from racism and ostracism by any means. It strives to understand how their tendency toward withdrawal and isolation, which exacerbate this state of marginalization and ostracism. This human interaction between a small and isolated group and another one is frequent. To illustrate, the Muslims face hardships in their integration into Western societies due to many factors, but one cannot ignore the extent of ostracism and racism to which they are exposed, the Rohingya's tragedy in their homeland due to the religious majority rejecting them, and the roots of several ethnic and religious conflicts in Africa, South America, and elsewhere. They get isolated as whole groups from their surroundings and are simultaneously exposed to preconceived notions, denying their entitlement to belonging or equality. Two parties are involved in this episode of injustice and unchecked violence, one of whom is overly authoritarian while the other is excessively isolated and detached.

Generally speaking, Sociology and psychology have conducted extensive research on the internalization phenomenon. It is a subconscious mental process through which characteristics, beliefs, feelings, or other individuals' or groups' attitudes are immersed in the self. They are generally adopted as specific to a certain individual. The intellectual features of those oppressed groups are the domain that lacks sufficient research in these disciplines. After understanding the structure of the negative identity imposed on the Nawār group, it is paramount to delve into the intellectual dynamics of its members and how they crucially shape their behavior.

A life of role-playing

Given that social rejection undermines a basic human need, its effects on multiple emotional, cognitive, behavioral, biological, and neurological functions are not surprising. As for the emotional responses, it triggers an increase in various types of negative emotions. Feelings of hurt are among the primary emotional responses, along with anxiety, anger, sadness, depression, and jealousy.

Social rejection impacts cognitive processes in two principal ways. First, it leads to the underperformance of intellectually challenging tasks, as proven by multiple studies. Second, it cognitively attunes people to socially accepted sources as a highly probable means of gaining others' acceptance. Moreover, socially rejected individuals show hypersensitivity to any signs of danger. By way of explanation, outcasts respond to a hostile stranger with correlative aggression, even within one group and all live within the same borders. Through this response to the aggressor, they often fulfill the aggressor's goal of being completely detached and alienated, facilitating their dehumanization by the aggressor.

Social exclusion extensively changes the cognitive and behavioral responses of the individuals, along with influencing the whole group of Nawār to regain social acceptance or avoid further social exclusion. Once those uninvolved in the primary disagreement are excluded, they activate what is known as the external "social monitoring system," which enhances perceptual and cognitive responses to social cues and information. Several studies[120] have confirmed that social exclusion triggers social behaviors demonstrating self-aggression against that community.

The behavior of the oppressed and excluded individual reveals their mechanisms to reduce the sense of oppression, which helps find an alternative affiliation for their protection from the ones to which they aspire. For example, the aspiration of belonging to the intellectual, wealthy, or white people categories leads the Nawãri to one of two actions. Firstly, the attempt to identify with the tyrannical oppressor by embracing the same degrading perspective forms a shield to avert the effects of that rejection. While this internal perspective reinforces the external injustice from which the oppressed suffer, it helps them attain differentiation within their group, giving them a sense of redemption from the "deficiencies" perceived and rejected by the oppressor.

Secondly, the cohesion with the oppressed and the construction of a collective identity, as per the real or imagined grievance, is founded upon the root cause for excluding that group and making it what it is. Skin color, religion, region, countryside, social class, and many more are a few of the causes. In this scenario, the deficiencies lie at the core of that group's identity, the bonding matter, and the unifying baseline. And thus, this nucleus of identity is embraced to the point of being celebrated as part and parcel of the collective identity that this new group constitutes.

In these actions, the introspection of an idea or its practice becomes inseparable from the intellectual functioning of those individuals. In this instance, they fulfill the role they assigned themselves. Shortly afterward, they are fully reincarnated. This role, initially established through a mechanism of psychological protection and resistance to oppression,

---

[120] For more information, see the following research papers:
1-   Twenge, J. M., Baumeister, R. F., Tice, D. M., and Stucke, T. S. (2001). If you can't join them, beat them: effects of social exclusion on aggressive behavior. J. Pers. Soc. Psychol. 81, 1058–1069. doi: 10.1037/0022-3514.81.6.1058.
2-   DeWall, C. N., and Bushman, B. J. (2011). Social acceptance and rejection: the sweet and the bitter. Curr. Dir. Psychol. Sci. 20, 256–260. doi: 10.1177/0963721411417545

becomes the principal intellectual axis on which these individuals base their thoughts, feelings, and identities.

As aforementioned, introspection is the internal intellectual reconstruction of an external stereotype. The sequential stages of this journey begin with reconstructing the process of an external activity internally triggered. To elaborate, oppression is externally practiced by the oppressor. Then its scope is extended through the interaction among the oppressed group members. Similarly, racism and sexism become internal practices within that group. Internal sexism is manifested in the sexist behaviors and attitudes of women towards themselves or other women and girls. At this point, the interpersonal processes of social exclusion are formed.

The second stage starts with transforming what is interpersonal into an intrapersonal process where the excluded individual becomes self-hating, believing in their inferiority. The transformation of the personal process into an intrapersonal process occurs through a long chain of events, of which a detailed discussion comes in the next chapter.

Consequently, the introspection process begins with learning the criteria, i.e., race and ethnic oppression, gender and sexism, social class, and class identity. Afterward, the individual gradually understands the reasons for their value or formation, which is finally incorporated into their view. Internal standards are said to be part of one's personality and can be manifested through one's moral actions. Nevertheless, a distinction between an internal commitment to a standard and what one externally practices or demonstrates is a possibility.

The sole influence on what an individual internalizes is their role model. Usually, such role modules accelerate the process of socialization and encourage assimilation. If someone respected by the individual demonstrates an endorsement of a specific set of rules, those rules are more likely to be accepted and assimilated. This process is called identification. Assimilation helps individuals identify and create their identity and value within a society that has already established a normative set of values and practices.

Taking all this into consideration, introspection is the integration of attitudes or behaviors into one's nature through unconscious learning or assimilation. People learn and internalize stereotypes through which they accept a set of criteria and values pre-established by other individuals, groups, or society. Hence, since dehumanization is agreed upon, let us be "non-humans" as requested.

Landmarks on the Road

A quest for the inception point

The pre-Arab Spring period and the gruesome post-Arab Spring outcomes in the Arab region primarily motivated this book. The explosion of the Syrian Refugee crisis in Europe triggered the unfolding of the Syrian dilemma on the world stage. Widely described as the popular movement coinciding with the Arab Spring, the undeniable fact remains that the vast majority of refugees were fleeing an open battleground and imminent threats to their lives and their children. Yet, the economic motivation behind choosing Europe as their haven was often implied. Moreover, political analysts had significantly laid all the blame on economic causes as the leading trigger of the Arab Spring protests.

However, the early stages of the Syrian economic dilemma preceded the 2011 uprising for many years. Since its independence in 1946, Syria has suffered decades of an unstable and turbulent economy. In 1963, the Arab Socialist Baath Party came to power and expanded the nationalization policies of unity with Egypt, and the government kept a sizable portion of the economy under control. By the 1980s, Syria had reached a point of being politically and economically isolated in the midst of a deep economic crisis, and the real GDP per capita fell by 22%. In 1990, al-Assad's regime adopted several economic reforms that proved fruitless for living conditions, and the economy remained immensely restrained. In 2000, Al-Assad's son took over the country and implemented shallow economic reforms that increased domestic production. Nonetheless, the selective open economy resulted in a spike in inflation and a continuous decline in annual per capita income.

By 2005, economic and living conditions had catastrophically deteriorated due to numerous US economic sanctions on the Syrian regime that had taken effect because of its role in the Iraq war.

In addition, significant segments of Syrians were internally displaced due to a drought that hit the Syrian desert (the Badiya). This environmental disaster, which hit the Syrian food basket focused in Raqqa and Deir ez-Zor regions, destroyed 55% of agricultural land and killed nearly 85% of livestock. Meanwhile, a political crisis coincided with this natural disaster. Abdullah Al-Dardari, the minister of Economy at the time, announced transforming Syria into a social market system[121]. For the Syrians, this meant the "Ramirization[122] of the Syrian Economy!" bringing to a close the stranglehold of the Assad family on Syria's economic future.

This declaration and the rapid change in Syrian market trends marked the obituary of Syrian agriculture and sealed the fate of millions occupying the Syrian Badia (Syrian Desert). They ended up in tin houses in slum areas on the borders of major Syrian cities. Consequently, nearly 600,000 people were internally displaced five years before the eruption of the revolution. This was not the spark or the rise of al-Assad's son to power after his father's passing in June 2000.

Then, what triggered the Syrian dilemma? Was it the economic crisis, according to some strategic analysts? Why did not any slogans highlight such economic demands throughout the months of demonstrations? Even if the economic deterioration played that role, it would be unfair to refer to the dilemma entirely for this reason. First and foremost, the Syrians rose against tyranny and screamed for freedom and dignity, not for higher salaries or more government support for commodities. It is a revolt that persisted despite the starvation and siege imposed by the regime on the strongholds

---

[121] A capitalist economic system that adopts a market economy but denies the absolute capitalist form and revolutionary socialism. It combines acceptance of private ownership of the means of production and private companies with government controls.

[122] The term "Ramirization" of the Syrian economy was used to denote the control of Rami Makhlouf, Bashar al-Assad's cousin, over it and the fact that a partnership with him is mandatory when a promising economic opportunity emerges.

of this revolt for many years. Reductive explanations of such an enormous problem have always been standardized and adopted in analyzing the Syrian issue. Devaluating the human factor of the Syrian revolution, particularly, and of the popular uprisings, in general, ruins the ability to understand and solve them.

A history lesson

The study of history is a prerequisite to Investigating any phenomenon. It is a broad term corresponding to past events, memory and exploration, collection, organization, presentation, and interpretation of information about these events. Everything authentically recollected and preserved constitutes the historical record, some written or photographed and others orally disseminated. History's discourse functions by identifying sources that can usefully contribute to producing accurate accounts of the past. History is a crucial component of life and thought. Events, memories, stories, and characters are meaningless without history. As the historical context interacts with the details surrounding an event, it helps us historically analyze events to understand the motivations behind people's actions.

Many impediments stand in the way of making the science of history an effective tool for such research. While history books' chief domain is narrating events chronologically, they regard their details and contexts as secondary. This perspective on history indicates our failure to factually and thoroughly study it. After all, history is not just archived bullet points and headnotes.

In German, history is called "Geschichte," meaning story, which was the vessel and carrier of history for thousands of years. The importance of the narrative accompanying an event in history might precede the event itself, representing one stream of that context. History is a narrative, even if marred by bias, considering that this narrative ultimately shapes the subconscious and influences actions and attitudes, whereas the events are mere passing incidents. History's current approach is to first read and zoom in on the events and later look at the narrative. This reduces our perspective on this narrative to a superficial investigation and a justification of historical events in a retrospective manner. This distorts history and sabotages the understanding of human historical consciousness, which is the leading motive for their work.

Whenever I explore the root causes of the Syrian problem, I find myself probing more into the post-independence history of Syria. The political topography of Syrian history is exceedingly complex. Most of its historical analyses often simulate a timeline featuring historical events from the political scene's development in Syria, overlooking any considerations beyond them. Even when a writer or researcher analyzes a historical event within its context, they address the subject matter by justifying it through the coinciding events or the overall situation.

I first explored and read about contemporary Syrian history. Contemporary History of Syria: From the French Mandate to the Summer of 2011, authored by Kamal Dib, portrays the Syrian reality throughout nearly seventy years. Like other books, its scope was limited to tracing the same events caught in the limelight and disregarding what lies beyond them. It narrowed its focus on regional and internal political events and some economic and social aspects while neglecting many details. Despite the writer's brief review of numerous economic and social aspects in Syria in the second half of the last century—probably the most informative section—his holistic approach overlooked the human factor, making non-politicians' mere pawns in the world events board. This geopolitically based view deprives people of any role in their history, which makes it undoubtedly deficient to the point of aggravating the feeling of powerlessness among individuals.

The study of the role people play in shaping history is still in its early stages. Cognitive ergonomics has not yet been engaged with history's discipline to reconsider its development and the construction of historical events. It is a scientific discipline that studies, assesses, and designs tasks, jobs, products, environments, and systems, as well as their interactions with humans and their cognitive abilities. In short, it is interested in mental processes, such as perception, memory, thinking, and motor response, because they affect interactions between people and other system components. Meanwhile, studying history remains restricted to researching human interactions with the historical context and examining the causes of events. To elaborate, why did the Arab Spring erupt specifically in 2011? Why do West and Central African countries not witness a similar spring, despite sharing more desperate economic conditions? Is it possible to test the theory of economic motives in making historical events in a country such as North Korea and understand why it did not witness a popular movement against its regime? Therefore, it is paramount to reconsider the traditional structure of the collected and stored history.

As aforesaid, the traditional narrative of history is chronologically ordered and event-driven, with a tendency to focus on individuals, actions, and intentions. Let us consider the French Revolution as an exemplar. A historian relying on the traditional narrative may be more interested in the revolution as a single entity that transpired in Paris. The primary focus may be on leading figures such as Napoleon Bonaparte[123] or Maximilien Robespierre[124]. Conversely, modern narratives usually focus on social structures and general trends. The modern narrative technique of history may replace strict chronology if the historian believes it better explains the concept of the French Revolution. A historian who adopts the modern narrative may highlight general features shared by revolutionaries across France. Yet, such a historian would illustrate regional differences from those general trends, i.e., several comparable revolutions. This same

---

[123] Napoleon Bonaparte (1769-1815) was a French military and political leader of Italian origin who rose to prominence during the French Revolution events. He led several successful military campaigns against France's enemies during its revolutionary wars. He ruled France in the late eighteenth century as Consul General and then as Emperor after restoring the monarchy to France.
[124] Maximilien Robespierre (1758-1794) was a French lawyer and statesman, who was one of the most famous and influential figures in the French Revolution. As a member of the National Assembly and the Jacobin Club, he urged the establishment of the Saint-Quillot Army to crush any conspirators against the revolution. He launched what was known as the reign of terror, during which he oversaw the arrest and execution of a large number of political adversaries, and his inclinations shifted towards dictatorship. He was arrested with several of his allies in the Thermidorian coup on November 9 and executed the next day.

historian may further use different social factors to demonstrate why different types of people support the popular revolt.

Narrative history records history following a story form and tends to reconstruct a series of short-term events. Since Leopold von Ranke's[125] influential work on the professional history of nineteenth-century history, it has been associated with experience. In this way, narrative history overlaps with "histoire événementielle," coined by the French historian Fernand Braudel[126] in the early twentieth century, who promoted forms of history-writing for analyzing long-term trends.

Historiographers began to take context and narrative more seriously in their studies in the past hundred years. Nonetheless, this approach is synonymous with traditional methods of historiography and is event-based and event-driven. Its ultimate goal is to justify and understand the event.

In any case, the multi-faceted aspects of history are paramount, as exemplified in the contemplative historical philosophy or "dialectics" of Hegel[127]. He strived to comprehend history, adopting a dialectical method between the thesis and its antithesis, followed by their synthesis. According to Hegel, folk history is termed reflective history. He argued it is not time-bound, transcends contemporary culture, and summarizes the dates or actual

---

[125] Leopold von Ranke's (1795-1886) was a German historian (1795 and 1885 AD) who is the founder of modern source-based history. Ranke set standards for many subsequent historical books as he introduced ideas founded on primary, experimental sources and an emphasis on the narrative history, especially international politics (foreign policy).

[126] A French historian and one of the founders of the Annales d'histoire économique et sociale. It is a group of historians associated with a style of historiography developed in the twentieth century by French historians to confirm the long-term social history. He is considered one of the greatest contemporary historians because he emphasized the role of large-scale social and economic factors in the making and writing of history.

[127] Georg Hegel was a German philosopher. He is considered the most influential founder of German idealism in philosophy in the late eighteenth century AD. He developed the dialectical method through which he proved that the course of history and ideas takes place in the presence of the thesis and its opposite, followed by their synthesis.

historical events. In other words, reflective history records a particular culture, country, or era and, at the same time, is no more than a byproduct of its time and confined to its narrator's opinions and biases. The best I can say is that it is the only way to comprehend philosophical history. It is the core from which the soul of events is generated and through which philosophers create history's goal. My disagreement with Hegel pertains to the inability to resolve the issue resulting from the excessive focus on historical events while considering the absence of historical events to be "dead times." Decisive moments are retroactively identified and realized after their time. The passage of time preceding the event, without which it would not have occurred in the first place, defines it. In light of this, which is more worthy of consideration, the unexpected phenomenon or the cause?

The Arab region's academia pays little to no attention to studying the conditions of the population and their social, economic, and cultural lives. I diligently traced word-of-mouth narratives and the tales of eyewitnesses who disseminated them; bearing in mind their inaccuracies and biases, the narrative is constantly more central than events. What happened is less important in our minds than what we think happened. The woven narrative hence becomes paramount in shaping identity, individual and collective.

Historians' current view of the human element remains constrained to extrapolating and monitoring their interactions with the event and their impressions. Recognized as merely responding to an ongoing occurrence, they are placed closer to the object state or, at the very least, the causal object. Thus, they are neglected despite being the real actors in shaping the passage of history. Shifting the compass to the human element on the terrain of historical events produced by human interactions is still not standardized within the conventional academic practice of historiography. Motion pictures and dramas have widely pictured historical landmarks where the event is in the background, not the star. These works are arranged in two parallel paths: the first is where the historical event is in the background, and the second is where the human story is at the forefront, illustrating only short-lived clashes between these two otherwise separate paths.

History is a human record. It comes out of a human-made industry in which humans take the seats of producer, director, photographer, and actor. This explains the pressing need to take the human component out of the backseats assigned for the historical crowd extras. Easier said than done. Hence, examining the intellectual aspects at the individual and group levels at a specific historical moment is crucial for profoundly understanding the course of history and its events, deriving a more conscious dynamic, and envisaging and influencing the future.

The purpose of shifting this perspective might be doubted as shifting the blame from the regimes to the people. In the manner of the Hadith of the prophet Mohammed, "As you are, as far as your actions are, so will be the rulers that will soon be set over you." The Holy Quran verse says, "Because of their sins, they were drowned."[128] It is not the intention of this book and is unacceptable to justify the injustice done to the oppressed by blaming them as the sole cause of their tragedy. To comprehend the historical context, we must understand how individual and collective thought developed among people living in systems similar to Syria. The course of historical events experienced by those populating a geographical area, such as Syria, profoundly affected their intellectual structure. These effects certainly played a role in determining the coming events.

The memory

I count it a privilege to come from a long line of centenarians. I witnessed three of the uncles of my grandfather born in Syria, never known to us. The eldest lived until the age of one hundred and four years. He was born in the Ottoman Sultanate in 1904, studied in the Mandate of Syria, and worked in Syria post-independence his whole life. Though he lost sight, he kept a sharp memory until his last days. Likewise, my late grandfather, may he rest in peace, was a quarter of a century younger than him. He offered me a realistic view of Syria in the 20th century as he experienced it. Considering these are subjective impressions, they still answered many questions about the social scene's development in Syria, apart from politics. I had not explicitly asked some of these questions and found none in the history books. Nonetheless,

---

[128] Surah Nuh—25

their word-of-mouth circulated tales vigorously conveyed historical image rich in details and implications of sizable events lacking in history books.

What distinguishes Folk History[129] is being fairly liberated from the temporal milestones profusely adopted by traditional academic history books. I do not recall coming across one of these centenarians talking about the 17th of April 1946[130] (the day of independence in Syria), as being a defining moment in their lives as such major event is expected to be. The Six Days War[131] is also marked upon as an insignificant, passing moment. Its political and military implications hardly have any effect on their lives directly. It was only noted in instances such as saying, "Before the Nakba, it was so and so" and "Since that coup, the case was such." Described in history books as grand, those events have no significance. My grandfather's uncles have never mentioned any unique recollection or specific incident that left a mark on their memory on the day of the coup of Hosni al-Zaim or Adib al-Shishakli. The margins of memoirs and calendars should have been filled with these events, not the minds of Folk historians and eyewitnesses of that era or a popular celebration of the launch of Damascus Radio or that of the establishment of the Syrian national football team.

Contrarily, folk memory perceives history as a series of complex, gradual interludes rather than pivotal turning points. Grand events do not outline folk history but individual and public conditions and their gradual transformations through time. These periods mostly hover across time without a beginning or an end. In folk history, certain narratives are found to structure the timeline with social phenomena instead of events. Such as mundane expressions about "when the women ceased to go out wearing sheets tied around their waists" and "when young men were arrested en masse from the mosques." Many of these are economically triggered, as in

---

[129] Folk history is a broad literary genre that falls under the historiography of a popular approach based on narrative, personality, and vividness of details.

[130] April 17, 1946, marks the commemoration of the evacuation of the last French soldier from modern Syria. It is an annual national day known as Evacuation Day.

[131] The 1967 war, also known in both Syria and Jordan as the June setback, is the war that broke out between Israel and Egypt, Syria, and Jordan between the 5th and 10th of June in 1967, where Israel was victorious.

the sayings about "when the dollar was equal to three liras" and "before they nationalized the sugar factory".

Despite the inaccuracy of these historical contexts, they indicate the perceived change and foretell the inception of a general phenomenon at some point. The exact moment of that change is not significant, but the sensation of its impact is the focal point. This change does not necessarily come about through a dichotomy of being or not being. Incidents such as a woman going out without a headscarf or a government employee accepting a bribe are not the least unusual. This social variable changed in terms of these incidents' frequency or the prevailing sense of their impact among a group. It is not conditional that the correlation indicated in their "folk tales" denotes a connection or a causal relationship between what is said and the events that might be attributed to those conditions and their outcomes.

History is not to be perceived in isolation from its very witnesses, who are none other than humans. Whether by action or inaction, this factor was primary in defining the path that history took from that moment.

Ailing Syria

Before the rise of al-Assad the father as an absolute ruler, Syrian society manifested signs of its affliction with a disease. His atrocious acts in the late 1970s and early 1980s irrevocably altered Syrian collective memory and consciousness. Politics apart, specific actions caused far more destruction than the 1982 events in Hama[132], which history ignored and lacked reliable figures. These events' beginning, frequency, and development cumulatively established a country primed for an absolute dictator to hijack. This caused the newly independent state, endowed with abundant natural resources, to regress into a dictatorship and acquiesce to the first military coup against its president, who sought to amend the constitution to maintain his position of power. In less than two decades, this young republic turned into a

---

[132] The Hama massacre occurred in February 1982 when the Syrian Arab Army and the Defense Companies, under orders of President Hafez al-Assad, besieged the town of Hama for 27 days in order to quell an uprising by the Muslim Brotherhood and resulted in tens of thousands of victims.

degenerate dictatorship, kidnapped by military men through pre-breakfast coups[133] and ending up in the hands of the Assad mafia family.

A brother killing a brother was far from the peculiar master scene of our human story, considering the backdrop of history stained with blood. What is shockingly peculiar is the prevalence and normalization of such a phenomenon, be it at the hands of Genghis Khan or Stalin. These events sometimes vary in quantity and violence without much change in severity. Murder is murder, regardless of its methods and motives, as well as arrest and torture. Normalization leads to its inevitable proliferation. Gulag[134] prisons inspired tyrants worldwide, bringing about Tadmur[135], Sednaya[136], and many more. In any case, torture acts are not limited to the confines of prison cellars in such countries.

During the past fifty years in Syria, documented systematic torture and killing were not committed within prison walls and intelligence basements but found their way to schools and even hospitals by none other than doctors and nurses, a most unusual and never-seen case in many other contemporary dictatorships. This case is not separate from deeper intellectual and psychological phenomena in Syrian society that led to the development of

---

[133] Since its independence, Syria has witnessed nine coups, which are: The March 1949 coup, the August 1949 coup, the December 1949 coup, the 1951 coup, the 1954 coup, the 1961 coup, the 1963 coup, which was later called the March 8 revolution, the 1966 coup, and then the 1970 coup that brought al-Assad to power. He called it the "Glorious Corrective Movement." All coups took place between 2.30 a.m. and 7 a.m. The joke was that whoever got up earlier had the coup d'état that day.

[134] The gulag is the name given to the Soviet concentration camps. It is a Russian acronym for Main Camps Directorate. The Soviet Union housed 18 million detainees, and nearly two million died.

[135] Tadmur Prison was a military prison located near the desert city of Palmyra and its ruins. It primarily imprisoned political opponents. In 2001, Amnesty International published a report describing it as "designed to inflict the greatest suffering, humiliation, and fear upon its inmates."

[136] These are military prisons near the Syrian capital, Damascus, operated by the Syrian government. It held thousands of prisoners, including civilian detainees and political opponents. It is affiliated with the Syrian Ministry of Defense and under the management of the Military Police. Amnesty International described it as the Human Altar in a report on its work during the Syrian revolution.

the idea and practice of this horrific violence by ordinary individuals. Furthermore, they were socially normalized and lost their oddity, which typically made them shocking and unacceptable. The absence of any forms of protesting, along with their justification or welcome by much of the Syrian public, cannot be exclusively linked to authoritarian violence.

The collective interaction with the tyranny of authority contributed to its normalization and legitimization. This normalization was another tool for criminalizing and double punishing the victim. When a person disowns his brother only because of his arrest by the intelligence service and fearing a similar fate, this distinctively signals how society is infested with repression and brutality. The victim would be released to find themselves ostracized due to their suffering, not despite it. This is the height of extreme cruelty. It cannot be excused or overlooked, especially when addressing how the social contract disintegrated, and society fragmented under tyranny.

Some actions are detested for what they are or for their effects. There might be a lot to observe about a phenomenon such as widespread bribery. Among these details are its moral corruption, the devastating economic impact on some, and its outrageous benefits to others. The target of discussing such a phenomenon is not to separate it from other factors and impacts that shape the collective consciousness of a nation. In an era in which bribery and all forms of government corruption are an open everyday practice without much of a blink of an eye by anyone involved or present, it has become a means of sustenance for millions. This indicates deeper problems within the relationship between that human group and its surroundings. The advent of that era signals that this group is poised to be seized.

I illustrate bribery as an example not out of moral righteousness or an ideological stance but for its representation of a critical aspect of social disintegration where collective identities mostly fail. In this context, the system enables the oppressor to legally reinforce their injustice, and the right-holder must defend their natural rights by habitually asserting them. Bribery consists of two independent crimes where the briber exploits the process to achieve their own interests rather than those of others. And the bribed party prevents the vulnerable from exercising their rights and favors those who provide a direct benefit.

An intentional crime by an unpremeditated duo. The achieved benefit does not certainly address the two primary social problems of poverty and vulnerability unsatisfied with government job salaries and suffering from the neglect of the administrative structure that, per definition, should protect and guarantee individual rights. In different scenarios, roles swap in people's minds between who is "usurped" and who the "usurper" is. In any case, the victim of this crime often remains oblivious.

The social rejection of political prisoners and the wide acceptance of bribery are among the most horrific things Syrian society achingly experiences. Though secondary to the book's context, these acts are not the sole intention of noting them. I aim to demonstrate how, in the 20th century, Syria suffered a societal regression that was not exclusive to the Syrians, but they symbolized this role in the minds of many. Also, my purpose is not to place the blame on the Syrian people or justify what they have endured over the past decades. These two aspects might have coincided with al-Assad's rise to power, appeared during the earliest period of his rule, or preceded him for several years. Irrespective of the beginning of their outbreak, their prevalence in society is correlated to being captured by the totalitarian regime established by al-Assad.

This is no moral sermon but an attempt to highlight some of the prevalent aspects of societies caught in the web of oppressive regimes, in which the social contract between its members collapses. This collapse paves the way for authoritarians to take charge. It is not an overnight process, nor does it start with an event to mark the end of the old world and herald a new one. Stealthily creeping up on society, they would wake up to a worsened reality.

In my opinion, it would be invalid to causally link the corruption demonstrated in Syrian society with the rise of a dictator. It is unfair to regard this complex issue reductively; needless to say, it would mean directly and utterly holding the victim accountable. Besides, considering repression and political atrocities to be solely responsible for the prevalence of these phenomena would be equally reductive and unfair. Such a denial of responsibility is similar to denying the eligibility for the human component.

Hence, other factors and reasons could change the viewpoints of the two sides, namely human corruption and the exacerbation of oppression and tyranny. It is prime time to deem them the results and symptoms of a much deeper problem in these people's social and intellectual structures. I attempt to project this dialectic onto modern Syrian history in certain sections of my book.

Therefore, it is significant to recognize the individual and collective role of our convictions and practices in shaping the outcomes of our experiences. For that reason, we must escape the dichotomy of criminalizing or victimizing the individual in this context. The oppressive tyrant would choose the first option to be rid of the blame or the second to be a supporter out of sympathy. Each of these two approaches guarantees the continuity of the status quo. Due to how history is documented, I believe events were our means to build grievances suitable to our situation. This inverted approach to history deprives us of many possible lessons to have learned. Rich in events and eras, history metamorphosed into an ideological weapon meant for justification instead of reserving wisdom and valuable lessons. In essence, it is not to be made by emperors and intellectuals but by people who make the most of the opportunities available to establish an approach that eventually serves their interests.

The illustrated intellectual and moral factors are not emerging cases for humanity, meaning they did not materialize out of nowhere. Monitoring their emergence as an isolated phenomenon or their prevalence in a society is not the goal. On the contrary, other tangible variables that coincided with their spread are the focus. Thus, this book monitors and analyzes behaviors and practices to determine the significance of tracking these phenomena and the periods of their prevalence. Once again, the goal is not to pass moral judgment but to track other concurrent changes that are inaccurately defined. It does not adhere to scientific standards for studying and measuring them. Notwithstanding, it is worth noting that monitoring individual behavioral phenomena and their prevalence in society positively impacts this book's relevance to the proposed topic, which is the concurring changes to these phenomena in Arab societies.

To elaborate on this connection, I illustrate an example frequently featured within mosque walls in Friday sermons and scholarly messages. They totally blame people's weak religious faith for their suffering from widespread poverty. In doing so, they utterly reduce many concurring factors to these two phenomena that might be mere symptoms of a more profound transformation in the reality of those societies. This attitude reads causality backwards or confuses correlations for causality.

In history, there is no ground zero. People's consciousness has no tipping points. Instead, humans hold on to recollections of detours under no specific dates or within no definite geographic borders. They get a wake-up call to a different reality, and these once-detours are finally recognized. History is not a spur-of-the-moment event and thus is chronicled under no date of effect. It creeps upon us amidst the hectic movement of life. No specific moment of any nation's decline or progress or fixed triggering phenomenon is known for these states. In this context, the advanced or degenerate states of society in an era are marked by the prevalence of some social phenomena. To explore a causal relationship between these phenomena and states would be a dead end. The much-aspired zero point exists only in our minds. For individuals, each zero point is unique to us and our experience. It cannot be transformed into a reference in the mainstream of general history. As for the phenomena under observation at a specific stage, these are more reliable references.

There came Spring!

Like the majority of my generation, I was thrilled to witness the first massive popular movement ignite simultaneously in seven Arab countries[137]. Besides, Jordan and Morocco had widespread protests and demonstrations.

Though unpremeditated, the spark of the Arab Spring was a decisive moment. Great expectations awaited this moment, which would have been pivotal in the history of the Arab region and the world. These popular movements were spontaneous based on their slogans, lack of organization, and absence of stated demands. Yet this sense of spontaneity had a deeper

---

[137] Tunisia, Egypt, Libya, Yemen, Syria, Bahrain, and Iraq witnessed popular movements during the Arab Spring in 2011.

mark on our interaction with these movements, stimulating our collective role as expatriates. Sooner than later, this sense of spontaneity spiraled into an issue that hampered their growth and development.

It is not difficult to answer a question about when the Arab Spring first started. The resounding answer is when al-Bouazizi[138] set himself on fire in a public square in Tunisia. However, it would be gullible to say that this action was the drive and cause of the Arab Spring, believing nothing paved the path to it. Despite its symbolism for the movements, this moment of al-Bouazizi self-incineration is a coinciding phenomenon manifested on the surface of Arab societies. The real reason is too deeply embedded to be laid over this book. What can be discovered here is a reference to these invisible factors, which is one of the book's significant goals. When does the spring season start? Before checking the calendar, we must agree on what this season is. If we refer to the 21st of March of every year, say, as the time for the vernal equinox and its start, this may suffice as an answer for some people. However, what if that day is chilly and snowy? Would we still call it springtime? What if a warm day in the heart of February precedes spring? Does this mean spring starts earlier than usual? A host of features, including the flowering of trees, the mild weather, the length of the day, and their persistence, come together to create springtime. One or two warm days or buds on tree branches do not announce the arrival of spring. It is difficult to determine its beginning except when we feel the weather has certainly changed.

This is how the precursors of the Arab Spring revolutions felt, especially for the residents and citizens of those regions. Ironically, most observers anticipated the coming spring in neighboring countries before experiencing it in their homeland. During my first visit to Egypt in 2008, I was appalled by the extreme poverty and unexpected levels of social injustice, besides the unfathomable livelihood disparity between slum dwellers and palace residents a few yards apart. More than anything else, I was in awe of how a

---

[138] REF xy: Ṭāriq aṭ-Ṭayib Muḥammad al-Būʿazīzī; (29 March 1984 – 4 January 2011) was a street vendor who set himself on fire on 17 December 2010 in Sidi Bouzid, Tunisia. His action ignited the Tunisian Revolution and the wider Arab Spring movement against autocratic regimes in 2011.

generation of well-educated and enthusiastic youth could take risks day after day to make a better reality. The forms of social class hierarchy and the obscene wealth of a small leading group in that country were grotesque to the naked eye. As I was leaving, I felt the revolution in Egypt was past due and fully eligible. Most of these indicative factors might have been similar in Egypt and Syria. However, in my assessment and that of many others, it was far from likely that Syria would witness a widespread popular movement with any momentum. Then the Arab Spring proved us all wrong. These same traits were present and prime in Syrian reality, unnoticed by me as a Syrian citizen at the time. Communicating with the revolutionary, educated youth in another country was more accessible for me than it was with my fellow citizens in my country.

This paradox alerted me to reconsider how I, as an individual, view society. My inability to infer the general status of my society was shocking to me; I am one of its members who fully know its conditions. However, as an outsider, I could identify similar phenomena in another society. Looming on the horizons of these two societies, I could spot them in one and be blind to them in the other. I miscalculated the human component of this equation. In this aspect lies one of the most crucial reasons for the delay and failure of such a revolution.

Amidst the roaring Arab Spring, the Syrian movement stands out notably for its long-term duration and the five stages it underwent, transforming it from a peaceful popular movement to an armed one. Then, as a civil war, it swiftly devolved into a regional conflict run by proxy until its recovery, at which point the state reclaimed what was out of its control with the support of its foreign allies. In a 360-degree spin, it ended where it began with peaceful demonstrations and movements, albeit landing on a small scale in a constrained territory.

This shift in the movement's form and structure intensified the outline of the intellectual aspects that led to the status quo. From a simple, reverberating slogan of Allah, Syria, and Only Freedom, the Syrian movement soon brought forth several courses, each having its own goals, agenda, individuals, and financiers. No matter how hard we tried to blame these divergent paths on outside forces, several internal forces exacerbated our tragedy. Although all the external actors on the Syrian scene, including the intervention of foreign armies and militias and the emergence of extremist and nihilistic jihadist movements, regenerated their courses, internal factors regenerated theirs. After ten long, bitter years, our hearts bled at the slogan Allah, Syria, and Only Freedom resurfacing in Daraa and As-Suwayda in 2021 and onward. On that note, it might be tempting to blame geopolitics for the course and conclusion of the Syrian revolution. However, the assumption that the Syrians were mere pawns on the regional powers' chessboard is categorically unacceptable. A popular movement with such momentum and perseverance cannot be powered or driven like a herd. Being their own decision-makers, does this not entail these people having a say in setting their course? They must be responsible for its creation, even if partially. Accordingly, I explore the depths of the individual and collective mindset of my nation. I strive to understand how the Syrians found themselves in a state of displacement, defeat, and loss of purpose. This is done with full awareness of the myriad of outside influences that played a critical role in the destruction of this revolution. We, Syrians, could not stop or change our course away from the intervention of Hezbollah, Iran, and later the Russians and the failure of the "Friends of Syria[139]" group to fulfill their pledges or respect their set of boundaries. Everything that happened had an irreversible outcome. My quest is to probe our inaccurate attitudes and actions that detrimentally affected this popular uprising at its critical moments, especially since they are persistent behaviors and practices deeply rooted in the Syrian individual consciousness on a collective scale.

In the cradle

In 2012, Syrian civil activists focused on relief work or on supporting the militarization within the Syrian civil movement in response to the repression of Syrian voices and their demands. I was drawn to contemplating the

---

[139] The Group of Friends of the Syrian People is an international diplomatic collective of countries and bodies convening periodically on the topic of Syria outside the U.N. Security Council. They are often referred to as the 'London 11' (Egypt, France, Germany, Italy, Jordan, Qatar, Saudi Arabia, Turkey, United Arab Emirates, United Kingdom, and United States.

reconstruction phase amidst all that was happening. At that stage, my idea was met with sarcasm and denunciation. As a Syrian, I closely experienced the economic and social conditions before the spark of the Syrian revolution. Therefore, I believed economic factors took precedence and required more attention at that time, regardless of where the conflict was heading. Economic factors and sustained development were not included in any agenda nor part of any plan, though they exceedingly influenced the revolution's outbreak and were critical in affecting the country's stability in war and other times. The 2011 Syrian revolution was not driven by hunger under any circumstances. Yet, economic injustice, in my opinion, partially accounted for driving the youth to take to the streets and protest against the regime. The injustice in wealth and income distribution was rather the cause. Additionally, this regime was built on rampant economic corruption after strenuously eliminating all forms of political action and political and intellectual awareness in its foundation of horror. The economic insecurity in any of the liberated areas will bring about their destruction. Unfortunately, my doubts have come true over time.

In 2013, we named a small development project the Mihād (Arabic for cradle). It was established through the collaboration of experts in economics, sustainable development, and human development. Its area of work was building individual capacities identified by Mihad's specialists and directly requested by activists and local managers within liberated Syria. The project worked closely with the target groups, who explicitly acknowledged the need for training but showed no interaction with this civil initiative. No funding institutions involved in these courses cast doubt or concern in the case of collaboration, and no international or regional forces would bring accountability or discredit! Established as a small talent bank, the founding group of Syrians planned for Project Mihad to develop multiple administrative and organizational capacities and skills commonly used in the public domain and necessary as part of collective duty.

Out of more than two hundred registered attendees for the first workshop, only ten showed up for the first workshop and five for the rest. In the post-session evaluation, the vast majority of the no-show individuals responded that these skills are immensely significant for all activists, especially when they do not know any of them. Yet, the respondents affirmed their knowledge of these same skills! Coincidence! We stumbled upon another one in the following stage: it was a competition in which the participants would provide project studies and win funding from the initiative. The performances of each participant demonstrated their absolute lack of knowledge of the skills which they believed were present in no one else but themselves! Being oblivious to one's inadequacies was a familiar trait among fellow Syrians, who are well-acquainted with each other. On the other hand, it was a shock to those who had not dealt with Syrians previously. It was a revelation of an aspect of our character and collective consciousness.

Our short-lived experience with Project Mihād was not unusual. Several institutions that previously exerted the same efforts shared similar observations. These had nothing to do with the circumstances of the Syrian revolution or its urgency at the time. Our colleagues who previously collaborated with the United Nations Development Program (UNDP) and the Aga Khan Foundation encountered similar interactions with various local communities in Syria. Whether the target group was university students or farmers in rural areas, irrespective of geographical, social, or economic status, we had the same response and outcome. That interaction was mutual among versatile target groups, who also showed identical mindfulness of what they found defective in others without realizing its existence in themselves, even if such defects were evident to others!

Before Project Mihād, my understanding of the Syrian economy and how the human factor is positioned was lacking. Syria is one of the few countries that still has half-century-old cars buzzing around its roads. In a closed economic system, Syrian labor had no choice but to be skilled enough to operate, produce, and continue to function with whatever low-tech or old equipment they possessed, without government development and devoid of any quality standards.

Nothing is beyond the Syrians' skill at fixing anything! It is quite a marvel in many Gulf countries. In neighboring and oil-rich countries, people have long heaped praise on how the Syrians are dexterous and can do wonders! They are skilled craftspeople! They are good with their hands! For them, nothing is impossible! However, there is a different facet to this blinding aura of superhuman capabilities, lurking away from the public eye and strange to many. Despite this widely attested manual and technical dexterity, if the Syrian master craftsman or craftsperson meets anything outside their expertise, a disaster is imminent. Syrian master craftspeople may repair a seventy-year-old machine, yet they cannot provide contractors with specific pricing or a definite timeline. In these matters, one would get confusing answers, such as something between ten and fifteen thousand! or probably two to three weeks! Amidst this predicament of inaccuracy and non-commitment, there is only the master craftsman to run the show.

In Syria, blue-collar laborers are ranked as master craftspeople and apprentices (called boys in Arabic). Not above or beyond. Also, for two master craftsmen to co-work, it is close to taboo. It would be a risky cobweb in which no one would wish to be caught. Even if one had a gathering of five master craftsmen, group work is nearly impossible. There would only be five individual master craftsmen. The only alternative is to have a master craftsman and four boys (apprentices). These two work scenarios reflect authoritarian tendencies in labor relations.

Labor relations in Syria demonstrate an authoritarian and victim dichotomy that has influentially destroyed all forms of joint action, whether in trade and business or civil and charity work. A caricature of how an entity suffers division among siblings or heirs after their father's death or that of its founder can be found all over our marketplaces and in satirical TV shows. This translates into a tangible failure in the Syrian-Syrian action, resulting from the inability to interact and criminalize everyone under the pretext of a few. In Chapter 4, I elaborate on this aspect in detail.

Once again, the Syrian revolution was not out of hunger, despite the general economic vulnerability that Syria experienced a decade before. The movement was diverse in its participants' social and educational backgrounds and particularly more forceful in rural areas than in cities. The front rows of the demonstrations had holders of higher academic degrees alongside merchants, farmers, and blue-collar laborers, signifying that it was not a marginalized or rabble movement. While not in the best shape, education in Syria is not worse than in any other Arab country.

Technical know-how, favorable economic situations, and educational opportunities were not the decisive issues for the collective Syrians. The Achilles heel of any possible Syrian Renaissance does not lay in education, funding, experience, or technology. It must also be noted that these factors effectively triggered the path towards the aspired-for renaissance and reconstruction—the first since Syria's independence or the first ever in more than five centuries. At this point, the social behavioral factor is worth highlighting. On this basis, we had to address this critical factor, even amidst an all-out war ravaging Syrian geography and social structure. Whether it is a matter of a common nature, a culture, or a collective consciousness, we must stare into the abyss. Hence, my book comes as an effort to trace some factors that make these behavioral phenomena common in our society. Accordingly, I outline some common behaviors demonstrated in other communities with which I interacted. These may be specific to my experiences, my society, and the temporal frame of producing this book. Also, some readers may have seen a few of these in their own societies.

All in all, I present my personal perspective on human experience that will give an account of mutual, general aspects. The Nawāri's features are, unsurprisingly, relative to what some observers could detect in other communities, such as East Europe or North America. The distinctness of these aspects in our society does not make it exceptional in and of itself, but rather their overlapping and intertwining in our fabric within historical, political, and civilizational conditions. I spare no effort in underlining them to introduce my observations without excessive exaggerations or blind generalizations.

Project "Mihād" was not an exceptional experience in any way. Throughout relief work and political activity, a set of recurrent instances gradually revealed how a human tragedy could undermine any efforts exerted on the Syrian issue by the Syrians. These were carried out in the opposition's National Council, the opposition armed factions, and the local councils that emerged in the liberated areas. They manifested how intellectual failure and what resulted in organizational, political, and moral dysfunction substantially sealed this revolution's fate. Accordingly, one of the most promising human revolutions lost its confrontation with the brutal and criminal machinery of the totalitarian Syrian state affiliated with Al-Assad's name.

This book was initiated by a limited experience supporting popular movements within the context of the Syrian revolution. It continually expanded in complexity to include the history of the human journey and in-depth aspects of the rise and decline of peoples and civilizations. It started with the depiction of the Syrian Nawãri until it progressed to comprising the intellectual features of any human group. Naming Syrian society is set as an example merely for its relativeness to my experience. This does not restrict these phenomena to just Syrian people.

Shifting gear

In 2013, people lived overwhelmingly grievous moments, watching the Syrians killed and displaced, losing their homes, livelihoods, and futures. This corresponded to a dead end for any solutions in the political and military arenas. At that dark moment, I was watchful for signs or clues to help me read into the destiny of Syria and Syrians once the regime had fallen and stability prevailed. Several questions were looming over our horizons. Shall we "Somalize"—follow the trajectory of Somalia after its civil war—or "Germanize," following in Germany's footsteps post-World War II? Are we on the verge of a prosperous reconstruction phase that will transfer our country to a post-industrial economy? Or shall we end up at the mercy of international organizations without much development or solid reconstruction foundations?

It is an extraordinarily challenging endeavor to forecast fate since it is a matrix of interwoven, complicated components. An economic "Marshall Plan" does not represent a crucial construct in all post-war and disaster reconstruction experiences. International concessional loans were also not an instrument for activating or discouraging economies during recovery. It is the people who have always been fundamental in seeing into the future of countries during recovery and decisive in this equation. This human factor is dependent on two primary criteria. The first is their training and technical preparedness, which I consider secondary. The other more paramount criterion is a social formula that interconnects people and interlocks their land into a shared social ground. Yet there is an eternity-absent code of conduct that must take precedence.

In 2013, the Syrian revolution underwent a transmission phase, similar to shifting gears in cars, where it was unsustainable to continue at the same pace. The opposition political system's transmission incessantly revolved around fueling militarization at any cost and urging international intervention to back the Syrian revolution. Other attempts pushed towards saving what remained of the civil movement and constructing a national pact. Besides these, some had a smaller scope and were more secondary than the previously mentioned. I was honored to have taken part in one of these similar small-group projects.

Global-scale events followed that milestone, each of which could be considered critical in its own right. These include the proclamation of the Islamic State in Iraq and the Levant (ISIL or ISIS) and the international intervention against it, without much compromising the ruling regime in Damascus. These coincided with an escalation in Iranian and Lebanese military interventions and, later, Russia's military intervention to support the regime. These were massive game-changers that tremendously affected the Syrian revolution. Yet, there was always another flip side to that on the news bulletin. It reflected the highly divided interactions of the Syrians in response to those events. They were integral to the process of addressing the issue and substantial in concluding the final scene. It is the sole and irreplaceable factor that we—the individuals and the human group—have in our hands to decide.

Derailing from its peaceful course to a militarized phase may seem like an outcome of impromptu circumstances, geopolitical implications, and an escalation of al-Assad's state terrorism. On the contrary, it was due to a long and accumulative experience with the Al-Assad regime and an accumulation of individual and collective experiences recorded in the collective memory. Consequently, the revolution's course reached this fateful transformation. The book aims to extrapolate how this collective memory and its decisions were established. It may have started with individual convictions and eventually streamed into a path collectively taken by a human movement at a historical moment.

The Syrian tragedy preceded the revolution for several decades. And similarly, it is more likely to continue for several long years, even after the fall of the dictatorship in Damascus. This turn of events cannot be changed, and in such a case, the span between the effect and its resonance must be given due respect. The only thing to do is control the factors involved in shifting gears from one speed to another. The Syrian revolution has left an indelible mark on the totalitarian state's future. A long time will pass between this event and its resonating consequences. The most important and decisive factor in making change comes from steering its direction and altering history's course. In trying to alter Syria's fate and free it from this totalitarian regime, we have to shift the context. Accordingly, instead of exploring the events that shifted the course of the conflict, I am primarily focused on the human factor, believing it to be the real context of Syria and the Syrians. Thus, the outcome of these events will be determined. To focus on human factors is to change the context in which this brutal regime was able to dig its roots deep and set up better approaches to the Syrian dilemma, leading to a long-anticipated positive change in the course of events.

Where to go?

The study of history is a discipline that eventually traces change through examining and interpreting human identities and the transformations of societies and civilizations over time. As previously mentioned, historians utilize analytical techniques and instruments to answer questions about the past and reconstruct an array of human experiences. This diversity reveals the profound differences in people's ideas, institutions, and cultural practices, the versatility of human experiences according to time and place, and their ways of struggling in a simultaneously unified and divided world. Historians use multiple sources to weave individual lives and collective actions into tales that offer critical perspectives on our past and present.

It is a study necessary to fathom and address complex questions and dilemmas by examining how the past has shaped and continuously shapes global, national, and local relationships between societies and their people. It provides insight into how to understand our world and appreciate current events. This is facilitated by constructing knowledge and perceptions of historical events and trends, especially those of the last century. So, understanding history is not an intellectual luxury but an obligation to grasp reality and extrapolate the future.

In Max Weber's perspective[140], society incorporates human relationships and interactions, and studying them constitutes a mechanism for understanding their causes and consequences. The study of people does not only focus on eminent figures but also the perspective of ordinary people in light of historical events. Thus, we can better understand the direction of history by undertaking this task. Social phenomena cannot be reduced to one that is only set by psychological boundaries. Cause and effect in psychoanalytic studies are often confused. Several mental concepts and principles, besides intellectual and moral values, compose the collective conscience, which is the set of beliefs and feelings shared by ordinary individuals in society. Acquiring a deeper perception of these social phenomena is an instrument for comprehending historical contexts and a key to accurately viewing the future.

Studying history offers a thorough insight into two aspects: the course and fate—or becoming—of human beings. The word "course" (sayroorah سيرورة) stems from the verb (sayr) "to walk" in Arabic, indicating motion; it is the understanding of movement through which humanity translates its course or denotes the course of society, people, or nation. It may be optional, based on a group's beliefs and shared goals, or imposed due to historical or geographic conditions or the control and brutality of a tyrant. As to becoming (ṣayrurah صيرورة), its origin in Arabic means to be rendered as; its concept indicates what the course ends to. It is how the state of the course and its outcome develop, besides how humans transition over time, how a historical stage continues, or how a historical regression or transgression develops. The course and its outcome are inseparable because one cannot fathom one without the other.

In my quest to explore the course, my purpose is to envision our fate. The thinker Ahmed Barqawi[141] demonstrated that historical possibilities have

---

[140] Weber is a German sociologist and philosopher who is regarded among the founders of modern sociology and the study of public administration in state institutions. He was the sociologist who defined bureaucracy. His most famous work is The Protestant Ethics and the Spirit of Capitalism.

[141] Ahmad Nassim Barqawi is a philosopher, university professor, thinker, critic, writer, researcher, poet, and Syrian-Palestinian. He participated in the Syrian events

several types that must be distinguished[142]. According to Barqawi, a realistic possibility is created and developed at the heart of objective reality due to an unprompted change in the reality's conditions. When the individual or collective consciousness recognizes a possibility, including its cons and pros, some form of correspondence is created between the mentally perceived version and that in reality. This correspondence may lead the positive version to success and transformation into a new reality similar to the initial mentally perceived one. Later, it establishes new versions. In another scenario, a possibility identical to the one visualized by the conscience may be rejected and hindered from its realization due to a substantial factor. Hence, there is a near-realistic possibility; it is visible, available with the least effort and will to transform or prevent it, and accessible for stable societies.

Regarding the remote-realistic possibility, it unfolds over time without any opportunity for pursuit or awareness before its ultimate realization. Being the fruit of abstract reasoning, it is mentally constructed and then evolves into reality. It was only envisioned by a few before materializing and spreading. Its realism is derived from the historical experience of societies and is related to the issues that witnessed several transformations through which this realistic possibility had room to exist. Its examples include the liberation from colonialism and the Arab Spring revolutions. This possibility, having no necessity or inevitableness, appears due to the link between the logical and the historical.

Al-Barqawi developed another type he called pseudo-possibility. It is a figment of imagination thought achievable, though impossible due to being discordant with reality. This type is produced by a false awareness of history and reality and is often the product of ideologies. The horrors of ISIS, the

---

in 2011, and the decision for expulsion from the university was issued on April 9, 2014, by Syrian Prime Minister Wael Al-Halqi, which deprived him of his pension. He currently resides in Dubai.

[142] Yekiti Newspaper, Ahmed Barqawi, The History between Possibility and Reality, October 4, 2020, Issue 278. https://0i.is/YRv9

dystopia of the communist central committees[143], and the proletariat dictatorship[144] illustrate how this pseudo-possibility resembles a collective delirium disconnected from reality. It is an attempt at reliving the past, believing it is achievable by force, like enforcing the righteous predecessors' methodology and the MAGA[145] movement promoted by Donald Trump[146]. The issue with most fundamentalist movements is that they reject change and maintain an absolute permanent state, indicating a pseudo-possibility. Moreover, this is desirable for tyrannical powers to alter a reality-denying perception to the real life, apart from its infeasibility. The conscience creates these false possibilities in response to reality, not due to understanding.

Considering everything said, the historical course is the intersection of reality and historical circumstances with a sense of consciousness that expresses a vision of a historical outcome. The more the historical conditions are in tune with the conscious perception, the greater the possibility of reaching the mentally perceived outcome. To know our destination, we must first describe our reality as individuals, monitor our historical circumstances, and then approach our consciousness on the individual and collective levels. Hence, the book aims to monitor our reality and consciousness and probe into the depths of our collective consciousness and perception of each other. It is an effort to examine some of the most critical Cognitive aspects influencing our individual practices and collective behaviors.

---

[143] China and the Soviet Union had a Central Committee of the Communist Party as the highest sovereign authority. The catastrophic failure of its famous five-year plans starved millions to death and led to bankrupt economies.

[144] The working class controls the means of production and the state institutions through its elected representatives and labor councils, referred to in socialist literature as the proletariat's dictatorship. Under this pretext, the central committees overrule the states' administrations.

[145] Make America Great Again was Donald Trump's campaign slogan in 2016. It was used by the right-wing groups that supported him—previously used by US Presidents Ronald Reagan and Bill Clinton. It was associated with Donald Trump due to his supporters' racist practices. It became a right-wing movement in the United States that persisted even after he failed to win a second term.

[146] Donald John Trump (1946—) is the 45th president of the United States from 2017 to 2021. Before that, he was a media personality, and businessman.

CHAPTER 3

THE COGNITIVE ASPECTS OF THE OPPRESSED IN THE NAWÃRI SOCIETY: "BELONGINGS"

I started writing the book with a head full of unanswered questions. Are the executioners of Tadmor prison and Saydnaya detention center human beings just like the rest of us? How can a human being degenerate into such inhumanity and savagery? How did society allow them to go through kindergarten and school, live around their homes, and walk the streets to be where they are? How can they execute scores of innocent people and go about their everyday lives? Aside from the deranged psycho in the presidential palace, how did the soldiers at the barricades and the branch conscripts reach this point?

Perhaps there is no way to find satisfying answers or a logical explanation. Some perceive it to be mental disorders. Whether this is a mental disorder or a moral failing, these individuals live among us and are part of reality. They are as destructive as earthquakes and cancer, like senseless acts of destiny. I wonder: Are people like Al-Bouti[147] and Ahmad Hassoun[148] at peace with themselves, their intellectual crimes, and their shameful

---

[147] Muhammad Saeed Ramadan Al-Bouti (1929–2013) was a Syrian scholar specializing in Islamic sciences and one of the most important religious figures in the Islamic world. He was close to the Syrian regime and fiercely defended its crimes. He was killed while giving a lesson at the Al-Iman Mosque in Damascus.

[148] Ahmad Badr al-Din Hassoun (1949–) was the Grand Mufti of Syria and one of the regime's lackeys before being dismissed due to the disapproval of his interpretations of the Qur'an to conform to the ideology of the totalitarian regime.

attitudes? Is there a little voice aching within their conscience, even beyond the media screens? Does it even matter to know?

Stuck in a fait-accompli status, we must endure feelings of loneliness, isolation, and helplessness and devise a mechanism to live with this scourge. It is a burden we carry within our hearts and on our shoulders. These so-called individuals have their own isolation, resembling ours. To ignore isolation is to look danger in the eye. It is a grave, a coffin, and a mouth gag. It is incumbent upon us to escape and save our souls from their dead silence. For a society to be one, it must swarm out of its dungeons and vestibules into the open skies. Whether we converse, chant together, or fistfight, we must never leave anyone entirely isolated. Never shall we surrender to self-withering, striving to be rid of our pain. Isolation is what allowed that human monster to exist and helped him escape society's criticism. Undisturbed and uninterrupted, he got away with his disordered mind.

Tracing the cognitive spectrum of psychopathy is paramount to examining its extreme cases. It is critical to study the judge and lawyer who incarcerated thousands of innocent people in prisons where thousands were arbitrarily killed. What sort of humans are the doctors and nurses who shackle patients to beds to be tortured? What kind of upbringing did a person get to turn into a police informant and give away their own neighbors? Who is that person who spied on a friend's and neighbor's son and reported him? How was their childhood? What about the cousin who abandoned the widow of their cousin and childhood friend, who was tortured to death? Where were our voices as we silently witnessed the beating and humiliation for all those years? Why did we consciously choose bribery whenever possible?

As a society, we have taken small steps that grew into leaps toward authoritarianism and totalitarian rule. The start was a coup, dissolving the political parties, dismantling associations and labor unions, arresting intellectuals and activists, and cloning other totalitarian social organizations, such as the Soviet Union and North Korea. Student and revolutionary youth unions came out of nowhere, teaching young people to smother ideas and their owners. In this way, they fell into the clutches of external and internal identification with an imagined society, were reprimanded with self-criticism, and were trained to report to security forces. Eventually, the kids were not spared; the association of terrorist scouts and nihilistic study programs took their turns to break them Cognitively. The elimination of unions, the closure of forums, and the establishment of informants in all corners followed. After decades long journey that culminated in the 1980s, we were heading to the next station, adding three additional decades of societal collapse. It was 3 decades that separated that era from the scenes of barrel bombs dropped on markets and schools, mass murders and sectarian violence, more than 200,000 detainees and forced disappearances, 12 million refugees and displaced persons, and shabiha/thugs and Mutaybijiyya[149] (cult followers) in every corner incessantly and blatantly championing the regime's murderers.

A behavior is a set of social values, experiences, and concepts, and their interaction constitutes the personality representative of behavior. The deconstruction of human behavior into its principal mental features contributes to a thorough understanding of the underlying behavior and its motives. According to Jacques Derrida[150], deconstruction substitutes the appearance-centered strategy because the essence is mirrored in appearance. Moreover, its process resolves any manifested contradiction between concepts termed appearances and their meaning or content.

Conversely, personality is the structural unit of mental traits, such as intelligence, emotions, feelings, impulses, will, and original and acquired reflexes, which must be organized and integrated. Integration is the term for unifying these characteristics, and complete integration is the ideal model. In this chapter, the illustrated cognitive aspects are universal, cross-cultures, religions, and identity. They are beyond unique to the Nawāri people, though their prevalence and overlap are singular. Ignorance and exclusion

---

[149] The Mutaibaji in Syrian and Lebanese slang and the Mutayyabati in Egyptian vernacular refer to individuals employed to make an emotional scene to provoke people's admiration. They ecstatically shout "Oh, Allah" during classic Arabic song refrains. They overly expose their grief and outwardly exaggerate their supplication to Allah at funerals. Others have this in their nature, not for money.

[150] Jacques Derrida (1930–2004) is a French philosopher and literary critic born in Albiar, Algeria. He is considered the first philosopher to use the deconstruction concept in its new sense and within a philosophical framework.

The Intellectual Aspects of the Oppressed in the Nawāri Society: 135
"Belongings"

are highly exhibited in the United States, but not intellectual inclusivity. Loneliness and isolation are manifested in Europe and the West, though for different motivations than those of the oppressed Nawāri people. An accumulation of ignorance and the absence of differentiation, along with totalitarian approaches, exclusionary attitudes, and isolation, influentially directed our actions and practices. To analyze our thoughts and behaviors, I separately study each aspect and contextualize our reality.

The dual methodologies of deconstruction and integration facilitate detecting the social and cultural structures of support and dynamism. They enhance probing the analytical vision of the Nawāri personality in the contexts of push and pull, collision, and harmony. In this chapter, I deconstruct the Nawāri identity. Hopefully, this chapter provides the readers with an integrative-based perspective of the overall structure of the Nawāri personality. It also introduces and underlines some integrating standpoints by observing individual practices and behaviors shared among the Nawāri community. Thus, we advance from analyzing the individual personality by dismantling and monitoring its primary components to re-considering some aspects and practices. In this manner, their motives and cognitive manifestations would be fully understood.

According to Emile Durkheim[151], any human idea or behavior emanates from interacting with society and is external to the individual, and the social facts are external to the individual's awareness. The practices of knocking on wood to bring good luck, clapping hands in applause, the tenets of faith, and values are external thoughts and behaviors to the individual. Yet they are responsible for shaping and preparing the individual to act in a certain way. These social facts, as coined by Durkheim, have a coercive effect on the individual. These facts are adopted outside the individuals and are the product of their interaction within a group, apart from their actions. Though I primarily focus on detecting the cognitive and behavioral aspects of the Nawāri individuals, these aspects do not constitute their psychological or biological fabric. They are the outcome of their social reality and surrounding

---

[151] Émile Durkheim is a French philosopher and sociologist. He is one of the principal architects of modern sociology, for which he developed an independent methodology based on theory and experimentation.

circumstances. Extrapolated at the individual level, they are the collective work of the majority of society. Hence, they are not to be perceived as individual manifestations. The mechanical category, described by Durkheim, fits the Nawãri community's interactions. It is based on the great similarity exhibited by this group's members and functions in a non-synergistic manner as an individualistic work[152]. The spontaneous behaviors of the Nawãri individuals are social facts that are neither their creation nor their property. Due to being imposed by their society, they form their culture but are not individualistic expressions.

The deconstruction of culture and its segmentation into customs, traditions, values, and standards would facilitate their description and analysis separately for more accurate analysis and interpretation. Not to mention that this measure contributes to zooming in on human behavior derived from cultural motives. These motives are the driving force behind the actions of the doer's personality. Deconstruction offers a chance to differentiate between ideal inherited mottos circulating among people by analogy or by reminiscing about bygone moral ideals. This measure would further differentiate between the interests that substantially direct how individuals in a society behave.

The unity and integration of culture are deconstructed as we segment its most significant values and standards, which form the fabric of a personality cognitively, emotionally, and morally. Accordingly, the basic Nawãri personality is triggered by a set of central values interactions. This section traces the most crucial values and components constituting Nawãr individuals' consciousness. The power of values varies in motivating and guiding the behavior of Nawãri individuals within the limited contexts of life.

From this angle, I concluded that by deconstructing the Nawãri personality and studying the cognitive aspects, society's cognitive state and how it ended up would be more decipherable. It might provide an outlook on how the forthcoming scenarios will develop. Hopefully, these analyses

---

[152] Durkheim differentiates between a primitive mechanical society and an advanced organic one in which human efforts cooperate to become an integrated unit. This unit multiplies the outcome of this individualistic-based work for the common good of the entire group. In the same way, a part of a group renders the whole ineffective.

The Intellectual Aspects of the Oppressed in the Nawāri Society: 137
"Belongings"

contribute to establishing plans and solutions by incorporating these features to affect reform, which is our goal. It is no less significant than our liberation, the elimination of injustice, and the advocacy of the popular will for a better life and future.

Resolving injustice sets justice, advocates equality, and is a tool for breaking out of the leash of being oppressed and submitting to the obsession of that grievance. To openly declare, "I am not the one responsible for how I ended up! They made me the criminal I am," and to introduce their story without saying," I am what happened to me, I am what I was forced to become".

Fig. 3-1

"Docile, we were humiliated, and upon uprising, we were also degraded. Like our cities, we were destroyed from within; our light tents were too heavy to be fixed to the ground. Our lives were erasable, as if recorded in pencil. Our voices were drowned out just as the immigrants were in the sea. All paths were shut in our faces, leaving only two doors to choose from: one to death, another for humiliation, and no way to life. How scary the terrorist Syrians were to the meek world! We scared them by demanding our equality as humans, as ordinary people living an ordinary life and dying an ordinary death. How scary the terrorist Syrians were to the world with our brute demeanor, just like a world frightened at the sight of a prisoner thrown in solitary detention for fifty years who just came out to the light."
—Maher Sharaf Eldien

1- Ignorance

> Let no one feign ignorance, tackling us,
> lest we feign greater ignorance, tackling him[153]

We have to start by defining the concept of "ignorance" and differentiating it from "knowledge." Generally, considering that knowledge is the mental image of a thing, ignorance is its absence. Nonetheless, this deduced definition assumes that ignorance is the opposite of, or lack of, knowledge. From this perspective, can we describe a person who responds to a question by saying, "I don't know," as ignorant? And what is the lack of knowledge if it is not ignorance?

Many people associate ignorance with various inaccurate connotations. It is widely confused with stupidity and foolishness. Also, ignorance is commonly believed to be a lack of knowledge. The meaning of ignorance in assuming the meaning of the term ignorance—as the state of not knowing—distinctly elucidates this term. It is not synonymous with stupidity and cannot be used interchangeably; they have independent aspects. Ignorance is not the absence of knowledge of a thing; it is the belief in something contrary due to poor knowledge or a lack of it. Hence, it is different from idiocy, which indicates the absence of knowledge, and foolishness, which denotes a poor mindset. It is, often, the deliberate negligence of learning or a persistent refusal to seek the truth. Its precariousness comes from the fact that the ignorant feel no need to seek answers and no emptiness within caused by the lack of knowledge. Consequently, they rely on their own perceptions. The renowned Ibn Sina reportedly said, "Beware of truncated ingenuity", which alludes to compound ignorance.

---

[153] From the suspended odes of the pre-Islamic poet Amr ibn Kulthum, one of this form's first and best authors. He narrates about the killing of King Amr bin Hind after manipulating his mother to serve the king's mother and humiliate Ibn Kulthum. So Amr ibn Kulthum took the only sword hanging in the hallway and struck the king's head. He left and went to the Arabian Peninsula, chanting his epic suspended ode.

Obliviousness is the opposite of knowledge and takes two forms. The simple form is understanding an issue without fully knowing all its details or denying its unknowingness. In plain terms, one would overlook some details yet realize the lack of awareness. The second one intersects with ignorance; it is being oblivious to one's ignorance, frequently termed compound ignorance. Henceforward, for an accurate definition, we will call it ignorance. To comprehend a matter contrary to what it is, or to not understand it while professing to know it, is ignorance. Obliviousness involves awareness and acknowledgment of unknowingness, while ignorance is the belief that one has full knowledge despite its absence. In the first case, one lacks knowledge and is aware of this deficiency, whereas in the second, one does not know and is unaware of it! When one is conscious of their unknowingness of something, this indicates having acquired some knowledge by becoming aware of what they do not know about it.

Un-knowledgeableness is the tyrant's most fatal instrument to afflict the oppressed. They not only isolate the oppressed from facts or any forms of knowledge or transparency but further obscure all knowledge that may discredit the false image they instilled in the minds of the oppressed. This un-knowledgeableness is backed by torture for anyone who pursues knowledge of what is meant to be concealed. Al-Assad's executioners apply this same methodology by beating their detainees who dared look beyond where they were instructed. The oppressed had to stay blind to the innumerable defects of the tyrants. Exposing these defects reveals the tyrants' weaknesses and contradictions, thus undermining their absolute authority.

This forced un-knowledgeableness imposed by the tyrants pushes the oppressed to neglectfulness for self-preservation and averting danger. They deliberately remain oblivious to what they know to be a contradiction, defect, or error. This involuntary neglectfulness, being irreplaceable, increases the scale of the contradictions perceived by the oppressed. Since the fates of the oppressed are interconnected with each other, their actions become connected as well. This is because the penalty for knowledgeableness exceeds that for those guilty of the "knowledge" offense. The Nawār oppressed have nothing but to stop the rest from falling into the web of "knowledge" and stay within the safe boundaries of un-knowledgeableness as much as possible. Easier said than done. Considering that this became part of a legacy spread among the Nawār, in the case of the oppressed, they do not have the same power as the tyrant to force un-knowledgeableness. Nevertheless, by depriving people of knowledge, the tyrant creates a safe space from unintentional ignorance, given that knowledge is a crime, according to the tyrant, and ignorance is more submissive. This creation thrives because it enables society to conform to and coexist with it. As for the undeniable contradictions, the oppressed accumulate justifications and answers to erase them from their minds.

Ignorance, and the fear of punishable knowledge, forces the Nawār to submit to available answers under given convictions and postulates. They do not seek factual or scientific evidence of events, as they hold on to convictions that need not be scientific or plausible. Metaphysical and complex beliefs are sufficient besides what authorities, such as the government, media, or religious institutions, produce. It would be better if these convictions were illogical and based on external factors, meaning that their analysis and verification required specialized knowledge. Among numerous examples are the claims that fasting prevents cancer and that desertification in the Empty Quarter pertains to secret weapons experiments for the United States. This complexity of understanding and detail undermines studying and scrutinizing this unknown matter.

Usually, this ignorance is not an individual conviction but is common in underdeveloped societies. This might have to do with the sources those individuals collectively entrust as references to their credibility. On top of these is the religious institution, widely revered but equally believed to be a nourisher of ignorance. All traditional religious institutions generally pride themselves on having the ultimate answers. Upon tracing how the simplest means of social media exponentially disseminate ignorance, one would observe that it has generally become self-generating and does not need endorsement or support. The members of the oppressed society themselves turned ignorance into a self-feeding cycle, initially fueled by individual or institutional efforts.

Voluntary ignorance symbolizes many oppressive nations and underdeveloped countries. The populations of developed nations and Western democracies have likewise demonstrated this problem. Movements such as QAnon[154] and many far-right and racist movements exhibit this cognitive aspect. Despite its varying depths, ignorance is a worldwide characteristic, and the developed world is not excluded.

Compound ignorance does not mean being unaware of it or the incompetence of logical reasoning to confront and escape its hold. Its driving force is the inability to question matters, discrediting deep-rooted convictions. This incompetence perpetuates a cognitive legacy's immunity to criticism or questioning. Over time, the survival of this cognitive legacy evidentially validates it, which becomes part of the taken-for-granted knowledge to build upon this construct. Being old-established is evidence of this thought's originality, which induces its steadiness. The fact that this thought remains unshakeable is a testament to its credibility as the unchanging truth that beats all falsehood.

Ignorance must have a stream of what is regarded as "knowledge" and a mechanism for its dissemination among people. With the use of sanctified sources, its manner of study would prohibit questioning or judging its content. Moreover, the methods of their indoctrination must align with the same goals. In Syrian society, the phenomenon of "learning by ear" has its mark on the learning and education of ordinary people. It is similar to the concept of "playing by ear" in learning music, which is not as robust and does not provide a deeper understanding of the music or the ability to learn other instruments, let alone compose new music. Learning by ear similarly results in weaker knowledge that is not foundational, transferable to other fields, or generative! This education method is purely auditory, as the name implies. It depends on the audio narration, where the narrator lends credibility. There are no authenticated written sources, which might be the means to protect it against any scrutiny or questioning. It is acceptable even if this knowledge conflicts with logic and what is proven by experiment and

---

[154] The American far-right devised this conspiracy theory about an alleged secret plan of the so-called "Deep State in the United States" against US President Donald Trump and his supporters.

evidence. By way of example, consider the alternative facts cited by the advisor to former US President Trump as justifications for his lie.

The neighbors' news, jurisprudence, tenets, music, medicine, and politics are all auditory knowledge. To Endorse its credibility, every documented reference that may contradict this methodology is partially or completely excluded. It strenuously pursues the unification of the reported account and makes it as frequently transmitted as possible or at least abides by those versions fit for its purposes.

For example, Prophet Mohammed's migration (Hijra) story is a typical example of our auditory heritage. From a young age, Muslims widely hear about how the people of Al-Madina welcomed the noble Messenger by chanting about the full moon rising upon us from al-Wadaa mountain trail. Solidly taught in schools, this frequent anecdotal narration contradicts the authenticated documents in most of the later historical references. According to Ibn Hajar and Ibn al-Qayyim, two scholars of hadith and the later Islamic sources, this reception was after the Prophet's return from the Battle of Tabuk[155]. It happened nine years after the date of the migration. Additionally, this widely accepted auditory knowledge circulating among the general public and several religious elites contradicts ample documented proof in books and references. The al-Wadaa/farewell mountain trail (known as Thaniyyat Al-Wadaa)[156] comes from the Levant and Tabuk in the north, not from Makkah in the south, another piece of rational evidence invalidating this assumption. Most importantly, how can a group of people greet an unknown man, whom they have never seen before, and declare their belief in and adherence to his message and the "obeyed" commandment before hearing it from him? On these grounds, the later narration is more logical, revealing the widely overlooked shortcomings of the famous verbal narration. The founding pillar of this narration is the frequency of the narrative, which impacts making an objective cognitive judgment with no alternative or need to question it.

---

[155] The Battle of Tabuk was a military expedition led by the Islamic prophet Muhammad in October 630 CE. THe intention was to challenge the Byzantines for control of the northern part of the caravan route from Mecca to Syria.

[156] A trail that runs through mountains around Al-Madina in Saudi Arabia.

Aside from the abovementioned story of that incident, innumerable misconceptions and fallacies have entirely taken over the minds of young and old. These include weird habits, such as the absurdity of turning over upside-down shoes or knocking on wood to ward off envy and further destabilize the foundations of logical thinking. By establishing an integrated, seemingly scientific structure, it aims to rationalize and justify what might discredit the validity of any part of this knowledge. Anyone who challenges it must produce an alternative interpretation of everything within that intricate intellectual system. They must clear their minds to initiate a soul—and thought—straining process. It takes the same amount of time spent captive to this form of knowledge to "unlearn" the ideas instilled in them. In doing so, they do not challenge a scientific matter or a partial issue but defy an entire legacy that is a source of pride and the basis for the unique cognitive identity of the Nawār community. An identity that rejects being held accountable or scrutinized, and a community that is thoughtlessly proud of what it deems to be its culture. Nothing can blemish the slightest part of this legacy. To describe this form of knowledge as an "intellectual legacy" is unacceptable; they firmly adhere to characterizing it as "science."

Ignorance is endless and boundless. Its limitlessness complicates its observation and obstructs its examination, tracing its trails and detecting any change in its condition. The difference between ignorance and its opposite—let us call it "non-ignorance"—is not quantitative. Ignorance is not transient but has a relentless, firm structure. Under this state, underdeveloped nations stagnate away from the movement of history. The underdevelopment description, which implies movement, does not fit these nations. It would have indicated that they realized this difference and were pursuing overtaking others. Nations suffering from this state are unaware of leadership, filling a standstill category at the end of the world's procession. This ignorance, imagined to be a form of knowledge, is an unyielding obstacle to civilization and an impediment to advancement among nations. To integrate this ignorance with its opposites, the oppressed Nawār would have to bridge the abyss, revealing the contradictions of this ignorance with the perceived and existing reality. For this reason, what I call the "sciences of ignorance" were fabricated as an alternative to science. The following section explains how they were established, and the sequence of values, bases, and postulates currently exhibited in the Nawãri community.

Ignorance sciences

In Syria and the Arab states, all schools, institutes, and even universities are remodeled versions of Kuttabs—the old-fashioned elementary schools (commonly called Madrassas in English with disdain) a school based receptive learning style, or passive learning. This model has—of course—replaced the traditional subject matters and replaced them with what the worst of the colonial educational system contained. This disfigured schooling system is based on teaching pre-prepared, decades old, and fixed curricula sequestered from our accelerated time and age. The only skill students master is memorizing books or references, and their evaluation is based on what they have learned by heart. The tyrant controls their curricula to serve one goal of un-knowledgeableness. Having no laboratories, experimental or applied sciences hardly have any room in this process. Even final exams and school assignments require basic retrieval of content to be noted down in notebooks and pamphlets. This learning environment has no classwork or curricula fit for inquiry-based learning that would allow students to research a subject of interest and discuss the outcome of their work. This would be a luxury in sixty students' classrooms. It would also be overwhelming to a meagerly paid teacher who cannot afford to support themselves on hours-long job income. How can they execute a duty they have never practiced or trained to evaluate? This poor educational process is explicable due to certain economic and political conditions. What is inexplicable is how these institutions are entrusted and how these methods are respected and appreciated.

Syrian fathers pride themselves on their sons' adeptness in memorizing the Holy Qur'an or reciting a muallaqa (suspended ode) in public. Getting full marks in exams means genius, and the knowledge of a Muslim cleric having a well referenced response and fatwa (Islamic law ruling) for every issue is equal to none. The Nawãr cannot get enough stories about doctors making a diagnosis by the sound of footsteps. For them, these are indicators of unique mastery and abundant knowledge, though they do not differ from quackery and sorcery. I refer to them as ignorance sciences. Later, I discovered that the Saudi thinker Ibrahim Al-Bulayhi[157] had previously used it. I believe our views concur in this regard.

For the ignorant, postulates fill in the gaps in knowledge and details to replace conclusions apart from the data. Therefore, particulars are disregarded if they conflict with these postulates, and what is intuitive to them remains protected. Over time, they assume the form of a set of knowledge, methods, beliefs, or practices under the claim of being scientific, following no conditional rules of scientific thinking. This newly-formed knowledge is a pseudoscience that serves no other purpose than providing pretexts and justifications for the targeted intellectual outcome. No scientific conclusion is produced, but they inversely result from another, retroactively built to support themselves and prove their validity.

They utilize ambiguous language and superficially use incorrect scientific and technical terminology for a scientific edge. They use proactive and dogmatic ideas to prove ambiguous, indefinite, untestable, and conclusive claims. They support them by adamantly seeking selective evidence while obliterating, denying, and overlooking what contradicts their preconceived conclusions. Personal testimonies and peculiar tales are their principal means to prove their authenticity. The targeted outcome is reached through a set of scattered and fragmented data. Hence, their point of inception is the targeted conclusion, and they compromise any means to their discrediting by accumulating selective evidence. To no one's surprise, the discourse of these so-called sciences is imbued with supernatural events and conspiracies. It is characteristically written in an ambiguity-oriented style that relies on metaphors instead of directly communicating its ideas.

The lack, or negligence of, what challenges this pseudoscience is as essential to ignorance as it is to preserve the precarious equilibrium experienced by the ignorant. Ignorance and oppression share a mutually beneficial relationship to guarantee each other's stable and constant existence. Consequently, ignorance is more widespread in underdeveloped and oppressed societies.

---

[157] Ibrahim Al-Bulayhi is a Saudi thinker and writer for Al-Riyadh newspaper. He has some bold ideas in criticizing Arab and Islamic thought.

Ignorance sciences are complementary products of the complex ignorance of people, where two factors interact. One is the individual's ignorance of their non-knowledge and boasting about it, feeling confident it is truthful and righteous. This factor is the most rigid building block of the underdeveloped structure. The second relies on erroneous cognitive data that the ignorant intentionally overlooked due to ignorance and false postulates.

The oppressed Nawãri societies boast of their vast and ancient cultures, which delude them into thinking they are flawless and sufficient. Compound ignorance is the first and most enduring at the level of individuals and nations. Accordingly, studying the science of ignorance that humanity has produced throughout history is imperative. Unfortunately, these sciences are not grouped under a specific name. No science can be pinpointed as that of ignorance, but all human sciences, technical and humanities, are plagued with their products. Amidst the frenzy of oppressed people's lives, their only means to the simplest forms of science are pre-made and ready-made. In times of decline, the sciences, like anything else, become purposeless and harnessed to serve ideology and fill the void. No efforts are exerted to fill the void of questioning and the innate need to learn. The path to investigating and researching is blocked, a path that may lead to what society or the ruling regime wants to be unknown. At these times, the best semi-scientific alternative to satiate that need is the science of ignorance, which compels their justifications and means of formulation and preservation.

Mastering ignorance sciences grants the Nawãri a sense of security, pride, and the firm belief that they have an answer to everything. It is primarily established to bridge the abyss between reality and hypotheses. As previously mentioned, overlooking the contradictions plays a role in the Nawãri oppressed society's anxiety about knowledge. Armed with ignorance sciences, they can rely on an integrated structure of pre-made and ready-to-serve answers. Thanks to it, Syrian individuals moved from merely ignorant and satisfied with selecting what they wanted to know to complex ignorance. Hence, whoever owns this form of ignorance firmly believes in what is contrary to reality and incongruent with their surroundings. A quasi-scientific formula reinforces their position, asserts its validity, and justifies their belief in it. Nawãri individuals reach the point of showing off and extending their rigid knowledge.

It is not uncommon to have beliefs, whether true or false. What is outrageous is to expand on false views to be involved in the knowledge arena. A compound crime is to challenge the world and forcefully impose such a perspective. For those who possess this compound ignorance, some believe that it is sufficient to structure the future and have an answer to every question. They consider that it must be enforced and disseminated, and that people must bear the consequences of this ignorance. This form of individual ignorance—whether imposed by the totalitarian ruler, their supporters, cronies, or any Nawãri individual in a position of power—is not a personal conviction with limited effect on its believer. Its scope of impact is generalized over the entire society, including those who disagree with this false conviction or compound ignorance. No one is spared from its influence and consequences. The fusion between self-identity and its convictions on the one hand and the forced cognitive system on the other creates a general status, holding everyone accountable for the wrongdoing of others with no escape. To criticize ideas and defy this ignorance indicates a lack of identity and a betrayal of the group, which must be suppressed.

Due to their motives, ignorance sciences are established to provide justifications and propaganda to serve an idea and a goal, not knowledge. They are chiefly false and unchangeable sciences confined within fixed frameworks and are based on spoon-fed ideas to be consumed without proof, analysis, thinking, or discussion. They have no specific direction. Falling under no defined scientific field, they are a way of thinking—or not thinking—where the learner is a passive receiver. National Education[158] books, based on propaganda and demagogy, are not unique in following their approach, as all educational and intellectual institutions are based on investing in the sciences of ignorance. This would strengthen their position,

---

[158] National Education is a compulsory subject in Syrian schools and universities. It focuses on teaching Pan-Arabism and socialism. It defines the policies of the state and its leading party, the Arab Socialist Ba'ath Party.

facilitate their work, and reduce the cost of managing the educational process.

Under this time-defying mode, closed and uniformed cultural structures that remain complacently fixed govern the Nawãri community. Decade after decade, ever fixed and stagnant, an integrated ideology and culture emerged within these sciences' orbit, which the Nawãri unthinkingly boasts of as "inherent" culture. To challenge or change the science, culture, and society structured around these sciences is met with anger. The underdeveloped classification is entirely denied, believing them to be at the top regardless of their degenerative conditions. Fixedly believing it is forever the civilization's cradle and the first alphabet creator, their rational judgment freezes, and they expand and create more. These sciences amass their strengths, superiority, and distinction from others and equally accumulate the faults and weaknesses of others. The West is immoral, denuded, and suffers from a dysfunctional family system, whereas the Muslim East is authentic, characteristically generous, and gallant. It is the founder of civilization, being civilization's land and cradle! The East invented zero-figure and algebraic sciences. Hence, it is the source of ancient and modern sciences because zero is their most pivotal component! This approach produces two catastrophic cognitive outputs. One is the absence of a sense of underdevelopment and ignorance. The other is the lack of a logical and objective measure to differentiate between progress versus underdevelopment and truth versus falsehood. Through this lens, the Nawãri magnifies their achievements, even if it is the largest plate of hummus, whereas the "others'" achievements seem inferior despite the progress and prosperity they produce.

I have a funny story in this context. I witnessed a situation in which a lady body-shamed her neighbor's son. "He is bald and has large hips! My son is a top-notch science and physics schoolteacher," she said. She completely overlooked the fact that their son is a 24-year-old computer engineer, whereas her nearly-37-year-old son has the same physique! Not to mention that their fathers are cousins!

This selective set of facts and data formulates judgments. Facts are not to be measured according to a single standard. The temporality of scientific leadership, its conditions, circumstances, and evidence are irrelevant to this discussion. Some factors reveal the flaws and social disintegrations in the "strange" other, while these same phenomena are curbed and hidden in the Nawāri societies and their collective consciousness. As the others are flawed in morals and religion, we remain the only surviving nation. This explains why 86% of Jordanians agree that killing is a just punishment for the apostate or religious skeptics, and 82% of Pakistanis and Egyptians firmly believe in stoning fornicators and honor killing[159]. Regardless of the perspective adopted and its relevance to the authenticity of these rulings in Islamic law, neither of these two classes can even consider these situations as local phenomena exhibited in their society. From a distance, the Nawāri think they did not personally meet that devilish atheist or skeptic. None of the 82% of Egyptian respondents came into contact with any of those immoral fornicators. Shockingly, some of those sent to death might not be strangers; they could be in their houses or among their most cherished ones. Those "others" sentenced to death for disbelief or immorality might be their flesh and blood.

The homogeneity displayed among the oppressed Nawāri society underlines two matters: an intense fear of the outside and a tendency towards higher homogeneity and greater identification among the clique's members. The ghettos[160] they live in are closed spaces with no light to reveal their flaws and no gate for others to penetrate. This is because, within their ghetto walls, minimal interaction with others is allowed. Given this, the possibility for another perspective to be viewed within what is normal and acceptable is denied. These factors reinforce the sense of the world's Orthodoxy in the eyes of the Nawāri, and whatever contradicts it is considered an extreme danger. The isolation, identification, and differentiation from the other strengthen the Nawār's sense of belongingness, slackening their will to exert efforts to identify with the other group. The Nawāri person can connect

---

[159] Pew Research Center, December 2010, Muslim Publics Divided on Hamas and Hezbollah. Support for Severe Laws.
[160] A ghetto is an area where a group of people willingly or unwillingly live and are widely considered a minority belonging to a particular ethnicity, culture, or religion. Its origin goes back to Venice, Italy, to refer to the Jewish ghetto near the metal foundry. Ghetto means foundry in Venetian, hence its name.

to their roots, simplicity, and the past through oversimplified forms of science, solutions, and conclusions. In this sense, black seeds cure cancer, and Ivermectin[161] cures COVID-19. One conniving group is the source of all evil. Once it is eradicated, the conspiracy is stopped, then good will prevail again.

Holding a society back from civilization is not the worst evil of ignorance and its sciences. Compound ignorance hinders societies from pursuing it. The path to self-questioning and openly discussing its issues and defects is blocked. It provides an imagined alternative form of civilization that is fit for purpose. The Nawãr society does not classify as part of the developing nations, as it remains stagnant and helpless, even unaware of its impotence, shortcomings, and underdevelopment! This explains how underdevelopment is a permanent structure and not a transient phase. The intellectual stagnation of the Nawãri community is part of a close-knit structure that denies and resists any change! This resistance constitutes their identity and, in their view, makes them the bright light against an ocean of a misguided world. Ultimately, they are that piece of light!

The most ignorant authenticity and the authenticity of ignorance

For all oppressed people, memory and the collective consciousness reminisce with dreamy eyes filled with nostalgia. The Nawãr takes pride in its authenticity and longevity. They boast of their legacy of beliefs and traditions, holding them as dear as the gift of humanity. Any challenge or destruction of that cognitive reservoir is next to impossible. Similarly, the Nawãri cling to their historical ignorance because it is the foundation of their identity; it is their survival, and they would go to war for its protection. It is the arena for their struggle with the West and modernity—the land of resistance, self-actualization, and free, independent existence. If this identity is challenged, its authenticity might be tarnished and eventually undermined. Preserving intellectual heritage plays a crucial role in keeping

---

[161] US right-wingers widely refused the COVID-19 vaccine. Instead, they used Ivermectin—designed to eliminate parasites and commonly used in livestock—to prevent and treat the disease, despite the absence of any scientific evidence of its effectiveness and the fear of its adverse effects.

the Nawār individual as an example, and the underdeveloped person in general, in balance with the world from which they are distinct. In this case, ignorance is an existential necessity and a deliberate choice because it is their shield against change that is to be avoided at all costs. Change disturbs the balance, and imbalance takes away the sense of security. It is a feeling to which all vulnerable, oppressed people desperately cling.

For its conservation, historical ignorance must be connected to the identity dimension, which needs a compass; otherwise, it is lost. The Nawāri individual resorts to this historical dimension through their own narrative. The formulated bond would endow them with rootedness and authenticity, making them beyond accountability—a sanctified rootedness that has its self-reference. They made their memory history's sanctuary, a mainstream for all that was good, and a lifeline to escape their harsh reality. Reproducing mental images of that history is highly revered, such as wearing a turban or sarouel (traditional Arab clothing), cupping[162], and treatment with natural honey. Additionally, rootedness underlines a crucial characteristic. It is resistant to time and remains an ever-unchangeable, fixed fact. The Nawāri individual hues the mental image relevant to this ignorance with noble and sacred historical roots. Throughout history, neither its image nor its characteristics have changed. Hence, this persistence indicates the authenticity of that act or belief, proving its validity. There is no need to re-question them; they are self-proven. The greatest minds have long ago found these acts or beliefs irrefutable and undeniable. How can anyone, at present, dare challenge their validity? This must be unjust, meaning every attempt to re-consider their validity aims at its destruction! Hence, all questioning is primarily out of malice. Consequently, these not-so-innocent attempts and malicious plots must be confronted and fought.

To consolidate this historical understanding, the Nawār individual resorts to producing sciences to record and theorize this contrived historical perspective. Besides, they are used as a foundation suitable for projections of their contemporary reality. These newly-developed sciences are branches of ignorance sciences whose halo of sanctity gets wider. The wider it grows,

---

[162] Cupping therapy is a form of pseudoscience in which a local suction is created on a cut skin with the application of heated cups.

the more questionable the outcome of its logic and content. Subsequently, the harder it is to incorporate into a debate.

This ignorance first manifests in overlooking logical fallacies and then being oblivious to them. Over time, a second layer of conclusions is formed based on the data of the erroneous ignorance sciences, and later other layers follow. If there is a logical fallacy in the fourth layer, the conclusion's validity is inferred by reviewing the next one. Through this mental judgment, what one considers a fallacy in that conclusion is deemed unjustified because the conclusion drawn from the introduced data is correct. This explains why numerous human issues did not get justice long ago, including the liberation of slaves, women's equality, and the shape of the earth. Accordingly, all the mental judgments adopting that train of thought established starkly flawed logical conclusions, believing them to be justifiable and assured of their validity. How were these ignorance sciences set? What was the cognitive sequence for the values, inception points, and postulates we, the Nawãr community, have now?

Ignorance: the gate to evil

According to Socrates[163], it is not in human nature to choose to act in a way that one believes to be harmful or evil instead of a good way. He claimed that every mistake or evil is only done out of ignorance and not to do evil. His view is controversial because people occasionally commit evil deeds out of self-interest or acting on impulse, against their best. However, the concept makes sense upon observing the logic behind human behaviors and motivation.

Socrates indicated that people act out of self-interest, arguing that this instinct keeps them from deliberate harm. Also, if people commit harmful deeds, it is only out of ignorance because they do not know what is most beneficial, the right way to attain it, or how not to fall into harm's way. He saw no conflict between self-interest and morality. On the contrary, virtue is the highest benefit, and immoral actions harm the agent. Therefore, it is

---

[163] A classic Greek philosopher and sage (470 BC–399 BC), he is one of the founders of Western philosophy.

only committed due to ignorance or misunderstanding of the most significant interest. In the "Al-Ilahiyat" (Theology) section of his famous book "The Healing", Ibn Sina/Avicenna[164] dedicated a chapter to how evil infiltrates everything through ignorance. He elucidated how evil occurs and that it exists and results from having to be, which is for good and right and causes no evil or harm.

This chief premise significantly transcends ignorance (evil) and knowledge (good) based on the stance adopted. In other words, we can either expand what we have of knowledge (good) or live on our ignorance (evil) to further solidify it. To proceed with our ignorance (evilness) is effortless. It takes a narrow mental approach constructed on self-deception and self-confidence. On the other hand, it takes a lot of effort to expand our knowledge (goodness), most significantly to have open minds and be freed from narrow, self-imposed viewpoints. We constantly see how people easily cling to their narrow-mindedness, ignorance, and evilness and refuse to take the wisdom path misguided by their own ignorance and arrogance.

The evils of notorious criminals such as Hitler, Stalin, Bashar al-Assad, and many other war criminals and criminal perpetrators might not find ample cover in ignorance. However, this stark evil is not my focus of observation. Instead, I delve into less severe, more widespread, and commonly acceptable evils that are not held accountable or governed by laws in most systems. It is exhibited in the daily actions of bigots, racists, fanatics, and the deeply rooted thoughts of fundamentalists. Their ignorance (evilness) is flagrantly evident when analyzing their behavior. Under a code of narrow-mindedness and ignorance, they pointlessly seek to appear righteous while unaware of doing the opposite. They deliberately extend their own ignorance (evil) to desperately prove their wisdom, still oblivious to further confirm it. This is similar to those who believe in the myth that the earth is flat and not spherical. And just as Mark Twain[165] said, "It ain't so much the things that

---

[164] Ibn Sina was a Muslim scholar and physician (980–1037 AD) famous for his works in medicine and philosophy.

[165] Mark Twain (1835–1910) was an American satirist who wrote poetry, short stories, and essays. He authored The Adventures of Tom Sawyer, one of the most

people don't know that makes trouble in this world, as it is the things that people know that ain't so".

Not to assume a reductive approach, it is more optimal to say that ignorance is among many other sources of evil. Various adverse consequences would be less probable if people were better informed. Yet, the extremely wicked can infuse knowledge into evil ends.

We must grasp that all forms of hatred and evil are not just the absence of good and that ignorance, whether intentional (conscious) or unintentional (unconscious), is not just incomplete knowledge or its absence. This would entail that we are all ignorant to some extent. Hence, our wickedness is relevant to the degree of ignorance and our desire to hold on to it, besides our inability and will to depart from it.

As regards the dichotomies of ignorance/evil and knowledge/good, we must also address one of the most critical logical fallacies throughout our decades-long intellectual discussions, namely the hypothesis that enlightenment is a solution. Just as ignorance opens doors to evil, so does knowledge or enlightenment open doors to good. Unlike ignorance, which results in the inevitability of evil, there is no inevitability in finding the "good" through "enlightenment". There are countless examples of thinkers, learners, and academics whose "enlightenment" did not stop them from being tyrants and despots. It is enough to witness the groups of professors and intellectuals who failed to see the evilness of a regime like Bashar Al-Assad's or the Israeli government in its genocidal war on Gaza. Names that are now too many and too well know to mention here.

Ignorance creates evil, whereas knowledge is not necessarily its cure or the gateway to virtue, a common belief among the philosophers of the Enlightenment Age and most contemporary intellectuals.

---

famous novels of the nineteenth century. His real name is Samuel Langhorne Clemens.

2-Indiscretion

White are our deeds, black are our battles,
Green are our fields, red are our swords.[166]

The "age of discretion" is a legal and statutory term referring to the age at which someone can discern right and wrong, independent of their parents or guardians. Although my use of "indiscretion" overlaps with the legal and statutory definition of the word, it further explains and defines its meaning. These terms are general in scope and add nothing to what the general public would say when judging an issue, i.e., they are broad and lack identification. For example, saying theft is haram (forbidden) in Shariya or a legal crime, naming the capital of a country, and so on. To broadly discern right and wrong is also referred to as the age of maturity. The age of discretion might draw the line between sensible adults and those less conscious in a particular group, but it cannot measure its total consciousness. It does not identify the wise from the foolish, though it aspires to do so. Setting an age limit leads to specific expectations about the ability to exercise discretion. As far as the term goes, there is relevance to comparing two things to decide which is more distinctive or distinguishing one person from the other in terms of rank. This measurement might be qualitative or descriptive, for example, based on race, color, or religion.

The term I seek to formulate in this section is closer to what is known in neurological and scientific terminology as "Two-Point Discrimination". It defines one of the characteristics of the sensory system—as in touch or sight—and its minimum distance for discriminating between two nearby objects. When two points are relatively close to one another, their distance decreases. That sense loses the ability to distinguish between them, resulting in the perception of the two points as one. The more that sense can discern between the two points separated by the smallest distance, the sharper, more accurate, and abler it is to make the distinction. By applying this ability of discrimination to thought, I can better clarify the meaning I want. The high sense of discrimination in an individual is demonstrated in the ability to

---

[166] A verse from the poem "Saly al-Ramah" (Ask the high-rising spears) by the poet Safi al-Din al-Hali (677–752).

compare two things that initially appear similar in form and type. Through this acute sense of discrimination, the best option is selected.

The distinction between right and wrong and truth from falsehood might be widely believed to be self-evident, innate, and straightforward. Regardless of this widespread belief, illustrated in some highly general and self-evident cases, the matter is extremely complex and arduous. Most of the projections of these cognitive, ethical, and legal issues might widely fall within the gray area between stark truth and utter falsehood. For an individual, passing judgment on a matter within that gray area is laborious, individualistic, and varies from one person to another. In the end, it is the most challenging measurable ability. Besides, taking a position on an issue requires assigning it either to the white category, i.e., true (right) or to the black category, i.e., false (wrong). When more details are known about a case, its coordinates change across a gray spectrum between black and white. This means the rulings on many matters shift according to their data, where they might be correct in some cases and wrong in others. Therefore, several issues lie across a gray spectrum, and its judgment is affected by its high subjectivity, where many variables constantly change. This changeable state obstructs taking a fixed and unanimous position on any issue, whatever it is, without a corresponding debate or argument.

Underdeveloped societies tend to adopt fixed ideas on many issues, whether under a religious, heritage or even legal facade, in which they exert the least effort in thinking and examination. These preconceived notions are transformed into valid premises and further extended. Also, the structures of these practices are set up for their preservation and to maintain balance and identity. They criminalize any attempt that defies their ideas, no matter how invalid they are or how accurate, correct, and solid the corresponding debate is.

Democracy, disobedience to a Muslim ruler, music, adultery, and positions towards non-Muslim countries are among the sub-issues of discretion and reasoning problems. Other less controversial issues include girls' education, male guardianship, beating children, superstition, seeking blessings, pessimism, fighting positive laws, and many others. These cases indicate a lack of discretion when passing judgment. They rely on a ready-made ruling or project it on any issue that arises but has no ready-made one. The Nawār communities vehemently reject the wrong positions on issues that have become self-evident. The lack of rationality and discretion hinders the Nawāri individuals from shifting the false positions adopted several centuries ago, despite their flagrant erroneousness and obscene injustice. Classifying issues into black and white is a dominant trend, besides passing broad judgments that guarantee easy decision-making and ingrain mental and moral lethargy. Subsequently, anecdotes and anomalies are generated to project the final position on the mindless black/white dichotomy.

These preconceived premises and divisions might cause this deficiency in discretion. To expand them, they must overlook the blatant contradictions of the ill harvest of the "black and white" fields and their differences with the values within their nature and thought. This might be mostly displayed across myriad customs, traditions, and some legal and customary prejudices, which are still considered absolute certainties, not to mention being a source of pride and cultural identity for those nations. Out of ignorance or possibly lethargy, the ignorant adopt ready-made ideas and pre-determined positions on issues they consider of no immediate and direct benefit or harm. To solidify their affiliation to their community, they share its opinions, or rather its leaders', on general issues, whether crucial or secondary ones, which have an impact on their agent. They forfeit their right to determine their position and identify what is right or wrong, despite being the biggest losers in the case of erroneous choices. When the ignorant are denied the role to think and judge, they lose the right to learn from the mistakes and experiences they should have undergone. Initially, this loss is welcomed as a benefit and a gain, facilitating decision-making and providing a chance to evade the repercussions of those judgments. They feel free from self-blame as they did not make these choices, but their society and customs dictated them. Eventually, they bear the brunt, and no lessons are learned.

The "age of discretion" determines when a person is independent of supervision and guardianship and exercises their right to self-determination after being prepared for this at home, school, and community. Providing a person with the faculty of choice is the greatest gift and the most precious supply for the future. It empowers all individuals with the capability to change. At a very early stage, the underdeveloped society commits a crime against its children, depriving them of the necessary advice, awareness, and deep insight. Hence, they end up immature enough to qualify for the discretion stage. Society continues to oppress its Nawār individuals, dictating their actions and predetermining their future under many pretexts that a few consider healthy and moral. These justifications include protection, consulting the wise, returning to the roots, and preserving heritage and customs. In this manner, the Nawār become submissive to their rulers and caretakers. In this light, society is a group of subjects to be managed and driven, exerting no effort to determine their destiny or form an opinion. Their life is dedicated to guarding society, or its façade, against change at any price, even if it costs them their future— it is a cursed cycle of tyranny and opinion privation leading to arrested development.

Though Nawāri individuals may reach the highest levels of development and advancement or find an escape from the ignorance that their environment created, they remain incapable of change or making a decision. Rational judgment is the foundation of liberation and development, regardless of having all knowledge at their fingertips. It is a skill acquired and evolved through only practicing it. To overcome mistakes, one must commit a few mistakes and learn along the way. Faults are only determined through direct and impartial judgment. The Nawāri individual is denied all of this.

The intuitive and the learned

The thinking process is initiated when one gains a portion of knowledge within the axioms or necessities—the intellectual postulates upon which thought is based—without re-reviewing it due to being intuitive. This is exemplified by recognizing the whole as larger than the part. Or it could be acquired knowledge that entails thinking and reasoning.

Additionally, there are self-evident, necessary perceptions that must be part of consciousness to introduce the process of logical thinking. These perceptions must be self-evident for existence, possibility, and nihilism, for instance, believing a whole is larger than a part and two opposites never meet. On the other hand, acquired theoretical perceptions occur through logical thinking, such as realizing that the earth is stationary under our feet while rapidly rotating around another celestial body and that cold is the absence of heat. Not everyone knows all the axioms; still, some matters are self-evident, of which many are ignorant. Acquired knowledge must bring an issue to the perception and thinking realms. The aim is to make an independent, intellectual judgment to develop a conclusion.

However, people's conviction in false axioms is a real disaster, as it bears deep marks on our challenging reality. This is because the best and most accurate mental judgments may not lead to sound results. The deficiency in mental discretion is not exclusively caused by the imbalance that afflicts thought's ability to conduct sound, intellectual judgments but rather by relying on false axioms that result in false conclusions.

Most axioms do not go through rational processes; for instance, experimenting with empirical data, listening to audio, or seeing visuals—one would not exert rational efforts to learn how the white color looks or how running water sounds. This form of knowledge must be directly experienced to be established. On the other hand, adopting untested or unexamined axioms promotes acquired fallacies that eventually ruin rational judgments. Numerous ideological systems suffer from logical fallacies if these actually constitute their founding pillars. Moreover, they indoctrinate them and are further supported and produced through ignorance sciences.

These fallacy-based beliefs fail to overcome their flawed foundations, being infiltrated into their composition as an essential, taken-for-granted part. An even more complicated issue, they ruin other axioms and push them to extremes. The interconnectedness of Muslims, Jews, or any closely knit group, and their favoritism is not reprehensible.

Yet, given what was previously referred to as the "false axiom—dividing people into two camps: a believer and an infidel—or classifying lands into the abode of Islam (peace) and that of war, ideas such as loyalty and disavowal[167] were rooted. They got confused into including all those who

---

[167] Al-wala' (loyalty), according to shri'ah (Islamic law), means support, love, honor, respect, and connection with the beloved outwardly and inwardly. The Bara'a (disavowal) is dissociation, disownment, and animosity after giving excuses and warnings.

do not follow an overly customized form of belief. In this manner, the interconnectedness among believers was radicalized to reject the other and establish a narrow version of faith where it is exclusively approved and accepted. Consequently, one false axiom can entirely lead an intellectual system to extremism. This is because the subconscious attempts to combine what it regards as axioms and finds a moderate value in comparison. In this regard, a mathematical example comes to mind. Imagine a popular café full of middle-class working people of average income. If a billionaire joins them, the total average income of that group dramatically increases without an actual increase in theirs. The next day, the change will not be in closing the enormous income gaps but in a shift towards mimicking the rich man's appearance and drinks. When transforming an acquired false idea into an axiom within a belief or eliminating any rational judgment of this axiom, that idea would immensely impact the overarching cognitive system. It shifts the ability to distinguish the differences in a specific direction, similar to how the entrance of the billionaire affected the average income of the cafe's clients. This is known in data science as skew and distortion.

Sometimes, indiscretion is a result of a lack of an ethical reference or characteristic. This reference contributes to the judgment of a belief regarding its content. It also helps distinguish between what is self-evident or acquired and what is or is not acceptable. Other alternative measurements would replace that ethical reference, for instance, halal and forbidden instead of true and false. This does not mean that the classification as halal or forbidden is independently unsound. The issue arises from the rational fallacies introduced in light of these two categories that distorted sound judgment. Likewise, much of what falls under the halal/forbidden classification is no longer subject to any rational judgment or moral-based measurement. It is religious and not moral, making its application for recent issues more challenging and conflicting with the principle that "the lawful is clear, and the unlawful is clear."[168]

---

[168] From the hadith of the Prophet Mohammad, "That which is lawful [halāl] is clear and that which is unlawful [harām] is clear, and between the two of them are doubtful matters about which many people do not know." Narrated by Al-Bukhari and Muslim.

When logical or cognitive fallacies introduce an axiom-formulated thought, this leads to incorrect comparisons. It may perpetuate an approach to applying a false discrimination process, such as distinguishing between and choosing one of two exclusive, defective options. This choice becomes an essential and sacred element in that thought's structure, obstructing its review or criticism. A deviation and a distortion of that thought gradually take effect due to adopting these fallacies, and history bears witness. Not all readers may see eye to eye on this part of my argument, and the point intended might be lost amid contention. No attempt is intended to refute any one idea or garner support for another. This is an effort to clarify that even the most well-founded intellectual doctrines can get corrupted if the necessary mechanisms of criticism and observation are lacking when most needed for urgent or emerging issues. It becomes more of an invitation to adopt cognitive fallacies while rejecting criticism or debate. Some lessons might be learned from promoting discourse over how these fallacies infiltrated those ideologies.

There was not one time in all human existence devoid of some form of oppression affecting all or part of it. The inability to structure an integrated global ethical system has long been part of humanity's agonies. This deficiency might result partially from a weakness in the overall ability to exercise discretion. After all, not all people have the same level of awareness, knowledge, and will. One can also add the factors of oppression and tyranny. Humanity maintained a sense of morality by establishing various eclectic ethics. The Nawār were born into and lived among social circles deprived of demonstrating any free moral aspect and were constantly pressured into abiding by distinctive standards, as in white or black.

The integration of ignorance and indiscretion

Why do we read? A rarely asked question with a range of opinions, including expanding knowledge, stimulating creative thinking, and even enlarging one's vocabulary. Hence, "learning" is the widely agreed-upon best response, and knowledge is the ultimate goal of reading. Knowledge acquisition is the desired outcome of all forms of education, and reading is one of the learning processes and a common desired goal.

Why do we learn? The response has to be independently discussed. We must reconsider how to rephrase questions to get more accurate and better answers, which is exactly my purpose. If learning targets transferring knowledge, another level of this question can be demonstrated. It can be revealed if we recurrently pose the same question regarding the purpose of that specified result. In a maze-like quest, we seek the direction and ultimate goal of the process and its actions. At one point, we might consider this the absolute end of all the premises of that question and end up with misleading conclusions. Blaming ignorance as the cause of crises and conflicts initially seems correct. Some might even consider it an axiom. Acknowledging this assumption, then, what if ignorance was their outcome? What fundamentally led to the matter that caused ignorance? Do we know the root cause?

Science advances as if we witness growing distant islands amidst a vast ocean of ignorance; this explains the constant deficiency of science. We risk going on a wild goose chase if we set science as the ultimate goal. Bridging the gap entails a change in perspective on what is acquired via the advancement of science rather than being a goal in and of itself. Assuming that reading is a means of gaining wisdom and not increasing knowledge, we focus on the behavioral approach instead of the "purpose" or "end". My point is uniquely summed up beautifully in a Quranic verse: "He is the One Who raised for the illiterate ˹people˺ a messenger from among themselves—reciting to them His revelations, purifying them, and teaching them the Book and wisdom}[169]. The nexus of learning, i.e., "recitation of verses "and purification and later learning, and then comes wisdom. It indicates an associative relation without identifying the learning process as an endeavor to an end of purification or wisdom. Wisdom is a long and winding road. Observing signs and evidence—or data and information—does not necessarily lead to a sound conclusion. Eliminating cognitive flaws (via purging and purification) precedes gaining the closest perspective on the truth and eventually gaining wisdom.

As described in the previous chapter, ignorance unquestionably disrupts and undermines individuals' ability to discern. The absence of ignorance (the acquisition of knowledge) does not entail the ability to distinguish.

---

[169] Surah Al-Jumu'ah/The Congregation, Friday—Verse 2.

Following a sound moral compass, the interaction of knowledge with experience prompts gaining wisdom, i.e., discretion, besides having a collective mind that allows society to adopt rational approaches. One gains wisdom through this interaction. Despite its dependence on a combination of knowledge and experience, wisdom is not inevitable due to their overlap. Sciences and experience have often failed to leave a mark or lessons learned. Society must have a group of such thoughts or space for intellectual diversity, considering that totalitarian collective thinking is not the means. The third section of this chapter elaborates on this totalitarian thinking and its impact.

It is essential to differentiate between knowledge and wisdom, as they are two different entities, even if they are frequently conceived as one. Through memorization and reiteration, one may name all animals but be unknowledgeable of all their species. Once again, it is summed up with another Quranic verse: {Allah has revealed to you the Book and wisdom and taught you what you never knew. Great 'indeed' is Allah's favor upon you}[170].

Right and wrong versus reason and emotion

Setting a jurisprudential-based delimitation among minors involves the ability to distinguish between right and wrong as a first step for the individual to learn the approved principles and prohibitions. In these societies, distinguishing rules constitute moral pillars and must be supported by real arguments and logical explanations within a legal framework. There is no contention and little to no disagreement on these matters, for instance, denouncing lying versus those who try to concoct scenarios where lying is acceptable.

The discretion of the wise or the responsible must progress to differentiate between true and false. Going through personal experience, discretion advances with the accumulation of experiences and expertise. The ability to exercise discretion develops the ability to differentiate between doubtful matters and what is or is not acceptable. The ability to exercise discretion is an individual characteristic, and its results cannot be generalized in any way.

---

[170] Surat Al-Nisa/Women—verse 113.

People are free to adopt boundless positions in areas of doubt. In this area, differences are displayed according to the ability to abide by principles and avoid abominations and wrongdoing. It is a free choice based on personal motives and decisions. Similar to the variation in individuals' ability to discern colors, their judgments vary and are hued by their experiences and surroundings. First and foremost, their ability to be intellectually distinctive in society also differs, which is unattainable in societies that impose cognitive orthodoxy apart from mature collective thinking. Among all the mentioned cognitive features, discretion is the most arduous and individualistic regarding its effect and role, i.e., the individual is the one to accomplish it.

Given this, right and wrong are relative and governed by disagreement. Passing a judgment varies on a case-by-case basis and according to time and place. This underlines the importance of discretion, considering these are not ready-made judgments to be ruminated on and assigned when needed for any updates. This arduous mental exercise requires deliberate examination of each issue along with all its circumstances and consequences to derive a singular judgment that may or may not be helpful in a similar issue. Consequently, this entails acquiring and developing the judging tool and not merely recalling it from memory to be recurrently put forward as a solution.

Our decision-making is often emotional- and intuitive-driven; later, the reason is engaged to rationalize those decisions. In other words, we engage our emotions, intuition, and later rationalization instead of studying "rational" and "irrational" thinking. Psychological studies usually focus on the "dual processes" of thinking. The names given to such processes or types of thinking include dualities such as controlled vs. automatic processing, systematic vs. heuristic processing, or rule-based vs. associative processing. They are not necessarily "rational vs. emotional" treatments. Thinking automatically is neither better nor worse than thinking in a controlled way, for each differs in function, but both are of equal value.

Nobel laureate Daniel Kahneman[171] and his colleague Amos Tversky[172] discovered some of the biases in people when making judgments in everyday thinking. They clarified that people use shortcuts based on prior assessments and available inference methods. Initially, the researchers observed such inferential bias as a source of error and deviation, as it generally leads people to make errors in judgment. For example, the availability heuristic is when people use ready-made judgments that come to mind as evidence of its widespread or likelihood in the world. Hence, people tend to overestimate the probability of dying in a car accident when they hear of someone's death in similar circumstances. The likelihood of dying in a traffic accident exponentially increases in their minds. This increase is due to a relevant event that is easily recalled. Such thinking can certainly lead to error and bias. What is crucial in this regard is whether judgmental inferences are generally beneficial or harmful.

At times, reasoning might not be a preferred course of action. Heuristic thinking sometimes leads to error and bias, yet it is an adaptive method of engagement, as it is exhausting to rely on logical reasoning to draw conclusions and make day-to-day choices. In truth, if humans regularly conducted a systematic, conscious, and controlled way of thinking, they would not survive. Much more than commonly realized, thinking and acting are guided by resource management and circumstances.

Nonetheless, this conclusion assumes that the natural conditions allow the ebbs and flows of life. These changing conditions create a sense of anticipation devoid of excessive pessimism or optimism. On the contrary, the standard psychological status sets people in a mode of optimism, generally expecting abundant good but rare bad things. Studies estimate that the majority of people lean toward optimism.

---

[171] Daniel Kahneman is an American-Israeli psychologist who won the 2002 Nobel Prize in Economic Sciences for his work on prospect theory. He is best known for his book Thinking Fast and Slow.
[172] Amos Nathan Tversky, an Israeli mathematical and cognitive psychologist, and Daniel Kahneman, his co-researcher, discovered the human cognitive bias and risk-taking system. He is a co-winner of the 2002 Nobel Prize in Economics.

This conclusion differs from the harsh reality of the Nawār people, who suffer under the big shadow of repressive regimes. Their stranglehold allows no political, social, economic, or scientific movements, bringing the masses down to their knees while granting them a few of these rights as differentiating prerogatives. Hence, harsh, hopeless times go by, pushing them deep into pessimism under continuous woes and scarce joys.

Both optimism and pessimism affect people's experiences in times of trouble and how they deal with them. In the face of adversity, an optimist's expectation is positive, unlike a pessimist. Optimism effectively impacts an individual's engagement with substantial life changes.[173]

In a social environment where one's aspirations and attitudes conflict and oppression are prevalent in various approaches and forms; pessimism dominates the collective consciousness. This continually puts psychological strain on individuals and mainstreams their individualistic decisions to follow the general mood. At this moment, calamities are exhibited across all walks of life. If the oppressed have no favorable winds to establish their experiences, learn lessons, and gain wisdom, their journey toward change will be arduous and faltering. The oppressed must explore their path and learn lessons during the harshest stages of their lives, similar to the different stages of the Syrian revolution.

Indiscretion and Radical Determinism

The locus of control is another factor contributing to the judgment scale. In personality psychology, the locus of control of reinforcement, or locus of control orientation, is the degree to which people believe they have control over the outcome of events in their lives as opposed to external forces, i.e., beyond their control. Julian Rotter[174] defines the locus of control as the degree to which an individual perceives that reward or reinforcement

---

[173] For more information, see the following study: Rothmann, S. & Essenko, N. (2007) Job characteristic optimism, burnout and ill health of support staff in a higher education institution in south Africa. African Journal of Psychology, 37,1, pp 135-152.

[174] Julian B. Rotter was an American psychologist famous for developing theories of psychological influence, including social learning theory and the locus of control.

depends on their own behavior and traits. This is opposed to the degree to which an individual perceives that reward or reinforcement is controlled by external forces or other factors independent of their behavior and the outcome of this behavior in terms of reward or reinforcement.

There are two types of loci of control scales. One is internal and is based on the individual's resolution, determination, and being under their control. The other is external, where the individual has no role or will to influence that factor, exclusively dependent on external circumstances. Based on the internal locus of control, individuals attribute their achievements, successes, and failures to their abilities, efforts, and decisions. Whereas the external locus of control makes individuals attribute their successes and failures to outside factors such as chance, luck, and fate.

Individuals have varied capabilities to act according to their internal locus of control and willfully influence aspects of their lives. The ability to control their health is much higher compared to the social and political realities. Yet, when an individual suffers exacerbating repression, feeling crushed and broken, one of the key defense mechanisms is resorting to external factors and leaving matters to destiny and fate, forgoing the role of doers. Similar to how their ability to take action and effect political change is almost lacking, the same thing is true regarding economic and social change. This negative engagement with reality often extends to their health, social relations, and daily personal decisions.

Determinism has been a principal assumption in many types of behaviorism, including radical behaviorism. It is one of the types of radical behaviorism asserting the position of animals, including humans, as merely passive, adaptive recipients. This perspective fails to take into account the active type of behavior affecting the environment and that it is a consequence. Besides, individuals affect and are affected by the environment, and the result of behavior can trigger a series of events and changes.

How strongly people believe they have control over their situations is evident in their motivation for achievement or work. Given their awareness of how they are in control of their circumstances, those with an internal locus of control demonstrate greater motivation for achievement. As for the oppressed, they underestimate their control over their conditions and attribute all outcomes to external factors. Hence, the Nawãri individuals surrender to a radical determinism in addressing all challenges.

Believing to be at the mercy of circumstances and unable to control events, they avoid challenges and choose the easiest options. They easily surrender, feeling overwhelmed with helplessness and incompetence, which develop into an incapability of reciprocating feelings. Due to their lack of self-confidence and feeling inefficient, they avoid feeling responsible.

Pessimism is projecting past adverse events into the present and future due to previous failed experiences. Failure generates failure. The Nawãri individuals remain passive towards changing their situation, not distinguishing between what is under their control, such as health and personal relationships, and what may not be. This prompts their belief in the sole and central role of external locus of control factors because it is impossible to improve matters. A pessimist has a self-perception of lacking control over things. Likewise, a pessimist's beliefs, ideas, or way of thinking about their capabilities in handling situations and events play a leading role. They may have false beliefs about their potential due to a miscalculation of the future or generalizing all events. Hence, negative expectations lead to negative behavior and further increase the possibility of those expected fears in the first place, which reinforces the pessimistic perspective that contributed to creating this reality. As the joke goes about a man walking in the street carrying a basket full of eggs, upon noticing a banana peel on the sidewalk several meters ahead of him, he grumbled, Poor me, there go my eggs! Under this scenario, only the worst outcome can happen as the persistent factors of pessimism and loss of the sense of one's ability to action integrate and collaborate with momentary or temporary external factors.

From this viewpoint, a pessimist holding false beliefs about themselves and their abilities to change matters continues to receive positive feedback from their persistent pessimistic behavior. They attribute those negatives to external factors and anticipate the perpetuation of this negative approach.

If prevalent in society, pessimism becomes a self-fulfilling prophecy. Accordingly, everyone goes around feeling treachery lurks around the corner and their early-warning system is ready for an eye-for-eye response. At this juncture, the Nawāri mind displays a flawed ability to exercise mental discretion. It resorts to an emotional one based on alternative criteria for the subject of debate. Thus, the argument shifts toward the debater instead of the debating point.

Bias-based evaluation produces emotional decisions whereby the individual cannot take positions on independent matters. Instead, their judgments are formulated through general conditions and the overall social ambiance. Distinguishing between the circumstances of situations separately becomes impossible, and handling each situation would follow the dominant pessimistic mood. Even signs of breakthroughs and positive opportunities are perceived as approaching catastrophes that lead to ruin; the worst is about to happen! In this context, assessing matters shifts from their origin and circumstances to their actors. It is a foundation for distinguishing instead of judging things. The Nawār individuals form their judgment on any subject according to the actors and their positions, which denotes a lack of discretion due to emotional biases that disrupt logic. We accept and justify whatever a friend does, aside from its consequences. On the contrary, we deem an enemy's deeds as wrongdoings, even if they have positive outcomes. To conclude this section, it is worth mentioning a verse of poetry for al-Shafi'i:

And in the eye of the content every flaw is so small
But in the eye of discontent every little defect is amplified

The Context and comparing options

Understanding the context of what is under mental discretion significantly makes the comparison or distinction between options more complex. It is a challenging element, being crucial in the discretion equation. As the primary variable for cases that are similar, it is intricate to understand and analyze the context, especially in the case of studying the cognitive features and practices of underdeveloped societies. They wholeheartedly welcome absolute rulings and classifications that can be effortlessly followed and applied at the group level. This approach facilitates addressing issues that Nawãr individuals do not consider urgent yet important enough to take a side. Another bigger dilemma arises regarding who has the right to make a distinction in specialized cases. Does the individual deliberating over the discretion have to take a stance on all the issues they face? Or is there a gray area to be accepted as it is without exploring or deciding which is right and wrong?

Discretion also takes subtle forms in the wrong place. To illustrate, which is more harmful? Islamic radical jihadism or secular nationalist totalitarian regimes? Who is the lesser of the two evils, Bashar al-Assad or Abdel Fattah al-Sisi? These few examples come to mind, and I hope they explain and express this notion and its purpose. Deliberating over the least of two absolute evils is a pressing concern among the Nawãr people, like others, and numerous thinkers. To compare two things, one must choose an appropriate option without primarily focusing on selecting an unacceptable one. For instance, the Nawãri individual quantifies evil through their estimation to make a judgment. If one criminal killed five and another killed seven, the first is less criminal! This elucidates the non-discretional mechanism of thinking in the Nawãri mindset. Distinguishing between bad and worse behavior must be limited to a vast, preserved sphere. An issue is eventually determined by selecting one of these options! In particular, if an issue requires high-effort thinking, that could have been better spent creating alternative options and solutions. The worst is when this chosen lesser evil is then taken as a fundamental stance that is not just tolerated but also defended, justified, and eventually assimilated to the moral code.

Do we have to adopt a stance on all issues? We are often confronted with two choices, the best of which is hard to swallow. This is called Hobson's choice[175], which indicates the illusion of choice. One of its most famous examples is "take it or leave it." Multiple choices are not a good sign, especially if all options are bad. Hence, we would have to decide on one

---

[175] Thomas Hobson (1544–1631) had a horse stable in Cambridge, England, and rented his horses to Cambridge students. Not trusting them to take care of his horses, he forbade them from riding the best ones and offered only the closest to the stable door or none. So, Hobson's choice was not a real one.

action and not another, making us directly responsible for these choices, at least in part. This means having the choice to decide whether to take a bad or worse action!

We cannot blame others for making an unavoidable moral error so long as they opt for the best possibility. They are to be blamed if they could have chosen better. Yet, we may hold ourselves accountable in situations where we are doing our best, but still, there is an obvious moral taboo that could have been avoided if offered better options. I'd be a moral failure if I did this! This is what our intuitive moral judgment would tell us if we pondered committing an inconceivable action. What would be the correct choice? Would a needy person take or give up Diyya (blood money) from an equally indigent one? Sometimes we find ourselves in a predicament that can only end in harm, and nothing is to be done to stop it.

In my view, these judgments should not be rejected but highlighted. In doing so and finding that that bad option withstood logical examination and moral judgment and was the most appropriate solution, its actor would no longer be blamed. The transformation of this forced situation into a default choice is among the disturbing repercussions, like bribery or child labor. Perpetuated for economic reasons, these examples spread to the extent of becoming customary across diverse spectrums of society. If some situations lead to unavoidable moral violations, we as a community must firmly not expose people to them. Granting people choices is seemingly good, but offering two types of moral failure is ruthless.

This passage shortly preceded the farcical presidential elections in Syria, where the pathetic dictator and some sham figures ran—a typical example of being offered two bad choices. To hold anyone under the tyranny's tight control responsible for taking part in this farce would be improper. They were not choosing one of the candidates but either to fill in a puppet's role in this farce, granting false legitimacy to the dictator, or boycott the elections and be subject to arrest, torture, and murder. As for the involvement of the Syrian citizens in Europe in this sham, it was a moral degeneration far more than the crime of a conscript forced to shoot civilians during the war, in my view at least.

Subtle discretion in the wrong place is demonstrated in undetermined matters due to a lack of accurate measurement means. The most prominent example is comparing qualitative criteria, as in saying, which is a better form of generosity or a worse form of stinginess? Preferring one answer or option to another is reasonable. Unlike adopting it as a cognitive or moral criterion, it contributes to intellectual deception instead of enhancing the faculty of discretion. What are the minimum and maximum forms of generosity? How can this unit be measured?

Conjointly, ignorance and indiscretion leave people without a cognitively guided moral compass who are passive victims and not real actors. It supports tyrants, charlatans, and swindlers in various fields. I came across a funny story a close acquaintance witnessed. It demonstrated the negative interaction of these two infections and how sound discretion may be beneficial even for the ignorant. During the nineties, a scammer called Al-Kallas[176] claimed to be a businessman and investor while running a Ponzi scheme[177]. My acquaintance was one of his victims, who came to collect interest (monthly dividends) of up to 15% monthly and 535% annually! As he and several clients were in Al-Kallas's office, a Bedouin man came in with a big sack. The Bedouin put it on the desk and told the so-called businessman, "Here is 9 million Syrian Pounds (worth half a million dollars back then). I want to invest with you. Do your count." The fraudster replied, "Bless you; no way will I recount after your, blessed Sheikh! You seem like a very trustworthy old man". The Bedouin insisted that he must count it, but Al-Kallas expressed his trust in his count, saying he had an honest face. In response, the Bedouin carried his bag on his shoulder and said, "Money not counted is money not to be returned." Then he left, to everyone's shock. They even pitied him, believing his stubbornness cost him a great

---

[176] Muhammed Al-Kallas was one of four founders of the Kallas & Amino company in Aleppo in the 1990s. It defrauded more than two hundred thousand people. Several swindlers carried out similar work several years later, whereof the most notorious were the Jarbou Group, Al-Dairi, Al-Kweifati, and Al-Bayanoy Company.
[177] A Ponzi scheme is a false investment marketing scam that generates returns for earlier investors using the money obtained from later investors. It is similar to a pyramid scheme as both rely on using new investors' money to pay previous shareholders.

investment opportunity. Four months later, the fraudster ran away with a loot exceeding one and a half billion SYP, or 32 million US dollars, back then. The narrator of this incident, a merchant and businessman, lost ten million of his savings, plus double that amount from his relatives.

The Bedouin, more ignorant than the experienced and knowledgeable businessman, had the discretion factor on his side that determined who fell victim to the scammer. The victimized businessman overlooked all he knew about trade, achieving profits, and distinguishing between profit, which is varied in nature and percentages, and fixed interest. He altered exercising discretion from the investment and its rationality to the fraudster's identity. The fraudster cunningly played the pious, righteous man, on point in his appearance, demeanor, hospitality, and surroundings. He spared no effort to convince people that he was the epitome of piety and righteousness. Accordingly, the discretion element was altered from the fraudster' irrational business model to his religious façade. The scammer's victims did not base their judgment on his religious demeanor but on what he exhibited about Islam, a religion that prohibits fraud and manipulation. On this basis, a religious person would abide by these rules. Considering that the so-called businessman acted religiously and would not commit fraud or manipulation, subsequently, this cannot be a scam. Even if there is no explanation or bridging of the ignorance gap in this issue, and if accessible knowledge and experience stir doubt, the absence of discretion led to the catastrophe facilitated by ignorance.

Still, ignorance and a lack of knowledge of investment and trade exposed the Bedouin to manipulation. What saved him was the faculty of rationality and discretion. In contrast, trade knowledge did not prevent the businessman from falling victim to the scammer. How can an investment generate profits if the business partner is willing to give dividends of five times the amount of the capital in just one year? More accurately put, "Is this a real project?" The answer is either a conceivable or an inconceivable project. If it is inconceivable, then it is a hoax. Materialistic gain and greed led to overlooking the first question and deciding on a less obvious one. The ambiguity supported accepting what our minds refused. Over time, several mental alterations reduced the issue to wondering whether Islam permits fraud and manipulation, which was met with a resounding no. Hence, the solution would promote submitting to a reassuring answer.

Ignorance and indiscretion share a synergistic relationship. They expose thinking to manipulation and transform it from a decision-making tool into a blind follower, compliant with more predominant and ready-made choices. Unsurprisingly, imposters adopt seemingly religious modules, and populist dictators overly affirm their simplistic popular affiliations and conservative religiosity, bringing them closer to their ruled commoners. Indiscretion affects the ability to make sound decisions and pushes toward following the herd's choices. Consequently, collective consciousness plays a bigger role in individuals' judgments, apart from being forcibly imposed. These two cognitive infections allow for totalitarian cognitive solutions; they entrench the pillars of political, military, and economic totalitarianism.

3- Totalitarianism

> Ours is the world, and all who dwell upon it,
> And we assault we assault in power.
> We are called oppressors; we never oppressed yet
> But we will preemptively strike our oppressors[178]

Totalitarianism is commonly defined as a form of government or political system; it prohibits all opposition and exercises excessively high, if incomplete, control over public and private life. It is the most extreme and ultimate form of authoritarianism. In totalitarian states, political power is often in the hands of autocrats (dictators or absolute monarchs). They employ all-encompassing campaigns to tighten their grip on all spheres of practical and intellectual life by disseminating supportive propaganda in state-controlled media while silencing the voices of all who dare to express criticism or opposition.

Totalitarianism is not just a political project; it is cognitive system that facilitates authoritarian control over societies through imposing brutal, collective thoughts, destroying freedom of thought. Exceeding the role of

---

[178] From the suspended Ode of the pre-Islamic poet Amr bin Kulthum.

hierarchical ruling systems, totalitarian governments have a cognitive system that governs all aspects of society. This totalitarian thinking conceptualizes law, religion, and culture and gives birth to society's heritage following the ruling totalitarianism.

Hannah Arendt[179], the German-American historian and political theorist, pointed out that the Nazi and Soviet regimes did not come about overnight. They were a product of cultures imbued with popular ideological movements in the nineteenth and twentieth centuries of imperialism and anti-Semitism. Hence, the most dangerous demagogues in history share the blame with the masses who adopted their ideology and established their cults.

If we may use this term, cognitive totalitarianism is founded on rejecting the concurrence of contradictions. The discrepancy between the various dimensions of personality is inconceivable. For instance, just as a pious individual cannot be a fraudster, nor can a defiant ruler compromise with the enemy, a heroic soldier cannot be a thief or a traitor. This would utterly reduce all the complexities and align them along one dimension.

All complex ideas within totalitarian thought are reduced to fit into its logic. All intricacies and discrepancies are filtered out. Ideas are diminished into plain, superficial projections. Likewise, these projections can be generalized to everything associated with that idea. Accordingly, the destructive American policy in the Middle East assumes all that is American is destructive, whether a cultural or technical product, a medical vaccine, or whatever bears an American brand. This projection establishes a comprehensive reaction to everything relevant to the main point, meaning the USA. Rejecting any aspect relevant to this point (USA) must be thorough and absolute. This repetitive simplification on several points eventually creates an identity for the Nawāri individual's intellect as resentful of the world.

---

[179] Hannah Arendt (1906–1975) was a German-Jewish political theorist and scholar. She is best known for her work on violence and power. She authored a book on the origins of totalitarianism.

Totalitarian thought prepares the mentality of those under control to push society into identifying with the "masses" and create a grouping termed "the divergent and deviant." It goes beyond the "us" and "them" division into "the all" and "the adversary." The other group is contrasting, external, and opposed to all we represent. It is our unquestionable, indisputable antithesis and a direct existential threat. In this section, I focus on how cognitive totalitarianism is established in the Nawãri society, its impact, and the relationship dynamics between the ruling tyrant and the oppressed.

When a group perceives another through the "us" and "them" lens, there is meager space for recognizing the peer element. In other words, they are plurality-based and not individual-based. Also, they are equals, although at fault, guaranteeing them the minimum level of humanization. Contrastingly, the entirety and the contrariety concept are based on monopolizing the plurality and denying it to the antagonist. It is based on denying all that is "we"-based on this "antagonist". This immensely befits dehumanizing that antagonist.

The discrepancies between authoritarian and totalitarian regimes contribute to understanding the totalitarian mindset by switching the administrative system features to an ideological one. These regimes are based on a single authority, be it an individual dictator, a military council, or a small elite group monopolizing all political power. Contrary to authoritarian regimes founded on state power and the absence of popular will, totalitarian regimes desperately need popular involvement and participation. Totalitarianism goes the extra mile to set ethical and cultural standards and regulate all social, cultural, and economic aspects. Authoritarian regimes are established and continue to be so without interfering with or controlling the economic and social systems. Besides, they do not rule under a specific political ideology and rank as excessively corrupt, whereas totalitarian power is ideological and includes an orthodox intellectual dimension.

The tyrants' self-image is another difference. Authoritarians' self-image underlies the desire and preservation of power. Totalitarians perceive themselves as not mere tyrants but epics with a mission to change and reshape the world and a message to convey at any cost.

Therefore, authoritarian regimes are not less tyrannical. However, they do allow for a considerable sphere for private life and pluralism in social organization. Lack of ideology is translated into their inability to mobilize their subjects to pursue national goals. They exercise power within relatively predictable limits.

In contrast, totalitarian regimes exceed administrative governance to affect all other social, economic, and cultural aspects. With an inspiring leader on top, they develop a charismatic cult of their personality among the masses. Following a populist model, it formulates a bond with the masses, strengthened by manipulating the masses' consciousness, where the leader creates a sacred halo around their personality. This role is fulfilled using repression and state control over businesses, trade unions, places of worship, or political parties to create its myth.

Historically, religious influence and heritage supported totalitarianism. Until recently, Christian religious organizations in Europe had an authority comparable to—and sometimes surpassing—the monarch's. Therefore, dominating and later domesticating them under the ruling system was vital. Throughout history, European authoritarian regimes based on ethnic or social class were cloaked in a religious mantle. Or, they opted for a secular, military ideology that opposed everything related to the sacred metaphysical perspective, such as the communist regimes in Eastern Europe and Asia.

In the colonial administration, exploiting religion proved highly beneficial to managing un-modernized societies. Hence, the ruling regimes, prior- and post-colonialism, harnessed religion to attain its sanctity and avoid any challenge or change. The totalitarian idea was spread over all aspects of life, undermined development, and killed the establishment of any future field by preventing or restricting it as much as possible. Even "secular" regimes such as Assad's and Saddam's resorted to religious legitimacy blatantly and unscrupulously.

Absolute righteousness

Absolute righteousness is a Christian principle based on the idea that God endows the sincere believer with uprightness and righteousness under the

Lord's will, just as He did with Jesus the Savior. In the Second Epistle to the Corinthians, the apostle Paul said, "For him who knew no sin he made to be sin on our behalf, so that in him we might become the righteousness of God. (II Corinthians Letters, 21)[180]. This true believer becomes the executor of God's will on earth.

The idea of a righteous individual God uses to carry out His will is found in Christianity and other religions, where this absolute righteousness means meeting all legal and moral obligations. From the evangelical perspective, it is related to how close the individual is to the Lord.

There is a similar image in Islamic tradition regarding the relationship between Allah and His righteous worshippers. The following Hadith Qudsi[181] refers to this saying: "Whosoever shows enmity to one of my devotees, I shall be at war with him. My servant draws not near to Me with anything more loved by Me than the religious duties I have enjoined upon him, and My servant continues to draw near to Me with supererogatory works so that I shall love him. When I love him, I am his hearing with which he hears, his seeing with which he sees, his hand with which he strikes, and his foot with which he walks. Were he to ask [something] of Me, I would surely give it to him, and were he to ask Me for refuge, I would surely grant him it."[182]

These religious traditions solidify those pious worshippers, motivated by the right causes and dedicated to the ultimate virtues, become God's servants on earth to carry out His will and all that pleases Him. These religious traditions outline a perfect image of how believers can affect the world, challenging the conviction of absolute fatalism. Yet, in the meantime, this is a store of material for creating human practices that endow whoever implements them with divine holiness. Instead of God being the source of this righteousness that the righteous servant pursues, that creature becomes God's independent voice and the sole, ultimate source of divine wisdom.

---

[180] The Epistles to the Corinthians are among the New Testament letters attributed to Paul the Apostle.
[181] Hadith Qudsi A special category of Hadith literature, where their content is attributed to God but the actual wording was credited to Prophet Mohammad.
[182] From Fath Al-Bari, vol. 11, p. 34041, Hadith No. 6502.

That creature possesses the absolute righteousness intended to prevail and govern the world. Often shrouded in this puritanical halo of holiness, tyrants carry out divine will, regardless of their apparent religiosity or immorality. Although numerous famous religious leaders exploit this aura, we barely see its effect in their close or public circles. This sanctity and the accompanying miraculous abilities only serve their owners.

Absolute righteousness in theology is a confusing cognitive dilemma since it is associated with divine will and wisdom. Still, rightness as a principle, i.e., right and wrong, and identifying which is more right out of two choices remain arduous. However, the one irreplaceable single truth where all else is wrong, even a sin, is what makes absolute righteousness a far deeper issue. When adopting what is deemed absolute righteousness, it becomes people's shield against being held accountable or investigated. By adopting this divine correctness with firm faith, their judgments acquire the divine touch.

Absolute correctness ideology is based on cognitive totalitarianism, where the ultimate truth lies in the sole absolute rightness. This undebatable and unarguable absolute correctness is part of fixed axioms that top a plethora of arguments, clear proofs, and conclusive evidence. The knowledge of absolute correctness is exclusive to an extraordinary few with good intentions and brilliant visions.

The totalitarian cognitive system produces a body of thought that includes several embedded contradictions. As an indivisible and selectable unit, its characteristic totalitarianism is underlined. It is also simultaneously a public and private system. If ignorance and indiscretion do not facilitate this system's acceptance or adoption, the Nawāri individual's need for self-preservation would force them to accept and act upon it in any event. It is a cognitive equality process through reprogramming individual thought and integrating it into the totalitarian system. Similar to how the calm and collected news anchor maintains a steady tone and demeanor regardless of the broadcasted news, the cognitive set becomes a single unit functional at all times. In every corner lurks an enemy. Every strange matter is undoubtedly a conspiracy. Every action of the regime reflects unparalleled wisdom and is unquestionably in the people's interest, even if something proves otherwise. It is the absolute correctness that everyone must see, even if they do not.

This absolute correctness stipulates several factors for its realization, as it denies any contradictory facts or skeptical ideas and opinions. Additionally, it entails a public pledge of allegiance, for which an cognitive identification essentially facilitates adopting this single truth. In the subsequent sections, I highlight some of these factors.

Absolute correctness indicates a timeless, unarguable, and ultimate, fixed truth. It is the cornerstone of underdeveloped thinking, whereby specific data become postulates beyond observation. Subsequently, the drawn conclusions become unchangeable and in-expansible. Similar to taking scientific evidence from religious scriptures to attest to the earth's flatness. Therefore, all information and data contradicting this idea is unquestionably false, and any assumption based on the spherical earth must be rejected by flat earthers.

These absolute facts create a stone blocking any way forward. For example, the advent of the savior of humanity, resulting from an incomplete or erroneous understanding of some religious scriptures, remains a centuries-long hope for generations. It also block any other solution for salvation. Only meeting the conditions for his advent is what they need to strive towards. These universal certainties and their counterparts compose the nucleus of rigid thought. Over time, they multiply, increasing the number of totalitarian opinions that serve their purpose, whether from scholars, preachers, or political leaders. This ceaseless growth is mirrored by a never-ending decline in this thought's correctness. Unscientific and selective in what it attracts, it disregards what is relative and theoretical and ignores change.

Likewise, the Soviet five-year plans ruined millions of lives. Yet they are rendered holy to avoid accountability, no matter how devastating their results are. For example, the Great Leap Forward[183] in the People's Republic

---

[183] An economic and social campaign that the Communist Party of China launched between 1958 and 1961. It aimed to use its large population to rapidly develop from an agrarian economy into a modern communist society through rapid industrialization

of China that Mao Zedong[184] executed resulted in the Great Chinese Famine, killing around 18 to 42 million people. The Soviet economy also suffered failure due to the Gosplan[185], responsible for increasing poverty and diminishing people to turn to the black market to buy what they need for their subsistence. A closer-to-home example is Abdullah Al-Dardari's economic plan; he was the deputy prime minister for economic affairs in Naji Otri's[186] government. His plan to abruptly turn to the open market economy—in a county with rabid corruption and a totalitarian regime—destroyed the agricultural sector in the Syrian desert within two years. They caused the internal displacement of two million Syrians and the loss of one of the most crucial Syrian pillars of self-sufficiency and food security by destroying millions of hectares of agricultural land and its produce of wheat and grain. These outcomes are not viewed as evidence of the failure of planning and its supporting rationale. Conversely, these plans are faultless, but the results did not turn out right; the results are irrelevant to these outrageous actions!

Contrary to absolute political correctness in totalitarian regimes, which catastrophically affects millions of lives, religious absolute correctness typically confines itself to theoretical issues. The rejection or adoption of religious absolute correctness influences individuals involved, whether the believer afflicted by its content or those denying it, who may be accused of disbelief and heresy, leading to probable killing or exile. Absolute correctness in totalitarian regimes goes beyond those directly involved to influence other unborn lives. All in all, absolute correctness accepts no

---

and collectivization. It failed to achieve industrial transformation. Simultaneously, the agricultural policies failure and farmers' transition from agriculture to industrial sectors, probably forced by weather conditions, led to a severe famine that killed nearly 5% of the Chinese population, according to some estimates.

[184] Mao Zedong (1893-1976), also known as Chairman Mao, was a Chinese politician, Marxist theorist, military strategist, poet, and revolutionary who was the founder of the People's Republic of China.

[185] The State Planning Committee, better known as Gosplan, was responsible for central economic planning in the Soviet Union. It was founded in 1921 and remained until the dissolution of the Soviet Union in 1991. Its main task was creating and managing multiple five-year plans governing the Soviet Union's economy.

[186] He was the prime minister of Syria between 2003 and 2011.

debate or approach except when identifying with or confronting it, bearing the repercussions of these attitudes.

One measurement and one Judgment

What sort of environment produces a totalitarian mindset? It is reality polarized into black- and white-categorized values and judgments. This totalitarianism did not naturally result from cognitive and social regression and underdevelopment. It is a product that reflects active decision-making and will in an oppressed society to formulate this totalitarian consciousness. Totalitarian oppression regimes effectively created unprecedentedly fragmented societies, suffering a social atomism never witnessed by humanity. Forced and not self-triggered, society is not responsible for its fragmentation. This penetration of social structures and their systematic destruction is unprecedented. It is not the aftermath of natural disasters or incidents but a conscious design of social construction that facilitates the tyrant's dominance over the masses.

Generally, social structure is based on the sincerity and solidarity shared among a group's members. They form relationships away from totalitarian authority. This network poses a direct threat that must be radically eradicated. Hence, all forms of gathering, even wedding ceremonies, are suppressed. In the tyrant's Syria, the General Intelligence Department has to approve and inspect wedding ceremonies to ensure that matters are in order. All public spaces and spontaneous gatherings are monitored, such as markets, schools, and places of worship. Informants brazenly infiltrate them all! For a totalitarian regime to ensure the utter subjugation of society, all forms of organization and collective action are eliminated; even families, tribes, and sects are not spared. Individuals must be utterly fragmented, and sincerity must be void of tangible meaning and content from which cognitive changes are naturally generated.

Unswervingly, the totalitarian regime creates a single monolithic narrative and correspondingly categorizes the "all" and the "adversary." The totalitarian regime constructs prefabricated recyclable propaganda using redundant and superficial language fit for all occasions and on repeat. This is illustrated in the discourse about the global imperialism conspiracy against resisting countries to break their will. During the information explosion era, where facts and data exposing traditional propaganda are impossible to hide, totalitarianism resorts to ambiguous language, speech, and words with obscure connotations. Doublespeak is the language used to deliberately obscure, hide, distort, or reverse the meaning of words. It may take the form of euphemisms, e.g., "downsizing" for layoffs and "servicing the target" for bombing. It disguises the nature of truth and obscures understanding of hidden meanings. At the same time, it silences all voices trying to explain and elucidate reality or reveal the contradiction in the totalitarian discourse.

The Nawāri individual is confronted with two options. The first is recognizing the official narrative's validity, regardless of its embedded contradictions. The second is the risk of falling into a mix-up of their inferences about circumstances and the message of the propaganda body. To exaggerate its narrative, influential figures are recruited, including imams of mosques, artists, intellectuals, and academics. This mobilization of advocating figures effectively pushes the Nawāri individuals to approve the official narrative validity, aside from how its lies are flagrant. Otherwise, there is only aggravated confusion and helplessness. Additionally, this media mobilization and the suppression of all opposing voices heighten individuals' sense of isolation if their convictions conflict with a belief seemingly prevalent among all actors in a totalitarian society.

The totalitarian mindset is duly created with a unified external reference; it is not the individuals' rational conclusion nor the outcome of transparent public discourse that discusses, explores, and constructs this reference. Conversely, authoritarian violence imposes this external reference that drives and forces identification with external behavior while enforcing self-isolation and silent suffering. Under totalitarianism, the Nawāri individual cannot even imagine any reality other than what the totalitarian-created mindset perceives. The totalitarian mentality forces identification with the surroundings, lacking well-established conviction or belief in their correctness. Not fearful of isolation, but rather the Nawāri individual's fear of being exposed as an adversary!

In many respects, cognitive totalitarianism is natural and effortless. Humans are biologically predisposed to align with broader group logic or the collective mind. It is easier to wholeheartedly embrace an ideology or ready-made narrative than to thoroughly sift through and systematize the inconsistencies and nuances of every political issue. Thus, one can uncomplicatedly discredit our political adversaries and glorify our heroes with a fixed, unified mindset instead of recognizing strengths and unavoidable weaknesses. It is millennia-old knowledge.

The totalitarian mentality is rooted in the belief in an immune and sacred reference for managing and settling all aspects of life. It develops a closed-society system where reference is under the authority of one individual, group, or faction privileged with unlimited powers, striving to organize all aspects of public and private life as much as possible. Whether it is a state or a religious institution, they fulfill the same function of framing and even crushing public life. The totalitarian mentality creates ultimate generalized judgments that are standardized and become basepoints for their logical arguments. Hence, the totalitarian regime's popularity among the masses stems from its rigid ideology, providing convenient answers to all past mysteries and present and future challenges.

This holistic approach is reflected in the collective consciousness of the Nawãri community—its primary practitioner. It requires neither exploring the basis of any action nor putting it through a logical judgment. This explains its appeal to the general public and their exemption from responsibility or repercussions. Moreover, it provides a set of ready-for-any-question answers. The Nawãri person follows their community by adopting a single, unchangeable answer to all questions. The expansion of science and knowledge does not incite holistic thought approaches to produce updated responses; on the contrary, previous answers are generalized to fit more than one question. "it is shameful", or "every innovation is a misguidance"[187], or "this is a foreign conspiracy" are effortless justifications to deny responsibility and avert change. In using them, any discourse or emerging matter is set as part of a waiting list for the high and mighty

---

[187] A blurb from a hadith attributed to prophet Mohammad and narrated in "Sunan al-Nasā'ī" number 1578.

cognitive totalitarianism to integrate them into the ready-made propaganda to be later disseminated among the masses for them to follow.

The totalitarian authorities impose blanket answers, and over time, these involuntary shallow answers, though intellectually unconvincing to those spreading them, are circulated. Its frequency escalates with prolonged oppression. Due to a combination of forced cognitive totalitarianism with the incipient ignorance of clueless youth and indiscretion, the lack of alternative answers becomes an undeniable fact. Moreover, society lacks the knowledge and ability to provide an alternative perspective for their own affairs or establish answers to what totalitarian authority constitutes.

Identification

In psychology, identification refers to an emotional bond between two parties linked to a perception of a common characteristic. The greater the importance of this common characteristic, the greater the success of this partial identification that represents a new bond between those involved. This mutual bond lies in the nature and strength of identification based on a significant shared emotional quality.

Therefore, identification is an cognitive state based on the cohesion of a human group in terms of a common characteristic, such as ethnic or religious identity or a binding relationship. It is integral to human harmony that forms human groups. Hence, it is a positive element, being the building block for group identity in the collective sense, besides enriching the individual personalities of its members. However, there is a total, unconditional identification that affects a human group. This totalitarian form obliterates personal identity, replacing it with a prefabricated alternative, usually based on a total-identification one. Founded on imitation and simulation and imposed by violence and coercion, ultimate totalitarian identification denies the personal identity of subdued individuals. It is only possible by eliminating individual identity and taking the forms of family, tribe, sect, and other examples.

All forms of thought are domesticated under the shadow of absolute power to establish totalitarian ideology in society. Hence, the so-called National

Progressive Front[188] took over the Syrian partisans, consolidating the one-party system, eradicating political life, and keeping domesticated parties as lifeless ruins. This corresponded with eliminating all intellectual forums resistant to and challenging the totalitarian scheme, such as the Syrian Communist Party (the Political Bureau) and the Muslim Brotherhood movement in Syria. A "skimmed" religious identity was created with carefully selected religious leaders as its representatives. A false revival of religious organizations in public life gradually came to be, such as the Qubaysiyyat movement and some Sufi schools. All forms of intellectual diversity were eviscerated through this domestication process, and the cognitive totalitarianism project was completed. "Rogue" organizations and parties were forced to accelerate their identification with the current regime, regardless of any intellectual conflict between their foundations and the ruling totalitarian regime and its practices. Consequently, Baath's doctrine[189] became the sole form of affiliation against utterly drained opposing identities.

Total identification most prominently characterizes Nawãri groups mired under the iron heel of totalitarian rule. It is facilitated through shifting the imposed totalitarian identity of the Nawãri community to a negative intellectual one, opposing whatever lies outside the totalitarian belief boundaries. This negative identity consolidates the founding pillar of cognitive totalitarianism: all versus the adversary, which is its nucleus. This clarifies why it is a widely influential instrument for identification among the Nawãr. What ideas they share are insignificant, but what they are against matters. They are against imperialism, narrow-mindedness, treachery, capitalism, globalization, Western moral decadence, and later Bashar al-Assad. This cognitive totalitarianism based on a negative identity shields totalitarian beliefs against osmosis with other ideas. In the Nawãri view, all that does not fall within this bubble is a strange and hostile thought! It is

---

[188] A coalition of nationalist, socialist, and communist parties in Syria led by the Arab Socialist Baath Party.

[189] Unity, freedom, and socialism—Baath's intellectual nucleus and its message—symbolize its ideology. My reference to these concepts is satirical, especially since the Baath Party, inextricable from Assad's Syria, was a mere shallow facade like all subservient parties governed by Assad's gang.

odd and rejected because it is globalist, imperialist, conspiratorial, and Western.

Individual space in Nawār society is impermissible; thus, their creative spirit and characteristic identity are lost. Additionally, its individuals are rigorously forced to identify with its ways, customs, sciences, and thinking. Given that all forms of difference and modernity are challenged, this society's responsibility extends beyond defining choices of vocabulary, dress code, and rituals of weddings and worship to governing the mechanism of individual thinking, setting its boundaries, and even its resources. The Nawāri individual exerts their best efforts not to diverge from the ordinary, neither in their appearance nor openly declared opinions, knowing that differentiation threatens individuals despite striving to follow the herd. With the looming menace that going off-track would inevitably expose them to social disapproval, one divergent case is the herd's target of elimination. Otherwise, another would follow suit.

People are the materialization of social legacies and are often victims of their surroundings. Try as they may, they cannot escape these manacles. It is only possible to elude them or avoid becoming entirely overwhelmed. Even if partial, emancipation from a group's bonds means offering the soul a unique opportunity to think outside the prevalent belief. Individuals must fight the herd's pull not to lose their absolute and free-of-restrictions humanity, allowing them a fresh breeze of free thinking and escaping stereotypes.

Differentiation and diversity in society usually enable its members to reconsider their reality and beliefs. In contrast, intellectual sterility and absolute identification eliminate genuine variation, where individuals fail to realize what they grasp or imagine for themselves. After a generation-long domestication and forced identification, it is inconceivable to perceive an intellectual and political alternative in Nawāri communities.

Nawāri individuals take up the exceedingly dangerous task of grasping the judge and executioner, or authoritarian, and their motives. It emanates from a desire to rationalize the Nawāri reality and understand the opposing party. Rationalized Nawāri individuals try to be objective in a comparison where they are not neutral or objective. Triggering an emotional reaction, Nawãri individuals are further infuriated over their reality. A more hazardous undertaking is seeking an equation for justifying the authoritarian's actions. Seats are swapped, and they play the authoritarian's defense attorney and judge roles. Thus, identification with the authoritarian is accomplished.

Called authoritative identification by Dr. Mustafa Hijazi[190], it is probably among the most crucial and prominent intellectual aspects of Nawãri individuals and is used as among defensive mechanisms for the oppressed. He/She defines it as usurping oppressed people who flee their world to be lost in the authoritarian's, expecting salvation[191].

According to Hijazi, identification takes three forms: identification with the judgments and aggression of the authoritarian, and dissolution in the authoritarian's world. This last stage is the most hazardous degree of identification driven by the desire to be lost in this world and not by external violence.

The rampant spread of total identification and its emergence in the Nawãri community are at the core of totalitarian thought that most characterizes Nawãri groups. Ruining their last opportunity for change, they are blinded to possible alternatives. Eventually, it leads to an outbreak of oppression, forcing them to normalize and accept it, even perceiving it as a form of heavenly or earthly justice. Thus, Nawãri individuals become guards at the gates of oppression, where the motive of identification with the authoritarian is self-targeted by society. Confronting oppression becomes useless and is a severely punishable sin. At this point, integration with oppression is the most optimal, and the group's best response is to accept it. Hence the motto of the Nawãri wisdom: "Put your head on the chopping block and cry, 'O, executioner."

---

[190] Mustafa Hijazi is a Lebanese writer, academic, and psychologist. His book "Social Underdevelopment: An Introduction to the Study of the Psychology of the Oppressed Man" (1981 AD) is a significant reference in understanding the impact of domination and oppression on the masses.

[191] Mustafa Hijazi, The psychology of the oppressed person, Arab Development Institute, p. 127.

"Cry out, O Executioner!"

A state of assimilated existence among the members of Nawāri society is forcefully urged to impose what or what not to believe. It also sets an intellectual reference stereotype that defines the standards of judgment. To join this society, individuals must submit to this stereotype and conform to the group. This intellectual conformity is conditional on involvement in this community.

Conformity with the group is a branch of modern psychology. It clearly illustrates the human tendency to override common sense and abide by collective wisdom, even in decisions held wrong by the same individuals. However, this group is based on narrow-minded affiliation, family or region, and a counter-identity, making everyone outside that group the other, an opponent, and an enemy! Nomadic tribe and clan values resulting from the desert diaspora, successive famines, occupations, and series of tyrannies in their history probably contributed to establishing the Nawāri reality of an environment hostile to life. Regardless of the prosperity witnessed in the Nawāri community, the narrow group system persisted.

These narrow groups have excessively complex relationships. In adverse times, their individuals are connected in a manner that makes their decisions an interactive series, reiterating a decision unaware of having this cognitive bond. The Nawāri society shares grounds but has conflicting interests. Although its members tend to act selfishly and subjectively, they often settle for the "wisdom of the crowd"[192] on crucial and daily issues. In the unconscious conformity context, the Nawāri collective is gathered around existential threats, besides minor matters such as customs, rituals, and social etiquette.

This intellectual conformity consequently establishes a cult within the Nawāri society based on blind submission to a unified reference; it produces a herd whose mentality lacks individualism and whose behaviors are modulated according to the opinions of their group. It might be an ethnic-, religious-, regional-, or class-based group or a mixture of those. Subsequently,

---

[192] Wisdom of the Crowd is based on the collective opinions of a group of individuals to answer a specific question rather than an expert's.

individualistic dissolution exacerbates, and identification and integration deteriorate on the cognitive and doctrinal level and across external appearance, language, race, and all other criteria for identification. At this stage, individuals are lost in the group's crucible. External and often internal identification preserves the group to the point through which tyrants alternate, attitudes change, and business-as-usual modes are effortless.

Joining an cognitive herd of worshiping leadership symbols results from a deeply rooted instinct in the animalistic origins. Like all creatures, the human race is driven to follow the herd mentality for self-preservation. According to William Hamilton, the British evolutionary biologist, each group member primarily serves their interests by engaging in this herd. To reduce any risk to their lives, they become part of it, practice its behavior, adopt its ideas, and defend it.

Subconsciously, individuals know that exploring and observing their challenges do not bear direct fruit for their interests, so the herd leader is delegated to discuss such matters and provide answers. Research, examination, and discussions are arduous, whereas imitation is more accessible and far less tiring. People generally comply with norms without thinking twice about defying them. It grants them a fair sense of psychological security, and they are exempt from the responsibility of forming and owning an opinion.

The danger of this identification is in treating it as a sacred imposition that endows people with euphoria, contentment, and tranquility. They are tamed to submit to and reconcile with the fait accompli as an unchangeable fact. In a herd, individuals increase in number; thus, the responsibility is confused, dispersed, and relinquished. This submission results from reflexive actions that undermine rational judgment. The unconscious produces these personal and collective actions, as directly demonstrated when recalling violence and unplanned oppression extensively spread across their life aspects within the herd. Hannah Arendt ascribed the evil practices of ordinary Europeans towards the Jews in World War II to the "almost total inability ever to look at anything from the other fellow's point of view." The Nawãri herd's submission is similarly due to its individuals' inability to perceive themselves outside the all-encompassing violence and the victimhood context that justifies submitting to reality and involvement in its corruption. This is attributed to their passive practices as part of the collective rituals of the herd.

The herd and the rise of the "Good Shepherd"

A central reference and an alpha leader are integral to a herd. The herd mentality constantly awaits a leader to think or act in its place, especially during crises. Conscious individuals are absent through this pattern in a predetermined way to follow decisions, but not due to oppression or usurpation of the leadership of the herd leader. The moment a herd vigorously relinquishes and obviates responsibility, it marks the making of a dictator. Though this process is fulfilled through the dictator's violence to impose their authority, it begins with the collective withdrawal from leadership and responsibility, besides the rise of someone aspiring for leadership.

Nietzsche[193] linked Christian morals with the rise of herd mentality. He considers Christian values a slave morality that arose in the Roman Empire to help people abandon their goals due to their inability and helplessness, which obstructed their way to the life they wanted. Also derived from Christian culture, the term good shepherd, which I borrow, comes from evangelicalism's designation of Christ and his role in leading believers toward salvation.

This term is used in the Gospel of John to describe Christ's role in restoring the Temple. The relationship between the shepherd and his sheep is known in the ancient East and among the ancient people (descendants of Israel). They considered themselves the flock of God—their own shepherd throughout history. Two aspects of power are conveyed in the shepherd's metaphor, simultaneously reflecting the leader and the companion.

This philosophy contributes to establishing an cognitive—and not just an organizational—need leadership. This leads to the urgent need for the birth

---

[193] Friedrich Wilhelm Nietzsche (1844-1900) was a German classical scholar and philosopher who became one of the most influential modern thinkers.

of a good shepherd at any time or age. A herd without a shepherd is a propagation of misguidance, and the shepherd's absence only signals divine wrath. The shepherd is not merely functional but indicative of the special care of divine providence represented in the resurrection of this kind and good shepherd in his wisdom and firmness. Hence, the necessity of the shepherd—any shepherd—is linked to the flock's survival and the only guarantee for salvation and achieving goals.

Given that the shepherd is connected to divine providence, the shepherd's character is insignificant during the selection process performed by metaphysical providence. Therefore, the qualifications and ethics of this shepherd are minor details, being the divinely chosen one. The universal wisdom made this choice, and there is no need to look further. Be it Bashar al-Assad or Donald Trump, nothing changes. Once the choice is made, this shepherd becomes central in everyone's life. His personality becomes part of their existence. He is irreplaceable and has a clean image and a unique personality. This now-symbolic leader is chosen for leadership without choosing or seeking it. Being The One with a singular character and exceptional traits, what these are is irrelevant. Their morals become the ideal model for the shepherd's morals.

Among the multiple forms of love is a deep affection for the idea of the good shepherd filling the hearts of faithful parishioners. It evolves into adoration for the one assuming this role in society, where the herd can be a religious or political group or a family tribe. Granting them magical powers, the beloved (good shepherd) enjoys immense freedom above criticism. Their characteristics are fully appreciated beyond their peers, to the extent that the shepherd surpasses their very selves before being chosen as the shepherd (beloved).

This imposed idealism is an internal tendency in the Nawãri society, distorting intellectual judgments and substituting the ideal self, unrealized by its individuals. Subsequently, the shepherd's adoration is for the aspects of perfection of which the Nawãri individual dreamed. By substituting self-narcissism, the shepherd's idealization exceeds the judgments of logic and conscience. It also develops into an unlimited commitment to glorify and serve the good shepherd, who replaced the self-ego of Nawãri individuals.

This infallibility and blind love qualify any leader as a candidate for the next tyrant. Whether their advent is through democratic systems or volunteering, it does not differ from taking over the leadership through hereditary succession or a military coup. It precedes any stage of tyranny and domination later practiced by the tyrant. This early stage of creating tyrants and authoritarianism is far from the limelight and is rarely discussed. It is barely mentioned that certain groups are susceptible to submission to tyranny, similar to how some groups are ready to be colonized[194]. Contrary to that, the susceptibility to tyranny, henceforth referred to as governability, precedes the spread of tyranny in these societies. The susceptibility to colonization results from the colonial act, that is, subjecting people to colonization, so it follows the act of colonization. Susceptibility to colonization is probably a deep internal submission to colonialism, as Malik bin Nabi identifies it. Therefore, submission led to the perpetuation of colonialism but was not originally its cause.

It is even safe to assume that governability and susceptibility to colonization are the outcomes of mental and psychological traits ingrained in a particular nation due to specific historical circumstances. Hence, their resistance is futile, or rather, not initiated in the first place.

Though the herd instinct's emergence in human societies is undetectable, there are undeniable, noteworthy factors when examining this phenomenon. To exemplify, comprehending the susceptibility to colonization is inseparable from the colonizer. Likewise, one can never understand the nature of governability and herd mentality if the good leader (shepherd) concept is neglected.

Given all this, the tyrant does not arise from a vacuum or is born gifted with their personality. Rather, tyranny arises from society's anticipation and mental image of the good shepherd. Their anticipation embodies a symbol that is the raw material for creating the tyrant, expecting nothing from them or holding them accountable for anything. The void, signifying the collective

---

[194] Malik bin Nabi discussed the concept of colonialism in his book "Conditions of the Renaissance," 1948. He addresses the responsiveness of colonized individuals to accept all the restraints, systems, and ideas set by the colonizer, defining the reality of the occupied.

withdrawal of intellectuals in particular, besides all members of society, accelerates the transition toward tyranny, initially entrenched by glorifying and deifying any leader. The solid emotional bonds displayed in the Nawãri groups sufficiently clarify the governability concept. A lack of independence and initiative taking among its members is highly characteristic of these groups.

The Nawãri communities facilitate creating good shepherds through relinquishing responsibility and attachment to flattering those in power. The shepherd might be the head of a group or the chief of a religious or scientific reference. The tyrant may not necessarily be a political symbol or a civil or military ruler. The dependence phenomenon has constantly been part of the natural constitution of human societies throughout history. Transitioning from a hunter-gatherer lifestyle to stability and agriculture stages, human roles have differentiated and gotten more specialized. Some chose to rely on each other to fulfill specific functions, such as agriculture, protection, and ruling. Hence, reliance on and delegation of group leadership arose. Due to the scarcity of initiative and courage to take such a position, and given the collective awareness of its importance, a sanctity aura was formed and surrounded whoever took up leadership, regardless of the merits and requirements of that position.

During the past century, several dictatorships emerged and developed before our very eyes. Though this is prominently relevant to Syria's political and social reality, it is equally applicable to many countries globally. Many of the political analyses conducted during the inception phase of these dictatorships implies to the reader that they were spur-of-the-moment events. The fact that they were simmering in front of our eyes. It is unfathomable how these dictatorships grew and thrived in an era of open skies and witnessed by people and the world's parliaments. We supported them, believing they were a democracy, national sovereignty, and a firm administration!

Leader of the age!

On an ever-high alert, Nawãr individuals brace themselves for imminent dangers triggered by cognitive totalitarianism. Hence, there is a lasting need for a "wise captain" to manage and steer the ship to safety. It is insignificant if it bursts into flames, killing its passengers. It is inconsequential whether these imminent dangers or scarecrows are real; they necessarily outline the journey. Approaching the danger zone instead of being indicative of the expedition's and its captain's failure proves their competence, genius, and foresight.

The dictator wages war on neighboring countries to distract the people besieged in their homeland. Moreover, they nurture a negative identity toward the world to guarantee the isolation of Nawāri people and to remain hostage to this reality. The totalitarian regime stirs problems in cases of impasse, recalling historical grievances and lurking conspiracies as a diversion from what is rotten in their own home soil. Fear shapes people—partly fear of actual internal oppression and potential external aggression. In this reality, the tyrant blatantly exploits whatever is possible to instill it. To contain this growing fear of the unknown, the Nawāri or society ignores their inner, known, and recognized fears (such as fear of poverty, sickness, and failure). Gradually, anxieties are integrated into one wholesome reality for them. Fearing the unknown and denying what is already in front of them, the autocrat establishes a forceful and active intelligence agency to infiltrate people. These bodies are reinforced by two key factors: first, the necessity of diverting attention away from and submitting to internal oppression and second, being watchful of the unknown. Finding it unbearable, the oppressed cannot just acquiesce to the reality of being held under the tyranny's grip, robbed of their dignity and rights. Instead, they seek solace in the illusion that the tyrant's regime represents their homeland. They become interchangeable. The security of this regime seals its security, and in defending him, they are defending it. The term "Assad's Syria" was used in reference to Syria for decades before the eruption of the revolution and the subsequent de facto partition of the country. The state of denial of the reality of oppression goes beyond directly targeting the oppressed. It includes the subjects of the brutal regime in the country and abroad. This is until the individual becomes a direct victim of that oppression. Powerless and helpless, they are abandoned by their own group, which turns a deaf ear to what will become of them. Thus, the dominant authoritarian decides who belongs to and who is expelled from the group or "herd."

What most astonishes me is how numerous activists and those involved in the Palestinian cause, whether Palestinians or not, interact with the Syrian revolution cause. How can those dedicated to defending the right to life and self-determination for a particular nation deny them to another because the ruling authority of a country witnessing a popular revolution declared support for their root cause? Among those is the Palestinian poet Tamim Al-Barghouti[195], a devoted advocate for the Palestinian cause who viewed the Syrian revolution as a "civil war" from its early days. He considered Hezbollah's participation in killing and displacing Syrians a "necessity" to protect the supply lines of the Israeli battlefield. Al-Barghouti deemed Syrians defending their land against Hezbollah to be Israelis and believed in Nasrallah's "honesty" in saying the road to Jerusalem passes through Qusayr and Zabadani. The British singer Roger Waters[196], a pro-Palestine activist, proclaimed that the Syrian White Helmets[197] are just propaganda and a front for terrorist organizations. Waters deemed the Syrian regime's chemical attack on Douma "staged". The list of this intellectual schizophrenia among celebrities and intellectuals around the world goes on.

The masses assemble around the Good Shepherd as oppression grows and intensifies, united and fortified in their response. Under oppression, they unanimously agree on a central, unifying identity based on avoiding confrontation with the tyrant or opposing the tyrant's actions or words. In choosing safety over confrontation, fear underscores the social feeling in a unifying manner. The authoritarian's aggression becomes a positive bond of identification among the oppressed. This emotional conversion is influenced by a mutual intimate bond with someone outside the group—the tyrannical shepherd.

---

[195] Tamim Al-Barghouti holds a doctorate in political science, but his poetry surpasses his political thought, so he is mentioned as a poet.
[196] George Roger Waters is an English songwriter, singer, bassist, and composer. In 1965, he co-founded the pioneering rock band Pink Floyd.
[197] The White Helmets is a voluntary civil defense organization operating in areas under opposition control in Syria. Established in 2013, it provides relief to those affected by the Syrian civil war. The organization considers itself neutral and impartial and pledges no allegiance to any political party or group.

The Intellectual Aspects of the Oppressed in the Nawāri Society: 197
"Belongings"

Focusing on the unknown, external "terrible", and disregarding the known, internal (local) terrible is an intellectual phenomenon worth studying. The internal suffering is not only a reason for controlling the herd and evading accountability for and opposition to the leader. It goes beyond to being a factor in the identification of the oppressed to becoming love and gratitude to the tyrannical shepherd, not for being the source of that oppression but for being capable of managing and legalizing it. The miserable subjects profoundly appreciate this much control over the herd. At this stage of my discussion of the dictator, I will take a different, untrodden pathway.

Does the answer lie in changing the perspective of these observers? Arguably, oppression, its extent, and scope are often arduous to realize by internal observers, given their limited level of free observation and the lack of a benchmark to compare their situation. Yet can an external observer examine a reality they never experienced or does observing from a distance make them an objective, impartial, and rational judge?

Saddam Hussein[198], a dictator for many of his people and a historic commanding leader for his devotees, most typically illustrates how varied humans are in pinpointing the tyrant and realizing the existence of tyranny. More than 17 years after his death, people are still divided on whether Saddam was a criminal tyrant, a resisting leader, or an honorable fighter from an external perspective. Some may admit Saddam's massacres of innocent civilians in Iraq. Nonetheless, his resistance to foreign countries and combating invaders justifies all crimes he committed against his people and his motherland. External observers widely share the perspective of the internally oppressed on the role of "savagery" and "brutal oppression" as a necessity in protecting "nations". They also agree on the necessity of unity in combating external danger, whether it is possible, actual, or simply imagined. Though both sides acknowledge the massacres and crimes committed, none dare openly admit that Saddam is a criminal and a tyrant

---

[198] Saddam Hussein Abd al-Majid al-Tikriti (1937-2006) was an Iraqi politician and revolutionary who served as the fifth president of Iraq from 1979 to 2003. He ran a repressive authoritarian government, which several analysts have described as totalitarian.

responsible for destroying his country; therefore, that "objectivity" of external observers often misses the target!

There are successive—and almost set—stages over the tyrant's lifespan. Yet, upon observing those timelines, one finds how the tyrant unexpectedly seizes control of matters or overthrows figures and symbols of opposition at certain junctures. Dictatorship imposes itself on the public stage at historical moments, seemingly as an unthinkable brutality that erupted in the minds of its victims. Conversely, a positive image is maintained among their supporters, especially when these unimaginable acts are committed under the guise of uniting the nation under their leadership. Violence does not protect the tyrant; public silence does, as popular support induces their superiority, empowering tyrants to command people. Analyzing these turning points in a dictatorship's history is focused on while oblivious to in-between events. This approach begets emotional analysis, lacking accurate conclusions. The oppressive transformation is due to historical moments and situations, regardless of what preceded or succeeded them. Hence, in Nawāri thought, judgments are related to positions justifying external historical events. The Syrian revolution devastated the country, and the second Gulf War destroyed Iraq! Contrarily, the Syrian economic recession was brought about partially because of the American sanctions, though it preceded the sanctions. This perspective contributes to submitting to these dictatorial transformations, which are difficult to anticipate and prevent, seemingly instantaneous, and justified for analysts. Subsequently, economic prosperity and freedom utterly declined before the Arab Spring eruption. They went unnoticed for years and were deemed insignificant until these revolutions started.

In the 2021 presidential election campaign, Assad's supporters chiefly portrayed him as a captain who steered the ship to safety! This caricatured description inspired this section's title. Why not! He bombed cities, destroyed the nation's infrastructure, and displaced more than half of its population, killing hundreds of thousands of them! He brought its economy to rock bottom, and its currency lost more than 99% of its value! What a great captain who truly brought his ship to safe shores!

Hence, self-dictatorship does not exist. Dictatorships are fabrications that rely on external factors to bring a dictator to full power. The famous saying "there can be no tyrants where there are no slaves" eloquently summarizes the ultimate mechanism for inevitably creating a tyrant. And whoever denies what the tyrant and his masses see is nothing but rogue subject that must be isolated and expelled to maintain the country pure and homogenous—a repeated proclamation by the tyrant. Opposing what the tyrant has done or is doing is taboo. Whoever dares to express their minds is compelled, within hours, to backtrack and publicly pledge absolute allegiance. They must reaffirm that they would sacrifice body and soul for the omniscient leadership, debasingly fearing the exclusion inferno that burns those not aboard the ship.

4-Exclusionism

We, the knights, assault all people
and kill people until the country becomes desolate[199]

As previously indicated, the totalitarian approach to thought and society produces an orthodox mentality based on the belief in an absolute truth, invalidating and combating what contradicts or challenges it. A single universal truth is imposed on everything under its jurisdiction, eliminating what challenges its narrative. However, individual inner thinking, for instance, does not fall under tyrannical totalitarian control.

Due to their inability to eradicate any opposing inner thoughts, totalitarian regimes resort to isolating any dissenting voices within their sphere of control. Totalitarian authorities do not merely address these dissenting ideas' influence but also fight to completely deny their presence. They take an active role in trying to prevent their emergence among people.

Despite the immense intersection between cognitive totalitarianism and exclusion, I chose to divide them into two sections for being successive stages of Nawāri thought development. The cognitive totalitarianism phase

---

[199] A verse from the pre-Islamic poet Al-Harith bin Abbad's poem is about his entry into the Al-Bassous war after his son was killed and taking revenge.

skims any intellectual and identical diversity in society. A vague identity replaces it, where the regime shapes its form and controls its discourse. Over a short time, the GCC-Israel relationship evolved from hostility and anti-Jewish rhetoric to comprehensive normalization and flattery of Jewish religious references. This was met with no opposition or objection within their societies due to the totalitarian thought phase of molding the oppressed into suppression tools for the adversary (other). Consolidating the vague totalitarian doctrine impedes identifying, judging, and criticizing its content. Yet, it facilitates identifying the opposite of that idea. With drums of war beating against the "adversary," the regime's media outlets disseminate the vague, indoctrinated identity. The oppressed would rush to suppress and exclude those "adversaries." Economic, social, and even religious exclusion occurs in media spaces or the dungeons of prisons and detention centers. Tracing how the relationship of many Arab states with the state of Israel transformed in 2021 and beyond would sufficiently elaborate this idea.

Exclusionism, on the other hand, is a product of cognitive totalitarianism that grew over ample time. The ability to develop a rigid ideology decreed by oppressive regimes. After living under totalitarian regimes for years, the general public is more like hounds wrapped around the masters' fingers, ready to attack any individual who chooses to control their thought-making. With the slightest of dissenting signs, they would howl or bark at anyone.

Excluding reality

Human relationships form an integral part in shaping human consciousness. These interactions create a social reality that becomes a postulate of a concept or principle. Social reality is the product of human dialogue, whereby the created ideas constitute more than just a living and shared reality for a group. It becomes factual in their conscience, setting norms to rely on for judgments. Social reality can be viewed as a component of the accepted social principles of a society. Thus, stable laws and traditions and a social identity are forged.

Social cognition is associated with a memory connecting past and present emotional experiences, perpetuating their sense of group awareness. This awareness becomes normative for individuals or groups. According to

Hegel[200], our universe has absolute truths separate from existence. Besides, individual consciousness creates a perception of this existence; this awareness, or truth, is sensory and simultaneously internal. It is partly valid, not for being an inner truth exclusive to individuals but a shared one with this sensory perspective. This shared perspective is a reality of social origin. It becomes a community-based practical "reality" that serves as its reference.

Social reality is formulated in an interactive process that produces common values. Bound by its temporal and historical contexts, it entails time and effort. Human knowledge is based on data corresponding to existing reality. It is not absolute but generally fixed and governed by standards that vary according to the environment. Although it may be scientific- and objective-based and irrelevant to the senses, human knowledge may also be subjective- and value-based. To illustrate, in any society, a cuisine relies on what is accepted and forbidden. For example, Christians in Syria and Lebanon did not consume pork products because they were prohibited among Muslims but because pig farming consumes large amounts of water, which is inaccessible. Likewise, bulgur is a centuries-long culinary staple in Syrian cuisine. Rice is relatively recent in East Mediterranean cuisine because it requires high temperatures and flood irrigation techniques. Nowadays, due to the availability of rice, it is possible to substitute it with bulgur. Though not that obvious, this change can be traced and put in context. However, no one denies Arabs their rice, nor do Arab Salafis demand a return to bulgur and wheat flakes.

Any concept has a universal and another-bound form specific to society and culture, linked to certain needs to be met. Let us take marriage as an example. It is defined as the union of two people as partners on legal, societal, religious, or cultural bases. Multiple cultures recognize marriage as the most acceptable framework for commitment, having a sexual relationship, reproduction, or adoption of children to start a family. Marriage, its motivations, and objectives are not necessarily shared across cultures. For instance, in Saudi society, marriage is the only accepted

---

[200] George Wilhelm Friedrich Hegel (1770–1831), a German philosopher, was one of the founders of idealism and had a significant impact on the development of philosophical dialectic.

framework to engage in a sexual relationship, unlike Norway or Portugal, which do not share this perspective.

Even if references are shared among cultures, the concepts resulting from social reality remain varied among peoples, within the same people, across generations, and at different times. Though believed to be the basic framework for a marriage contract in most Islamic countries, a nikah/wedlock contract in Islam is not synonymous with the concept of marriage. Marriage in Egypt is perceived differently from Saudi Arabia; in Saudi Arabia, some conditions in marriage contracts are not included in Egypt, for example, equality in lineage[201], though both countries share the same religious reference. Consequently, the social reality of marriage—presumably a concept recognized in a given society—varies according to time and people.

The legislative approach to regulating a marriage contract in different societies illustrates the extent of differentiation in each of them. In the United States, a marriage contract framework stresses the financial responsibility towards spouses and children. It does not necessarily promote having children or give any special support for that. Contrarily, in Japan, it entices families to have children. In some conservative countries, it is a mechanism for legitimizing sexual relations, while in others, it is a mechanism for legalizing sexual relations. In every social circle, marriage has an image imbued with its formula, goals, and laws. Though seemingly minor and secondary, such discrepancies hinder a person of a specific society from comprehending the purpose of a concept in another, regardless of how universal and unanimous it is.

Social reality's development into a "truth" shared among a human group is ever-recurrent. This transformation of common knowledge may be unconscious and enforced by social references. Lacking factors that bring this social reality to experimentation and the absence of opposing voices turn these realities into a primary—and probably the only—criterion among members of that group. The more closed a society is, the more resistant this

---

[201] In Saudi Arabia, the judicial authority has the right to annul a marriage contract on grounds of unequal lineage. Wives' parents usually resort to divorcing their daughters from unwanted husbands.

reality to be tested and changed. The greater the oppression practiced under the totalitarianism of the ruling authority, this social reality is forcibly modified to consolidate that authority, whether religious, political, or social.

The idea precedes the empirical stage, thus establishing an initial form of knowledge and producing a pre-experimentation hypothesis. Guided by reason and by senses, the hypothesis directs the experiment and carries out the knowledge forward. But if there was no experiment to test it this form of knowledge is still carried forward. Consequently, this initial idea becomes ingrained in the mind and consciousness almost as a commandment. Over time, this unchallenged and unrefuted commandment gradually grows into an intellectual axiom, further underpinning it—the human mind actively rationalizes and defends it against any transient doubts or challenges. Entrenched in consciousness and spreading over collective consciousness, this untested idea is transformed into a unanimous truth, above any questioning of its validity. Hence, logic—the tool that was supposed to guide towards accuracy and truthfulness—becomes a means that impedes achieving that. The rational interpretations that were to guide us to the truth are now a means of its distortion.

Some polls surveying issues that challenge norms prevailing in a given society reveal how the overall reality dominates individual and collective thought. Pew Research Center[202] polls found that more than 90% of respondents in Indonesia agree with the obligation of killing apostates; equally, Egypt and Saudi Arabia approve of stoning adulterers as an obligation; and 98% of Nigerian respondents and 97% of Jordanian respondents approve of rejecting and criminalizing homosexuality. Besides, in the United States, cousin marriage is stigmatized to the extent of being criminalized and punishable in five states. Such polls reveal some social reality features and how firm a belief gets in society.

Both opposing parties must be considered to examine any belief. But in a closed group, we encounter a different approach to weighing in the stances of each party. On one side, those of conviction do not imagine the existence

---

[202] Pew Research Center is an American research center in Washington that works in the field of peoples' research and publishing.

of an adversary among their own group, deeming them automatically as outsiders. It is not a thought-centered disagreement but rather that of the central identity uniting that group. From their perspective, the adversary is then defying that thought AND their identity; they are strangers, outsiders, intruders, and enemies. Therefore, they do not belong to that group, are unaccepted, and are shown no mercy. For them, it is unimaginable that an adulterer can be a son, or an atheist can be a daughter or a brother. They have a demonized image of the adversary; they are far from being humans, let alone resembling one of them. Hence, the idea of any dissenting thought, or its existence within, is exterminated. Inhibition factors applied in that society constantly protect this conviction to maintain its cohesion.

The other party, in turn, believes that its opinion is dissenting against collective truth and has no place in society. Outsiders' opinion is intimidated by social rejection, severe punishment, and the loss of belonging and sense of identity. Therefore, those on the dissenting side fear losing society's trust, facing its wrath and hostility, and losing themselves; the core of their identity and belonging are at stake, not just their safety or social image.

Across human history, there are some indeterminate and untraceable social truths that are incompatible with reality. Accordingly, an increasing gap grows between social reality and existing reality. When reality exhibits a change in data, the social reality is not subject to evolution and therefore inconsistent with that change. Instead, society pursues preventing change in its social reality, despite how detached it is from real-life experience. Some readers may relate to multiple cases relevant to religious heritage detached from present reality; these are innumerable, considering the extent and aggravation of this growing disparity in several areas. Living on their historical glory, that group continues to feel as a pioneer in this world. They feel that they are timeless world leaders on some level. This leadership shifts from intellectual and moral to military, according to emerging circumstances. They remain oblivious to a reality overflowing with opposing real-life data. Before the 2011 revolution, Syrians pride ourselves on being an educated and science-loving nation. Despite this being far from truth when you look at levels of high education per capita in that country over time. We cling to a self-image that defies evidence. If anyone succumbs to responding to factual reality, their right to belong to the group is lost. Hence, we live with the reality that "whoever denounces us is none of us."

Exclusionism shifts the point of discussion from disputed facts and the validity of beliefs or refuting evidence to the true loyalty of that adversary who is disputing that core societal image of itself. Steering discussion toward debaters is a defense mechanism against criticism. It is to maintain the homogeneity of the group and remove any impurities is the target to facilitate its total identification with the despot. Teaching Nawār individuals the concept of exclusionism itself is the most substantive for intellectual exclusionism. It is more accessible than indoctrinating them on the perceived social truths and how to defend each of them. Nawār are to get one thing into their heads: this disagreement indicates non-belonging, an unforgivable crime. Consequently, the perpetrator must be punished and excluded before examining the defect punishable for non-belonging. And later, this becomes the sole prerogative of the tyrant or their custodian to mind these intellectual conflicts among the Nawār.

Ideas are not judged by weighing them against evidence and logic. Instead, a checkpoint is established to inspect the debater's identity. At this checkpoint, this dissenter is excluded for being an outsider to that group, for which holding a debate with them is now pointless. They are from the adversary party, i.e., enemies and conspirators. The Nawāri society must identify and hunt down those who perpetrated the sin of being "adversaries." The sign at the checkpoint reads, beware, lest the faith slips out of your hands, where each Nawār individual becomes a gap in the wall of "us."

In this manner, Nawāri individuals deduce and transmit acquired exclusionary ideas themselves as recognized absolute truths. And so, the path to a journey for reason and social evolution is blocked with formidable guards who never disobey whatever the tyrant or the social commandment dictates.

I don't know who we are, but you are all against us

Back to reversing positions at light speed while continuing self-reconciliation and conformity to oppressed Nawāri groups, similar to the overnight changing positions on Arab-Israeli normalization. This example elucidates exclusionism and how it works to maintain unity, purity, and homogeneity. Such incidents in oppressed societies are identified as a wag-the-dog situation; the tail shakes off what's not part of it. Exclusionism is an uprising that uproots everyone who displays symptoms of dissent.

The exclusionary idea's content is irrelevant. It's acceptable to instantly alter your mind from prohibiting women's driving to supporting it. Its function in discarding dissenters is what matters. Exclusion is the goal, then, not pursuing doctrinal or fundamentalist puritanism. It seeks homogeneity and identification with the ruler in what is said and decreed.

Those with an exclusionary mindset are molded according to their societal reality. They will, therefore, continue to subject the next generation to the same totalitarian rule. Society now sees only through one eye and see only one color, believing it must ensure the analogousness of the collective perspective with that of totalitarian authority. Holding the right and tha ability to change that color, totalitarian power can reverse any stance overnight. The formidable guards of that soceity ascertain that everyone alters and conforms to this inversion. Cognitive exclusionarism is now autonomous self-dependent. Reality is one and must remain that same one. All else is baseless, absurd, and harmful and must be contained and removed at any cost, along with its believers and all it produces. Exclusionary discourse remains the same in religion, culture, politics, and economics.

Banning books and blocking satellite channels, apps, and websites characterize the oppressive regimes of the modern world. Surveys of countries with similar practices of infringing on thought and science never lack an Islamic or Arab country. This blocking and intellectual censorship exacerbates, according to how much military and security oppression is practiced against dissenters on land and abroad. The obstruction of opposing ideas adopted by the totalitarian approach creates the exclusionary ideology, which is the highlight of this section. What is blocked and accepted may change in a blink of an eye. Today's enemy can be tomorrow's friend, whether a channel, a country, or an author.

The exclusionary idea is ancient and deeply rooted in Nawār societies. People have sought to stand out since the early days of humanity. So, they created a barrier to distance themselves from the rest. It was initially an act of self-preservation to keep out enemies. Throughout history, traditional kingdoms and empires prohibited pluralism of thought at variable degrees; this was exclusive to specific domains apart from political and sometimes religious ones. Freedom of thought was bridled lest the resultant intellectual pluralism create a political challenge, threatening and contesting the legitimacy of that tyrannical administration. The elimination of political pluralism led to the gradual uprooting of intellectual pluralism in other fields. Subsequently, intellectual and religious trends merged to become one, and then expanded to engulf social norms and other aspects of culture. Accordingly, intellectual unilateralism in those areas became a direct result and guarantee of political unilateralism within a closed circle, which characterizes the region's history.

Cognitive totalitarianism is exclusionary by default, as the totalitarian authority must impose its vision, exploiting all its tools to dominate all aspects of life and isolating whatever opposes its absolute dominance. It outlines the "all" in that society. Similarly, cognitive exclusionism is everlasting and unshakeable. And the one who is excluded is irredeemable, as it was and is with the communists and Islamists in Arab countries. Its influence may even last for successive generations with no chance for forgiveness, let alone acceptance and openness in interacting with it.

Cognitive exclusionism is established by imposing a dominant pattern of thinking and behavior that does not necessarily abide by its intellectual content. As mentioned, its focus is to preserve unity and expose dissenters. The divergence from this pattern is considered disobedience or an abnormality that must be fought. And so, Intellectual unilateralism becomes dominant. The single-opinioned mentality of the Nawār community is the seed of exclusionism; our intellectual heritage, political history, and social history are conspicuous proof. Intellectual unilateralism is reinforced as integral to life and an unchallenged truth.

Oppressive nations go so far as to make whoever knows about the existence of these dissenting ideas accountable for crimes, besides stifling opposing ideas and criminalizing individuals who hold them. Similar to Arab countries, Syrian and Egyptian prisons swarm with inmates and detainees incarcerated for no reason other than having a forbidden book or attending a gathering deemed objectionable, or simply knowing that someone has done so and not telling on them. In Syria, owning Sayyid Qutb's[203] book "Milestones on the Road" or performing Fajr/dawn prayer in mosques called for arrest and trial. These acts might even be punishable by the death penalty. At any rate, punishing those criminals is not a lesson for them only but a message for the whole group. This brutality is not necessarily relevant to what is deemed a "grave" act because the violation, any violation, regardless of its nature and severity, is an unforgivable crime. Not only do perpetrators of these acts bear the brunt, but also their kin may suffer greatly. Consequently, society en masse responds promptly to eradicate all forms of dissidence and strive to maintain intellectual purity. Exclusionism is an instrument for cognitive totalitarianism to preserve purity and extract and filter out all dissenters. It works well against skepticism that questions the leadership's judgment or the validity of its convictions. In a Nawār society, the authoritarian ruler automates exclusion as a part of the functions and duties of good citizens towards belonging. It threatens their lives if they fail to cleanse society of impurities that threaten its purity and homogeneous structure. Hence, those "adversaries" must be secluded by banishment abroad, imprisonment, isolating them from society, or voluntarily isolating themselves.

5- Isolation

And I have among them a family that is isolated
and brothers who disdain the party of corruption[204]

Cognitive totalitarianism and exclusionism automatically lead to the renouncing of dissenters. There is no place for those outcasts who have a different understanding of the world. In some cases, they are exposed to

---

[203] Sayyid Qutb is an Egyptian Islamic writer, theorist, and a former member of the Muslim Brotherhood's Guidance and Executive Office. In 1966, he was executed in Egypt on the grounds of calling for overthrowing the Egyptian regime and the application of Sharia law. He was considered the father of Salafi jihadism.

[204] A verse from the poem "And his money is plundered by the question" by Lebanese poet Ahmed Fares Al-Shidyaq (1804–1887).

forced exclusion through expulsion and distancing from the group. Individualism is the practice of an individual's goals and desires as independent values from tis society. It is a personal choice there an individual creates a path of their own, setting themselves aside from the rest. They can live independently, and so they do.

When a Nawāri person's beliefs change, they pursue a subtle form of isolation, because they are unable to acquire independence from their group and have self-reliance. Being dependent on this group for their survival forces them to embrace a secret seclusion. Silenced and secluded, the outcasts feel anguish, leading a life of internal isolation unrevealed. Their opposing faith remains undisclosed to their group, fearing their wrath and being thrown away.

Here is revealed: many in Nawāri societies pay the dearest price: forced to spend their lives putting on masks unlike who they are. Many of them cannot bear the hardships of expulsion, banishment, and subsequent social and authoritarian punishment. Forcedly, they cling to their bubbles and distance themselves from a reality that denounces their entities and ideas. These loners see themselves only as divergent in contrast to the "all" group. They believe themselves sinners for being the only ones whose thoughts deviated from the rest. Some of them seek refuge in repressing their opposing beliefs. Dissimilarly, others firmly believe in their differences, making retreat not an option; they are ready to risk their lives in an existential battle.

Readers of this introduction might conclude that these isolated individuals are a limited anomalous group, believing in atheism, homosexuality, or other religious and social taboos. However, a long list of ideas and beliefs entails the punishment of exclusion. Many secretly declared their rejection of oppressive bodies and opposition to totalitarian regimes or watched their lives go by without having the chance to proclaim and develop their beliefs. Isolation in the Nawāri community is a plague too widespread to be ignored or deemed a mere exception.

Depriving the Nawāri community of voices opposing the totalitarian authorities and the homogeneous herd reinforces loneliness and alienation.

No voice echoes what reverberates in their hearts and minds. Therefore, they may suffer the lives of strangers, isolated from their peers under one roof or in one neighborhood. Surrounded by the tyrant's informants, they are perpetually apprehensive and suspicious that some clue will escape, exposing them.

Alienation in social relations is demonstrated through a lack of integration, the degeneration of shared values, or the growing alienation of individuals from each other or a group of people in society. It is defined as the powerlessness of being or the inability to be in control, where the individual expects or guesses that their behavior and work are futile. Several classical and contemporary theorists developed this social concept of multiple uses relevant to the discipline. It can refer to a personal psychological state—as previously mentioned in the Inner Solitude section—and a type of social relationship discussed in this section.

Sociologist Melvin Seeman comprehensively defined social alienation in his research, "On the Meaning of Alienation." He presented four features of alienation. The first is powerlessness: socially isolated individuals believe that their life events are beyond their control and that their actions are ineffectual. In this way, Nawãr people are destroyed. If their domestication is unrealized, like the herd, whatever is left of their human traits is broken, and despair takes over their consciousness and sub-consciousness. If they do not give in to domestication within society, they are objectified in dark torture chambers and prison cells.

The second feature is meaninglessness: when an individual loses the ability to derive meaning from the things in which they are involved, or at least not the shared or normative purport derived by others.

The third feature is social isolation: when a person does not have a meaningful connection to their community through shared values, beliefs, and practices, and/or when they do not have meaningful social relationships with others.

The fourth one is self-estrangement (or self-denial). Suffering from social alienation, people may deny their personal interests and desires to meet the demands made by others and/or social norms.

Isolation in the Nawāri community is a closely tied leash. This isolation, ironically enough, becomes the last remaining shared connection. As individuals, we choose to be secretly detached, not knowing that the majority of us keeps a secret for themselves while externally trying to assimilate in the group. Living in its shadows, we all conform to and identify with our society. This secret isolation is the way of life for the majority for various reasons and motives. They relentlessly attempt to survive and maintain a formal affiliation with an imagined group. Vague cognitive totalitarianism outlines this imagined community. The vaguer its collective identity becomes; the more Nawāri individuals isolate themselves. Hence, adapting to this silent, isolated reality is inescapable.

Syria has long been based on treating its people as a collection of loners, isolated, frightened, and trapped in the kingdom of fear created for them. Loneliness and isolation were criteria for succeeding in fulfilling this job. This explains the unbelievable transition from the small protest of March 15th, 2011, to the Friday of Dignity[205] on March 25th, 2011. It was a death declaration for the Assadist kingdom of fear. The panic in Hauran[206] and several separate protests erupted not for their grievances but in solidarity with the Hauran people's grievances. It was a new sense of belonging to the vague image of the Syrian nation. However, shortly thereafter, the ruling authority, multiple Nawār community leaders, and parties within the revolutionary movement co-suppressed this popular explosion. Nothing was left but to revolt in their way. Otherwise, they are either traitors, or adversaries to be exiled for the sake of revolution's purification from them and their misguided ideas, or to voluntarily quit and leave the arena to the "real" revolutionaries.

Ode to glorify isolation

For many cultures worldwide, isolation has an aura of reverence and glorification. In written literature, isolation is positively and fascinatingly depicted. It is true that, at times, individual isolation is beneficial for the

---

[205] Syria's "Friday of Dignity" had many local uprisings full of surprising dissent and immediate deadly repression by the regime.
[206] Hauran is a region that spans parts of southern Syria and northern Jordan.

soul and can purify the mind. As for adopting it as a permanent collective approach in society, this is the psychological and intellectual factor this section attempts to examine. When isolation turns into a life approach and a constant attitude towards the world, it changes from a temporary refuge to a whirlpool, throwing those within to lands beyond their world boundaries.

There is no denying that isolation is a temporarily positive space. Sages in isolation meditate and take up a temporal space—and sometimes a spatial distance—away from the noise and life's hustle and bustle. This "wise" isolation results in the individual's rebirth in the world with a clearer vision that may sometimes be different. In contrast, a sense of survival, seeking no prophecy, feeds Nawār people's isolation. It is eternal, with no attempt to come out of it. The isolation of the wise sage is perhaps a means to an end, while the Nawārs' are final, with no escape. The isolation of the wise usually takes a spatial form in a sanctuary or an office, or it may be a temporal one during the night. The Nawār has no time or space dimensions; its residents can be amongst thousands of people. Isolation is a double-edged sword. A person would emerge strong and insightful, or psychologically weakened and disabled.

History grants isolation a spring of credibility and fascination. Syrians often derive the sanctity of their isolation from Islamic heritage; Muslims deem isolation part of their heritage. The Islam Message saw the light out of the dark cave of Hira[207]'s isolation. Besides, several Quran verses support and emphasize isolation and distancing from violators and sinners. Contrary to prevailing public understanding, tradition chiefly advocates and classifies mixing with people as better than isolation, bearing in mind that isolation is for worship and to ward off wrongdoing. Hence, in Islam, mixing with people is more preferable than isolation. This is indicated in the Prophet's hadith: "A believer who mixes with people and endures their annoyance is better than the one who does not mix with them and does not endure their annoyance."[208]

---

[207] This site in the Annour mountain holds tremendous significance for Muslims throughout the world, as it is here where the Islamic prophet Muhammad is said to have received his first revelation of the Quran.

[208] The hadith is narrated by Al-Tirmidhi, (2507); And Ibn Majah (4032).

Comparing humans to animals individually, numerous animal species are more adept at adapting and surviving. In other words, animal survival skills significantly outweigh human ones. Let us imagine a man and his dog getting lost in the forest for days. The chances and ability of the dog to survive exceed its owner's. The same happens when comparing humans to mice or mosquitoes. Humans stand out in comparison to other living creatures not for their physical abilities—noting that humans' mental abilities are not what enabled them to rule the world—but rather their sole prerogative, which is the power of communicating, co-working, and trusting other humans.

Natural biologists widely argue that many animal species and plants communicate with each other using audio, visual, chemical, or even electrical code. They are recognized as languages similar to the diverse languages of humans. This is a limited view of human language and communication and how they differ from animal communication. Animals and plants naturally share signals of short-term semantics such as "Watch out! A wolf is coming!" or "Look! An apple tree!". Would an animal communicate with another about a matter, whether un-instantaneous, intangible, tangible, or perceived? Children are narrated a bedtime fairy tale about fictional monsters and events. Though completely a figment of imagination, it is interactive and would stay vibrant in their memory. Humans are the only species capable of using language in symbolic and abstract senses. We lie, interpret, and talk about past and future events; this does not comprehensively illustrate the intricacies and uniqueness of human communication and its capabilities.

The sound of isolation

Imagine that today one can review the ideas of Aristotle or Abū al-ʿAlāʾ al-Maʿarrī without ever personally knowing them or ascertaining they existed. You read a book written by someone you hardly know, printed with a machine assembled by people whose names are unknown, and eat food grown and prepared by strangers as well. You might even write down thoughts based on predecessors' work to devise an unprecedented idea or create a new product for folks you will never meet. Humans did not go over to the moon or examine the smallest of atoms due to an individual's genius.

These are millennia-long discoveries, shared experiences, and accumulated science.

Monkeys live in small tribes for communication and to provide confidence. A monkey in a tribe must fully know its fellow and ascertain its behavior, sincerity, and loyalty so that he stops harming him. Without this full knowledge, confidence is reciprocated. I highly doubt that many of us ever thought of one's tailor, whether they abided by their principles or were stealthily looting from the herd! It does not concern most of us whether the garbage collector is committed to the religious values we believe in or not!

Similarly, oppressed people suffering from isolation completely reproduce their judgments according to the relationship, or lack thereof, between them and those around them. Nawãri people replicate a monkey tribe's method, that is, dependence on exclusive communication, exclusive adoption of ratification, acceptance of what is exclusively internal to that group, and rejecting the unfamiliar. In the series of cognitive regressions in Nawãri societies, this isolation goes beyond being an outcome of exclusion to an active factor independently. Undoubtedly, it is far from lacking the ability to influence and determine a Nawãr 's behavior. To build a rational basis for these practices, the Nawãri mind discriminates against what is not the herd; it is centered on finding what differentiates others more than classifying them according to a basis. This approach outlines the "all" group in contrast to the "adversary" few without the slightest interest in who falls under it. From these cracks, racist and immoral practices emerge with the support of an intellectual philosophy established on superiority, mastery, and, to a large extent, conspiracy theories.

The state of isolation on which I focus, and estrangement share several similarities and discrepancies. On the one hand, isolation results from the conscious and intentional actions of individuals who deliberately dissociate themselves from those around them. On the other hand, estrangement stems from the inability to establish human communication, regardless of futile attempts. A lonesome person tries to communicate with the world from which the loner is escaping. Isolation is an individual distancing themselves from the noise, danger, and turmoil, while estrangement underlines emptiness due to a lack of human interaction. Isolation creates a sense of reassurance, deepening the chasm between a recluse and the world.

Specific intellectual and psychological elements sustain Nawāri isolation. In an intellectual and social environment where totalitarian and exclusionary tyranny rules and rejects all else, people lose the ability to communicate with those around them. Due to closely inspecting their surroundings, they increasingly drift towards being on guard and distant from all suspicions. These factors only produce a cognitive formula resulting in introversion, which cuts society away from its surroundings and what is beyond its ability. The group delves into introversion, and so does Nawāri lonesomeness. This introversion leads to exaggerated self-consciousness, which falls deeper into the hollow of estrangement. Over prolonged oppression and tyranny, this introversion heightens and increases what that individual or group considers "opposing." Nonetheless, if oppression is not prolonged or exacerbated, introversion is automated and continues even after that oppression's end, escaping its direct influence.

Ever independent from oppression, introversion generates isolation. As mentioned earlier, isolation is necessary for the individual to continue as a part of such a group. It is equally essential for such a group and environment to survive in a world of oppression. Being implanted in the psychological structure of Nawāri society, isolation, and introversion are excessively grounded and clear against a vast ocean of intellectual alternatives. At this point, isolation is unavoidable, evolving into survival and protection mechanisms on individual and group levels against the oppressive environment. Isolation becomes a membrane distancing the outer realm of different ideas and social surroundings. Nawāri individuals remain reserved when liberated from their group's tyranny to a more welcoming environment.

Amid isolation, thoughts are inarticulate, and emotions are voiceless. Nobody escapes and tells what happened in isolation. Nawāri isolation entails sacrificing our voices in an exchange: muteness for survival. Eventually, all our experiences will silently die, never being communicated or shared with anyone. Nonetheless, the cost of this survival in isolation goes beyond being fully paid in muteness; other senses are collected.

Senses are shut down and time is stopped

Numerous axioms require experience to be consolidated. Individuals in isolation have no opportunities necessary for sound, realistic, and logical thoughts. This primarily characterizes Nawãri minds—a limitedness of ideas based on limited knowledge and a lack of experience. Whatever this thought has of abilities and capabilities, it is bound by the ideas' limitedness, inefficiently and passively acquired. Fleeing from cognitive totalitarianism and exclusionism, Nawãri minds produce only vague, theoretical ideas. Deep in isolation, they cannot overcome the effect of cognitive totalitarianism. A negative identity is eventually established by exchanging ideas with those on their side of the argument against totalitarian ideas. A discussion or debate is unlikely. Thus, the Nawãri isolation establishes an intellectual formula simulating what cognitive totalitarianism imposed as being vague, theoretical, and inaccessible to a discussion. Equally passive isolation, it is a rejection in and of itself without identifiable essence beyond that point.

Change and progress are problematic in nations and societies afflicted with the widespread phenomenon of this isolation. One cannot affect change if disconnected from the rest of the world. An individual or a group cannot be something they cannot imagine. Isolation means time has stopped, space is kept, and doors are locked. It is an attempt to exit but not eliminate the time dimension, trying to abide by an epoch and desperately stop and prevent the hands of time. It is an invaluable age in a given society, based on the symbolism of what their collective consciousness deems an incarnation of a golden age. On individual and group levels, isolation does not necessarily reflect stillness and submissiveness. To exit time progression, one must continuously go against the course of time back to the past, simulating swimming against the current. This ceaseless reverse movement does not change or even leave its spatial dimension. In its relentless, persistent motion, it perseveres to stand still. This omnipresent isolation feeds on the Nawãri community's energy and attention—nothing else is in their sight.

In brief, this isolation is an escape from advancement. It is a journey of regression, going back to the past, to the golden age and the best of times, and a return to the imagined theoretical and the impossible utopian. It is a regression toward a general and personal historical past. They are not only trying to go back to being a child running after the ice cream truck, but to an imagined past they never even lived. Nawāri individuals do not seek refuge in the present (e.g., the wife) or the future (e.g., the offspring) but in their past and roots. "All I seek is your satisfaction, mother," is a motto not based on mothers' religious and sociocultural status. Having added value in the Nawāri community, mothers represent a time compass anchored in the past and a stabilizing relationship, which is fine. These are among several signs demonstrated and achieved in Nawāri thought, which develops isolation in defiance of time and reality requirements. Isolation in the Nawāri community is an attempt to exit and lose all meaning of time. As if still tied to the umbilical cord, Nawāri individuals cling to their parents. They seek safety in the mother's image—the sole reminder of comfort in a bosom that never lets them down—and run to find maternal love, a safe cradle, a warm embrace, and the good old days.

As illustrated, isolation is an attitude toward the outside world. It is escaping from advancing to retreating toward the past. In isolation, age and time lose meaning. Subsequently, isolation is chosen to deal with the world and is no longer a mere method of self-preservation. It became the nucleus and identity of the self. It transformed into a shovel to dig a grave for that individual's future.

Nawāri individuals do not lose the wisdom of the crowd when in isolation. As previously indicated, it constitutes a part of their unconscious understanding of many issues. Afflicted with isolation, Nawār thought degenerates intellectually, morally, and mentally. Introversion and social isolation, separating individuals from the world and undermining normal vital activities, lead to an atrophy of perspective, awareness, and conscience. It is an isolation capable of creating monsters instead of saints and poets.

Nawāri social structures grew out of the fragments of a severely atomized society whose competitive structure and its individuals' estrangement were controlled by membership in a group. Brutality and backwardness are not what characterize Nawāri or the "mass men", as Hannah Arendt called them, but rather their isolation and lack of normal social relations. Nawāri individuals are descendants of a nation-state's torn society, which is class-, regionalism-, and religion-differentiated, whose cracks are cemented with nationalistic sentiments and what cognitive totalitarianism laid down for popular cohesion. At the first vulnerability of their new experience, these masses unsurprisingly fell into violent nationalism or particularly abhorrent sectarianism. Rising Nawãr leaders yielded to their instincts and purposes for purely demagogic reasons and reproduced the tyrant and his approach.

Buried alive

Inner isolation is a long and winding road that millions of Nawãr endure. A more arduous one occurs when a sign of "dissension" is openly or unintentionally expressed, exposing Nawãri individuals to the oppressed society. Authorities must punish the openly exposed isolation and the general community before them. Those now "adversaries" must be exiled. Varying between imprisonment and killing, banishment is the ruling tyrant's expertise. If anyone survives the tyrant's punishment, society is no less adept at their forms of exile under one theme: to be buried alive.

Fig. 3-2: People's injustice made me hit the road! Cuties get their own way

Psychological and social deconstruction is increasingly needed in studying forced alienation affecting oppressed dissenters in the Nawãri community within or outside of their motherland. Save the homesickness and agonizing longing, the exiled or expatriate is in better condition than those exiled at home and inside their neighborhood. After all, they are far from direct harm and, if desired, may lose the sense of belonging to their original community and culture and to express a sense of individualism of their choosing. In contrast, for citizens in their motherland, alienation means harsh suffering if exposed and their dissension revealed. This alienation exasperatingly spreads during dire times. Victims of this form of alienation suffered even more during the "Muslim Brotherhood uprising" at the end of the 1970s and the beginning of the 1980s. Crises may end, but not this alienation, which persists as long as those individuals live. Their alienation is more dangerous than those displaced, regardless of the immense hardships of estrangement and issues related to psychological adjustment to a new milieu.

I chose victims of arbitrary detention to illustrate this forced alienation and isolation because we, the Syrians, lived through stories that make this case relevant to almost all of us. If not victims themselves of these arbitrary detentions, most of us would know a detainee and trace their journey from society, detention, and all through the last stop at the isolation imposed by society, if lucky to survive that brutal physical detention.

When released, the detainees mostly fear how they will be received. There are two contradictory scenes. In one, the released heroes and martyrs are received with celebratory ululations and joyous and proud faces. On the other hand, society, league, syndicate, neighbors, and the closest relatives turn their backs on the detainees as soon as the totalitarian regime announces them as "adversaries"—from the first day of professing their dissension. It gets even worse if the detained are females who are never accepted in society again. Over time, the number of doors locked in their faces increased.

Through acts varying between initiative and obviation, society entirely partakes in burying its victims alive. Shifting from jailers' torture to society's banishment of any dissenter, several individuals are forced to live in isolation, voluntarily or involuntarily. Once an abode for them, they are no longer welcome. All they have endured never fades from their memory, even if they try. It is an irremovable and incurable stigma and a sin for which there is no repentance.

Detainees do not just fear for themselves and their well-being but also for their loved ones, who are powerless in this confrontation. The dissenting individuals are not solely punished with expulsion from the group's mercy but also those directly connected to them; their parents may equally pay the price of exile. The wife and children suffer dearly compared to siblings, cousins, and even the father, who may have a way out by disowning the dissenter—an unprocurable option to the wife, even if divorced, nor to the children. In some Hindu societies, Sati[209] was previously practiced, where the widow would burn herself following her husband's death. In contrast, the Nawāri community wholeheartedly welcomes any opportunity to burn the wife and children of the victim. For a homogeneous society, all precautions are taken against whatever may blemish its puritanism, and any divergence is sacrificed.

Not with good intentions nor in compliance with regulations and legal mechanisms that detainees were released. Their escape from death in Assad detention centers was a mere twist of fate. Releasing them is a means to release detention stories and spread terror. The slightest hint of opposition to the regime brings up a store of detainees' stories and images of death and torture.

When Syria's greatest uprising in all its history broke out in 2011, the number of those buried alive increased right away, albeit unevenly across different cities. The more significant the city and the bigger its population, the more the regime worked on self-cleansing mechanisms. Several heroic stories circulated about a Samaritan merchant who hid wanted men or women, saving them from oppressive authorities' aggression, against the backdrop of hundreds of people who voluntarily reported on their neighbors. On the other hand, stories about neighbors telling on their neighbors and working to expel families simply for being from "rebel areas" or alienated and isolated them in their homes until they were forced to leave. They ensured that suspicious members were cut off from social solidarity

---

[209] Sati is the feminine form of "Sit" in Sanskrit, meaning truth. It is a religious ritual for some Hindus in which the wife is burned to death at her husband's funeral, voluntarily or by use of force. This ritual has become rare and was criminalized in 1829.

with the tyrant. Then came the green buses[210] and forced displacement of entire villages and towns before the very eyes of whole neighbors as the final scene in cleansing the homogeneous society that Bashar al-Assad repeatedly boasted of in his speeches.

I will not narrate the residents' lashing in one area or the meaningless arguments as I plead with them to stop the green buses and prevent the army from pursuing the purge of those villages. Only a few stayed, either regime supporters and army informants or those who chose to battle with death and detention over forced displacement and the risk of humiliation and privation. Population displacement and the exit of buses were the tip of the iceberg of a decades-long social disintegration.

Today, Syrians live varied nightmares within the boundaries of geography, circumstances, and challenges, but equally under oppression and helplessness. The Syrian diaspora extends from being held hostage in Assad's army-controlled areas and autonomous ones under Syrian Democratic Forces[211] and others armed factions in the north, to being refugees in Turkey, Jordan, Lebanon, Egypt, and elsewhere. Each of these nightmares differs in bitterness, isolation, and pain, and being buried alive is fulfilled at any rate. Initially practiced by the group against a few, being buried alive became collective, targeting entire groups. All Syrian groups eventually became victims of alienation and isolation, even those in their homes and were supporters of the regime in secret or public. Alienation initially has a limited impact on a few individuals who do not fit in a group. Over time, their impact dramatically worsens, gaining both momentum and severity, and turning into a vicious, inescapable circle. Syrian alienation no longer distinguishes between supporters and opponents of the Assad regime. Nevertheless, in the previous case, the punishment of being buried alive and

---

[210] During the forced evacuations of civilians in the government restored territories in the Syrian civil war, the regime made a habit of using the green public transportation buses to evict those civilians from the country and send them to other rebel controlled territories.

[211] Syrian Democratic Forces, referred to as the SDF, are a multi-ethnic and multi-religious alliance of Kurdish-dominated militias. They controlled a quarter of the Syrian territory in the northeast in 2021 when this book was published.

alienated was initially triggered by this differentiation, intended to be contained within society.

The surviving Nawãri is constantly in day-of-judgment mode, having their actions and thoughts more than cruelly judged. No wonder their haven is underground in a simultaneously metaphorical and tangible vault. Surviving Nawãr individuals quit the world, away from all their surroundings, including family, folks, and even their own physical bodies. In an impenetrable vault lies that survivor, withdrawn from the world and the violence they endured. Seeing beyond the fake and deceptive appearance, a barren and brutal world is the truth they believe.

Civilization and societies were based on pillars of co-existence, joint interaction, cooperation, and solidarity among people and between people and their surroundings. All is lost when people lock themselves in their vaults and underground cellars. Some Nawãr people confess a sense of ecstasy, running away from confrontation to a sense of security and believing that this hideout offers a rebirth, recreation, and a space to come with a response to the vicious world outside. Ecstasy is mixed with anxiety, but safety implies to Nawãri individuals that it is an opportunity to change the world out of their retreat. They expect their resurgence in the world will be stronger and better prepared.

Change one letter, and the word vault [Qabu] becomes grave [Qabr] in Arabic. The difference is that a person may rise from one and never from the other. Nawãri individuals turned their vaults into graves, bringing their doom out of their isolation. Similar to how some buried their Nawãri siblings alive, now is the time to voluntarily and unsuspectingly bury themselves in the hope of re-emergence. They are oblivious that someone else, not themselves, has to reach out for them. Thus, Nawãri individuals' life cycle is complete, and they are buried before their time of death.

In any event, isolation is inevitable by whatever means, regardless of their political affiliation or religious beliefs, even if they did all they could to assimilate and identify with the tyrant. It is a continuous, systematic destruction of everything on which societies can be built. This section aimed to customize the course of the self-destruction mechanism by accelerating social collapse and integrating social practices with those of the authoritarian.

Isolation is an outcome of extreme integration with the authoritarian. When individuals turn into jailers, incarcerating themselves, cognitive totalitarianism and exclusionism reach their final phase. Ultimately, Assadist violence is collective, sparing no one. Discriminatory and excessive, it took over our daily lives, infesting bread lines, governmental bureaucratic dealings, and school classes, where humiliation is purposefully utilized and not a mere instrument of subjugation. The victimhood it establishes pursues differentiating between itself and whatever constitutes an element in joining adversaries' ranks. All efforts are exerted by the Nawār to flee the circle of humiliation, not realizing it is inescapable. Such futile attempts breed more racism and exclusionism in that society's offspring. It degrades whatever morality is left in that society. and instead of serving self-preservation, this cycle—oblivious to them—is concluded with self- annihilation.

Even within opposition-held areas, Idlib under the Hayat Tahrir Al-Sham's[212] control, the SDF-held, or even immigration, Nawāri individuals carry the burden of isolation, ever performing simultaneous roles of jailor and police over themselves. There is too much to fear and too little to communicate with the world. With our early warning systems on, we are ready to destroy and alienate the other at the slightest hint of dissension. We are lost in this conundrum of why we are where we are, but all in vain. Despite our best efforts to dig our way into a world of open skies, we are stuck under the slab covering our graves.

Isolation in the age of social media

In 2008, I logged into Facebook and Twitter in their early days. As a well-off young man, I was privileged to start using the Internet at a young age. For me, like many Arab youths, social media was an excellent and

---

[212] Hayat Tahrir al-Sham, or Organization for the Liberation of the Levant, commonly referred to as Tahrir al-Sham, is a hardline Salafi-jihadi group. It was and is involved in the Syrian war. HTS is an extension of Al Qaeda in the Levant. Its current stronghold area is in Idlib.

convenient alternative to being active in personal blogs and forums we joined and participated in for daily, long hours. Offering an open space, previous activities on chat sites and interaction domains were replaced, and conventional means of communication were eliminated, namely face-to-face conversations. Everyone in this public square is a listening audience while simultaneously shouting into a loudspeaker.

Facebook was my working space and a field for activism, my only available means in exile. Organizations, action plans, demonstrations, and campaigns of all kinds were given life in Facebook groups. In this virtual medium, I made several friends, who became my best friends, and worked with many activists. I befriended wonderful people who later on became martyrs, forcibly disappeared people, and eyewitnesses to one of the most horrific atrocities committed in this century. I was introduced to a facet of Syria unknown to us. Social media was an opportunity to probe ourselves and our acquaintances in a deeper way. Through its discussions and heated arguments, I acquired knowledge that was never accessible before. These are hard facts. Nevertheless, this new interconnected digital world was not limited to only this rosy picture. We found out a different face of that world especially during the post-militarization phase of the Syrian civil war and after the neutralization of the movement's civil role. From then on, we shifted from activists with a big impact to observers barely commenting on what we see and cannot control. We shifted from being the actors and players occupying the first league to the bystanders occupying the far-end rows.

Social media played a key role in mobilizing and organizing the Arab Spring, especially among expatriates and those far from the fields, squares, and streets of Arab cities and villages. Emerging social networks such as Facebook and Twitter accelerated the downfall of Tunisia's and Egypt's regimes. Besides, these means contributed to social and political mobilization in Syria and Bahrain.

However, these means failed to affect social change for two primary reasons. First, the connections and relationships in these virtual spaces were superficial. This was attested to in the participants' ability to create a common political ground in a virtual medium, but they failed to translate it into reality. For instance, "Days of Rage" was declared in Syria on the 5th of February on Facebook but witnessed no participation. Similarly, the 15th of March was a poor protest, though it remained highly symbolic of the Syrian revolution. Despite the limited participation, it was the first anti-oppression mass movement to voice their calls for freedom in Damascus's streets. The mass arrests of the participants in the 15th of March protests heightened their symbolism.

Several factors thwarted both attempts. Besides, it is inaccurate to claim that the digital call for the Arab Spring triggered the Syrian revolution, no matter how much the media and activists persistently focus on the 15th of March symbolism. In all probability, the Children of Daraa incident[213] and the responsive demonstrations on the 18th of March sparked protests throughout the Syrian map. Similarly, the tragic suicide of Tunisian street vendor Mohamed Bouazizi set himself on fire after being humiliated by municipal officials. It ignited the Arab Spring in Tunisia and, from there, the rest of the Arab world. The human element remains more capable of initiating change than the bits-and-bytes digital actor.

The second reason social media's role was inefficient in the Arab Spring is that the decision-making process is complex to reach a consensus and inaccessible through virtual mediums. Therefore, these means were unfeasible in forming connections between its participants to be later translated into reality. Moreover, it was unsuitable for creating a unified public opinion or a comprehensive decision representing enough participants in the anti-totalitarian regime uprising. Of the ill fortune of the liberation movements in the Arab countries, Syria in particular, authoritarian states entered the digital arms race, strengthening electronic surveillance and internet censorship and establishing more effective electronic armies.

Given how matters progressed and advanced in the Syrian lands, social media arenas responded by shifting the discourse towards militarization. Besides the increasing number of fired bullets and guns in the squares of

---

[213] This refers to an incident where at least 15 teenage boys were arrested because of graffiti spray-painted on a school wall reading "it's your turn, doctor!" in reference to his turn to be ousted. The city of Daraa in the south then became the epicenter of the Syrian war.

villages and cities and the absence of demonstrators' voices, a similar transformation on Facebook and Twitter spaces ensued before our eyes.

The rise of Zahran Alloush[214], Abu Muhammad al-Julani[215], and others were mirrored on Syrian Facebook, where similar figures share the same military and repressive perspectives on the Syrian issue. The short and broken Syrian ranks began to be increasingly and regularly fragmented. What had once been expected—the origin of the Arab Spring—not only proved to be a vacant and insignificant phenomenon but became destructive to what those revolutions aspired to build. My view of this matter comes after numerous, long years of working in the virtual world. Like many others, this is where I had the opportunity to communicate, coordinate, enlarge my circle of relatives and acquaintances, and spread awareness. Nevertheless, I got caught in a web of pointless intellectual battles like those who ventured into the battlefield, fully equipped and sparing nothing.

In part, Facebook algorithms are based on constructing a black-and-white world, connecting its users with like-minded people, and creating echo chambers[216]. These glass chambers stand against other echo chambers with opposite ideas. In these chambers, small gangs exponentially grow and significantly identify over time. They differentiate themselves against their

---

[214] Zahran Alloush (197102015) was a military commander in the Syrian revolution. He was arrested on charges of his Salafist activism in 2010 and imprisoned in Sednaya prison, only to be released under a presidential amnesty early in the Syrian revolution in 2011. Later, he participated in armed action and founded the Islam Company, which evolved into the Islam Brigade and eventually the Army of Islam. Syrians' opinions are divided about him into supporters and accusers. He was accused of forcibly ruling the areas he controlled, killing and kidnapping civil activists, and carrying out an external agenda instead of the Syrian revolutionary agenda. He was killed in a Russian raid in 2015.

[215] Ahmed Hussein al-Shar'a, known by the nom de guerre Abu Mohammad al-Julani. He is the commander-in-chief of Hayat Tahrir al-Sham, formerly the Al-Nusra Front, the Syrian branch of Al-Qaeda.

[216] A term used in media to refer to situations in which beliefs are amplified or reinforced through communication and repetition within a closed system without challenge or scrutiny.

adversaries, preparing to expel them from virtual reality or win them over in a glorious victory.

The Syrian revolution was characteristically inclusive and loosely defined as anti-Bashar al-Assad's regime, allowing large cohorts of Syrians to participate. But over time, this characteristic led to its downfall, especially on the digital front, failing to mature into a unanimous, inclusive thought and a decision representing these large cohorts. The algorithms played a dirty game on a nation that had long suffered from intellectual stagnation, lack of differentiation, totalitarian thought, and exclusion. Living in silent isolation killed its chance to learn about dialogue, its methods, and its properties. Instead of facilitating the creation of a central identity and an inclusive vision, social media broke the Syrian rebellious scene into narrow intellectual cantons.

Out of more than a thousand military factions, we witnessed how four took over or obliterated the rest. Likewise, the diverse intellectual arena comprising all Syrians boiled down to intellectual brigades that had to identify and differentiate as much as possible. As for the vast space that once allowed diverse cohorts to approach the revolution, it culminated into rigid fronts: neutral, Shabeeha members, and revolutionists. These totalitarian classifications comprised spectra of intellectual trends eradicated by their groups to achieve unity and conquer the antagonistic enemy. Every Syrian, who once could have yelled their opinion, has now had to customize their tone and phrases according to the flow of the new league that usurped all else. The dichotomy of totalitarian, exclusionary thought and insidious algorithms made the Syrian digital intellectual war reflect the raging battlefield in ferocity and endeavors exerted to destroy the adversary.

Forums and written and audio chat sites were our assemblies for debating and arguing before Facebook and Twitter. Back then, intellectual intimidation was not unfamiliar to us, graduates of Ba'ath school and the one-party ruling system. It was ingrained in our consciousness and subconsciousness. Facebook and the Syrian revolution had a dangerous embrace despite being distinctive. In the old days of forums, debate arenas were smaller, with few participants under alias names. No one was bent on fervently waging war. It was not rare or impossible for two people to utterly disagree on one topic and equally agree on a different one on a separate page. We had the right to forget and be forgotten before the digital book of deeds age came to record every detail, small and large, for the public. Anyone was free to hold whatever position on any issue without jeopardizing their affiliation or acceptance by their electronic sect, which they found themselves part of on Facebook.

As social media users, we are an attempted image aiming to please an audience, not our true selves. Similar to celebrities' superficial and trivial stance—to avoid enraging their broad and non-homogenous audience—we fall into the same predicament of hiding our resentment. We must expressly name what we read to confirm our affiliation, use the same jargon, and take positions that guarantee our survival within our group. Thus, and only thus, we are affiliated with the order and can push ourselves to the first rows. This is how one can catch up with the first row in the Assad regime and his ruling party. We must hail, applaud, and overly acclaim the "all" that is exclusively us. Are our profile pictures and names not in the spotlight on social media posts? If we do not believe, we practice dissimulation or bear the consequences of defying the group.

These means of communication imposed a state of identification, to which our only alternative was social ostracizing and exclusion. Instead of building bridges among the intellectual spectrum of society, social media duplicated the totalitarian intellectual system in a more extreme and ostracizing version.

The Syrian revolution was not the only intellectual victim of the rogue social media phase. Several studies and research projects were conducted on its impact on Western societies, including Japan and the US, and their political dilemmas. Its adverse effects were proven in cases such as Brexit, Trump's[217] winning presidential elections in 2016, and the rise of far-right movements worldwide. Multiple examples took center stage due to the social media structure. Social media is not necessarily the origin of these

---

[217] Donald Trump is the 45th President of the United States, a populist with authoritarian tendencies. He held office between 2017 and 2020, lost the 2020 presidential elections, and refused to concede defeat.

issues. This indicates how its system focused on increasing interaction at any cost, positive or negative, contributed to accelerating the rise of such intellectual pestilences. Several countries have social and regulatory administrative protection networks to safeguard their social contracts from disintegration. In the Syrian case, its social contract was decades long lost before civil and Facebook warfare at the mercy of the Assad totalitarian regime.

The active participation outlook in social media, uploading material features, commenting on shared material, and sharing Facebook "likes" perpetuate the user sovereignty myth[218]. Social media users choose to be active, a form of conscious participation that ultimately leads to commodifying personal attention and information, being stripped of their users, and being reconfigured for targeted advertising. This prompted their developers to enhance the individualistic importance of their users in terms of likes, views, and other metrics. Besides, maximizing the limit of altercations between contradictory parties increases their interaction, even if it turns into a heated debate, bullying, or direct threats of death and assassination.

Consequently, Nawāri individuals live in a new state of alienation in another dimension of their lives, what was once their only opening to the world under a pseudo-identity to express, hear, believe, and reject whatever they want. A dimension where neither an algorithm filters their world nor a clique filters their words, like their living and breathing world, such as school and the street.

Marx indicated in his work *A Contribution to the Critique of Political Economics*[219] that alienation is considered a lack of awareness among members of a social class of their social role in history. Alienation theory

---

[218] User sovereignty, or consumer sovereignty, is an economic concept that refers to the dominant power of consumers; it is a principle indicating that the consumer determines the characteristics and quality of goods produced in society. This is done collectively and through the so-called mechanism of supply and demand.

[219] Karl Marx wrote and first published this book in 1859. It is an analysis of capitalism and the quantitative theory of money. Marx discussed alienation and its causes among the exploited working class.

entails a set of transformations from relationships among people to things, which are then transformed into material attributes. First comes objectification; relationships in social media are of two types: friends and followers. The only way to distinguish between their relationships is through the subsequent step, where ownership of a thing is transformed from its value to its equivalent in money. The number of likes, comments, and interactions is the value of what we produce, and the number of likes and comments shared reflects the strength of the digital relationships or lack thereof. The latter transformation is characterized by intellectual and digital products' growing dominance over actors or actions. The content or originality of an idea is no longer the criterion for judging it but rather the amount of interaction produced or that can be produced. Hence, when a person shares an idea, the interaction with the proposed idea is their concern, measurable by likes or comments. Similarly, this amount of interaction may discourage ideas that do not receive enough likes or comments.

Social media turns ordinary users into active participants and accomplices in the efforts to silo them into echo chambers by social media beg techs, deepening their isolation. Alienation means submitting to a system that deprives its users of their identity and freedom to be replaced with counters: one for views, another for likes, and another for followers. The offer here is to like and comment, or the demand there is to be collectively engaged in wailing, let us attack, or it is high time for awareness.

Varying between the exclusion of any "hail to" clan, be it "the Free Army" or "the Brotherhood of the Minhaj/methodology,"[220] and the alienation of damning "those animal Alawites," we witnessed how the revolution's masses were reduced to a much smaller part of the grassroots movement that could have been in its crucible. Yet, this small group has to be further filtered to be increasingly branched into sub-groups in its intellectual puritanism and purity until all else is eliminated and further re-fragmented. These intellectual lines, therefore, open the door to self-annihilation.

---

[220] Nickname for the Islamist armed groups.

The Intellectual Aspects of the Oppressed in the Nawãri Society: "Belongings"

The following is a funny dialogue between Abu Saleh and Abu Rashid talking about Islam and Muslims while watching the news on TV in their town:

Abu Rashid: What is on your mind, Bou Saleh?
Abu Saleh: It's astonishing how great Islam is! It's practically everywhere, see those Chinese Muslims!
- By Allah, you're spot on, Bou Saleh.
= I bet all they know of Islam is fragments. They act as foreigners, except for praying. Arabs are the only true Muslims who understand the Qur'an and hadiths.
- By Allah, you are spot on, Abu Saleh.
= Not all Arabs, that is; some do not even pray obligatory prayers! I kid you not! You see, true Muslims are the Arabian Peninsula and the Gulf people.
- By Allah, you are spot on, Abu Saleh.
= Well, not all of the gulf. Some Gulf countries allow alcohol. Saudis have true Islam.
- By Allah, you are spot on, Abu Saleh.
= Yet, in some areas, women show their faces; others smoke hookah and tobacco; and some have Bid'ah (innovations). True religion is here among us.
- By Allah, you are spot on, Abu Saleh.
= Yet, some people in our town listen to music. May Allah help us! Our alley is where true religion is.
- By Allah, you are spot on, Abu Saleh.
= Yet, I see in our alley satellite dish antennas, and they watch indecent channels. Only my house, yours, and our neighbors.
- By Allah, you are spot on, Abu Saleh.
= Yet, may Allah guide our neighbors; I do not see their children in the mosque or them in the mosque that often for Fajr prayer. To tell you the truth, Abu Rashid, none but you and I pray Fajr in the mosque in our neighborhood.
- By Allah, you are spot on, Abu Saleh.
= Come to think of it, Bou Rashed! These days, I do not see you fully supplicating to Allah in Fajr prayer!!!

(I found this story circulating on the Internet without a source or its original author).

6- In Conclusion: the non-self

Give your all for self-negation, fear nothing,
strive, and God will guide you to the right path[221]

Eventually, the psychological and intellectual transformation of Nawāri individuals culminates in a morbid state of denying the self, prompted by the reality of suffering extreme oppression and profound isolation. If they do not entertain suicidal thoughts, the way out lies in rooting out the only source of pain accessible to management. Pain and oppression delineate the human being's roadmap to self-annihilation and alleviate its burden.

In the Christian context, self-denial denotes altruistic abstinence or withdrawal, meaning the willingness to renounce personal pleasures or endure personal hardships for public benefit or interest. Selflessness, or altruism, is a moral act emanating from a higher human virtue. But my reference to self-negation underlines that it does not seek virtue and is not triggered by self-hatred. It also does not result from the existential nihilism afflicting Nawāri individuals. This is merely an attempt to alleviate their burdens. It is an act of pursuing their escape from reality, culminating in a steady, utter helplessness. Nawāri individuals intentionally lose their features and fade into their surroundings. It is the death of the ego and the total loss of the personal self-identity where individuals fade away and shed their selves. Hence, nothing remains of their identity except the victimhood they experienced, embodied, and became all they have on a path to a sealed fate.

Self-denial is a state of evading reason and conscience. For Nawāri's survival, what is required is to adopt a dogmatic, inarguable, and morally faulty set of beliefs. Self-denial becomes a must because individuals' actions—or non-actions—have no tangible effect on their reality, and their existence necessitates omitting their conscience, whether they like it or not. That person lost their freedom and now has no say in their destiny. Therefore, reason and conscience are obstacles, weaknesses, and sources of

---

[221] A verse from the poem, you are in the universe, a hidden spirit, by Pakistani poet Muhammad Iqbal (1877–1938). This poem was published in the Secrets and Symbols Divan.

pain without any tangible benefit. Why should one bear the consequences of something they feel no control over or hold themselves accountable? Conscience also becomes a prerogative, but not for oppressed people.

This alleviation of the self and its heavy load grants them stability, being exempted from the consequences of thoughts and actions if undertaken. In addition, it relieves Nawāri individuals of feeling responsible for their actions and non-actions, which is a form of action on their own. It is a declaration of the end of internal conflict and the beginning of decline after years of suffocating isolation—an attempt to fade away.

Unfortunately, the human soul is too complex and grand to fade away. Despite Nawāri individuals' attempts to negate the self to be rid of reason and conscience, what remains defiant are their instincts, emotions, feelings, history, and awareness of the bleak reality in which they seek to fade and dissolve. This human regression is not death because death is a final process after which existence ceases. What Nawāri individuals pursue is partial death and evasion from what is left of life. It is a wish to be free from oppression and restrictions without exposure to more pain while holding on to a small part that would give their existence meaning.

The self-negation process provides those previously incapable of integrating and identifying with society with a comeback, given that what once differentiated them is about to dwindle. In dissolving the intellectual self, a hollow carcass is left, formulated out of dimensions that connect a vanished individual within their society. Though appearance or religious affiliation might be a dimension for their reconnection with the Nawār group, the most binding link is still grievances resulting from decades-long authoritarian oppression and totalitarian tyranny.

The non-self, belonging, and grievance

When Nawāri individuals deny the self, their identity is equally lost. They lose all instruments that can distinguish them in society, allowing them to change their old self, grow, and mature. Their affliction of partial death incapacitated their ability for intellectual growth and maturity. Subsequently, a state of intellectual atrophy follows, in which, as aforementioned, there is no structure except what is inherited from the Nawār group. The grievance gives that structure its shape and design; eventually, it becomes a unifying matter and source of identification for that human group.

At this phase, individualistic identity is replaced with a negative sense of belonging, left to fate to decide its definition and aspects. This belongingness is no longer optional, fading away from reason and conscience faculties; instead, it is a regression of identity towards a major unifying one, awaiting its fall. That involuntary belongingness is not based on a shared ideology or a social contract but on a negative affiliation that assembles its members under a shared grievance.

The Nawāri grievance is comprehensive and fairly uniform among individuals to a large extent. This similarity is the root cause of a narrative hued by unity-based homogeneity. It resulted from a universal justice perceived in a collective consciousness that totalitarian culture and oppressive history molded. This is not a grievance exclusive to those in the gloomy dungeons of the Nawāri world. Its influence and affliction spread over those favored or at the outer perimeters of events and over those who barely witnessed or remotely heard about it. We—expatriates and immigrants—were equally brought up with injustice and oppression rampant in the "Motherland of Darkness"[222]. This dark narrative has largely forged our collective identity and has repeatedly proven to be its nucleus. Suffering the same affliction left no room for sympathy among those plagued. No one was spared! Likewise, there is no need to hold each other accountable (as third parties, at least!). In other words, one would expect the worst from everyone, and no one is entitled to theorize and condescend.

Detaching emotions, rights, and standards when establishing a collective identity or national or other affiliations undermines forming bonds. The ones that are naturally and gradually generated through continuous social interactions. Generally, social interactions in Nawār reality are transactional[223],

---

[222] The Land of Darkness is a trilogy of novels by Abd al-Rahman Munif that mainly focuses on Iraqi social and political history during the 19th century.

[223] Transactional relationships are between parties that act according to self-interest. They perform an action for the other party, expecting a certain amount in their best

imbued with skepticism and distrust. This relationship fosters a minimum level of depth and continuity and is based on self-preservation, following a quid-pro-quo transaction module, after which the relationship ends.

Extending the narrative of grievance serves the tyrant and consolidates their rule. It also establishes equality in injustice, a sense that holds the oppressed back from demanding its alleviation. However, equality is not in this injustice but in the grievance. After all, it is an imagined cognitive state. Also, extending this narrative liberates the oppressed from accountability, criticism, and correction. Are they not the oppressed, suffering at the hands of the oppressor? Those claiming the grievance are authentic and rightful owners, bearing no sin or blame for mistakes or crimes committed under the tyrant's authority or when they rose in defiance. Not only that, but they are also not obliged to change. Instead, the world must devise a different formula to alleviate injustice, allowing them to continue business as usual.

Multiple grievances may overlap in one society, each of which deems the other its oppressor. Alawite grievance considers Sunnis their oppressors. Similarly, Kurds hold Arabs as their oppressors. Successively, several grievances sometimes unite against a group, and through the victimhood narrative, they consider a group or an event fully responsible for what happened and is happening to them.

Grievance is a supra-historical complex. It remains unyielding despite the end of the injustice that produced it, whether by being emancipated from or escaping its shackles. It is transcontinental and resistant to change. These complex reshaped Syrian individuals, rendering them their moral trait and justification for whatever was committed. It represents their path towards fulfilling the grievance by fully surrendering to oppression or reproducing it by transforming the oppressed into the oppressor. Alawite's grievances led to Bashar al-Assad regime; the Kurdish one supported the PKK[224]; and

---

interest, regardless of the other party. It is zero-sum thinking, where one's gain is the other's loss.

[224] The Kurdistan Workers' Party (PKK) is a left-wing Kurdish armed group. It arose in the 1970s in the Kurdistan region of Turkey as a separatist movement with an intellectual mixture of Kurdish nationalism and socialist revolution, seeking to establish a Marxist-Leninist state in Kurdistan. It moved to Syria with the blessing

the Sunni grievance contributed to the establishment and entitlement of ISIS[225] to rule, and so on, respectively. How much support this grievance gets within the party that adopts it is inconsequential. What matters is its continuation and, consequently, the continuous entitlement acquired by ISIS, the PKK, or others to maintain the status quo. Besides, eliminating these organizations and regressing to a worse situation are interconnected, especially from an Alawite grievance perspective, which underpins the impending threat of extermination if Assad is overthrown. In this case, the fait accompli is tied to its victims through the grievance, which becomes the stake nailed into its victims' hands.

Nawãri individuals set out on a journey as a featureless and deformed crowd extra on the margin of a big screen, obscured further into the dark corners. Following a systematic process, all that is within us and everything that makes us normal, active human beings and owners of our destiny and decisions get exterminated. We are stripped of our self and humanity, lost in the wilderness of a gloomy landscape like a speck blown with the wind into nothingness until it gradually fades. The final scene of this tragic journey is the group's immersion in its grievance to the point of being its identity, where the individual becomes nothing but a limb in that grievance. In this state and condition, a muffled scream echoes, "I am not what I chose to be; I am only what happened to me."[226]

---

of Hafez al-Assad and established a base to launch his military operations. Later, Hafez al-Assad handed over its leader, Abdullah Ocalan, to Turkey.

[225] The Islamic State in Iraq and the Levant (ISIS) primarily founded its ideology on the Sunni grievance that the rulers of Iraq and Syria are not from Ahl al-Sunnah wal-Jama'ah (people of the Sunnah and the community). Hence, it is obligatory to restore things to normal—according to ISIS—through their rule of these areas, being the people of the Sunnah and the rightful group.

[226] German psychologist Carl Jung is credited with saying, "I am not what happened to me; I am what I choose to become." The above statement is the exact opposite of his quote.

CHAPTER 4

BEHAVIORAL ASPECTS OF THE NAWĀRI COMMUNITY: "LITTER"

Our experiences construct our beliefs, which we then express via actions, making a compass out of these beliefs. In the second chapter, I discussed the experiences of Nawāri consciousness. In the third chapter, I elaborated on some of the primary beliefs and intellectual foundations of Nawār individuals. Here in the fourth chapter, I introduce a few common behaviors in Nawār society.

In this chapter, I review six critical aspects of Nawār behavior that I believe are graver and more destructive to the self than their surroundings. My focus is not on the outwardly fatal shortcomings in personal behaviors, such as appearance and personal hygiene. My context does not include descriptions of nonsensical insults people throw at each other, but I chose a few expressions that embody a persona or an act that people use in colloquial Syrian Arabic to refer to them. Each section here is titled with a popular term that best conveys psychological concepts and practices relevant to each behavior. Frankly, I explored the origins of these terms and exhaustively elaborated on their denotations. I coined new connotations for these terms and behaviors to uncover their depth and layers of meaning.

The sole focus is transgressive behaviors caused by neglect, contempt, and intentional abuse of other Nawār individuals. These vary from a failed attempt to differentiate from the rest of Nawār individuals, purifying itself from Nawār, and retaliation from Nawār and the self.

This chapter was the most challenging for being the most emotional and derogatory to us, the Nawār people. It was the first part I wrote of this book, which took years to see the light. There is no intention to hurl reprimands or further insults at Nawãri individuals. The following sections explain some behaviors and their adverse effects on Nawãr individuals and their environment. Moreover, this is a criticism of a society that accepts and may even approve of many of them. For instance, if a Nawãri person is described as slothful or sly, that does not mean they stick to this behavior in every situation or that the behavior of that person applies to the entire society. The aim is not to stereotype Nawãr's actions by enumerating and analyzing these traits.

We must differentiate between a stereotype and its use on the one hand and discuss the prevalence of an cognitive or behavioral aspect in a society on the other. Assuming that one out of every ten men is killed in violent incidents in Guatemala is quite staggering. Still, 90% do not die for that reason. Out of this percentage, many do not concern themselves with the threat of being killed due to their economic situation, place of residence, or any other reason. Likewise, if one out of every nine adult black men in the United States was imprisoned last year, this does not conclusively prove their criminality. The spread of this incident could be because of external factors, such as systematic police violence against blacks, poverty, and the violence they suffer.

For the last 20 years, Guatemala was the most violent country with the highest homicide rates. Not for long as our glorious countries came in to compete! The prevalence of imprisonment and detention among blacks in America does not attest to their criminality, as mentioned above. This indicates several elements, including some outside their control and others closely related to circumstances that exclusively affect them. Discussing these behaviors or practices aims to comprehend the relevant psychological phenomena. Its purpose is to break the link with victimhood, which only leads to its continuation and corresponding bad conditions. My main goal in this chapter is to bring forward the adverse effects of these practices on Nawãri individuals, their community, and their surroundings.

Changing behaviors is excessively taxing. They developed from experiences and convictions built across a Nawãri individual's life. Besides, these represent an old, unyielding approach. However, changing behaviors can end the vicious circle that feeds the causes of unending situations. Generally, Nawăr people have an enormous grievance about living under repressive regimes in our countries. Another one is instilled in our consciousness, controlling our destinies and making us most suitable for victimization. It contributes to empowering authoritarians' oppression and their continuous grip. Additionally, it ruins our efforts to change our reality, as proven by the outcomes of our frozen spring in the past decade.

In this chapter, I address six behaviors characteristic of the Nawări personality; they are prominent and widespread in our society. Several of these are subject matters of discussion, monitoring, and analysis. Academia examines some of these aspects and their impact on education, civil peace, and reconstruction. Similarly, literature and the arts, ranging from serious fiction to soap operas, depict us following an outline of these aspects. Some of these behaviors intersect, but I discerned specific, independent features for each, enough to be separately distinguishable.

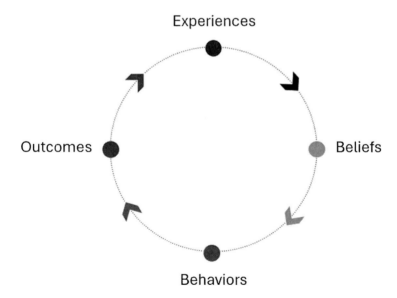

Fig. 4-1: A graphic demonstrates how experiences play a part in creating individuals' beliefs and affecting their behavior. These behaviors' consequences, in turn, lead to

developing new experiences. Some of them re-establish beliefs and repeat the experience.

1- Tanbal (Sloth)

Long have we boasted about active and productive Syrian workers and that Syrian society is a tireless beehive when reality constantly tells a different story. All attempts to overstate Syrian society's productive capabilities, leadership, and hyper-activity contradict the lackluster Syrian reality, with which we have been stuck for decades, at times loaded with mighty odes glorifying workers, construction, and development. There were countless stories celebrating Syrian resounding success stories, whether in international inventions, scientific breakthroughs, or high-tech handicrafts. However, Syrian scientific, technical, cultural, and developmental realities indicate how society lacks creativity and is deficient in production. Individual success stories could barely conceal the blatant reality we suffered. The unending pride in our individualistic successes does not erase an undeniable truth because of a high school degree or a patent achieved by a Nawãri person. Nevertheless, such individual successes that do not translate into action and further into collective success are a sad end to a story that could have been better.

In reality, the oppressed people highly fit the description of a tanbal (sloth). This colloquial term has a Turkish linguistic origin, tanbal, which means lazy, idle, and dull-witted. The Sultan's tanabala refers to lazy, ever-jobless people in his courtyard. In this context, this word does not refer to the inactivity required to work and earn a living but rather to an practical state that afflicts Nawãr individuals, which renders them incapacitated. The negative experiences they underwent partly caused this state. It becomes a comprehensive perspective, though subsidiary and often externally imposed. This emerging incompetence is a learned state; it affects a person's perspective on life and formulates their existence and actions. Under this condition, a tanbal is utterly afflicted with learned impotence, believing themselves helpless and powerless. Multiple misinterpretations of events cause this learned helplessness, making Nawãri individuals live in chronic helplessness and frustration. The first of these is mixing the transient with the permanent. The authoritarian system imposes transient impotence, which is mainstreamed in all situations. Hence, a misjudgment on the continuation element—a temporary emergency or permanent—develops a perspective for Nawāri people that events are due to permanent and excessively prolonged causes. The second is a miscalculation of the prevalence scope. Is the lack of resourcefulness exclusively relevant to what is against the oppressor or in general? In other words, does the failure to rise against the tyrant's oppression include all matters? The third is determining the responsibility for this incompetence and the ensuing failure. Is the responsibility internal, attributed to the individual, or external and out of control?

The American psychologist Martin Seligman carried out research on learned helplessness for over fifty years. What was and will be illustrated is substantially consistent with the findings of Seligman's experiments. Learned helplessness is a condition due to repeated exposure to aversive stimuli—failure in this aspect—where the individual learns there are no options, a possibility of escape, or even changing reality. Helplessness exists when an individual's actions have no perceptible positive effect on outcomes.

Learned helplessness is a psychological construct that significantly contributes to understanding what Nawār people experience in an oppressive society. Under this condition, aversive stimuli are ongoing crackdowns committed by oppressive power. The intensity of the stimuli, for example, killing and torture, is unimportant in inducing an effect. What is influential is the ubiquitous, repeated exposure to oppression, which is often small in scope and can cause learned helplessness. The object of these repeated aggressions eventually resigns and sees no possible alternatives. Similarly, institutional racism influences minorities' personal behaviors and decisions, leading to learned helplessness. This notable lack of options makes the current social and economic power structure seem fatal and unchangeable.

Our upbringing

Syrians grow up confined to an isolated intellectual pattern within their family circle, where the world seems overly simplistic and automated. In this clear-cut picture, every question has an answer, and every incident has its justification and wisdom. And, if not, there is a metaphysical vacuum to resort to for blaming and evading responsibility.

Nawãr resort to a cache of references for constantly unquestionable, valid, and applicable answers. Independent thought, taking the initiative, and conducting investigations are foreign concepts to Syrians. Serving a life of enslavement, they are to receive and obey the dictates of superiors and society in marriage, divorce, study, faith, talk, and appearance. In contrast, their positive energy is demonstrated when diligently working, studying, and memorizing. Society has defined the good person as a skilled worker, docile student, energetic peasant, or pious devotee. Listening and obeying always come first.

Hearing and obeying may be valuable faculties in prosperous and stable situations in Nawãri societies but destructive in crises and turmoil, which are not uncommon or infrequent in their lives. When hapless Nawãr individuals find no answers or solutions from their references, they wake up in isolation, as aforementioned. Moving from childhood to adulthood, the illusion of social cohesion diminishes. At this moment, the herd bursts, struggling to reach a haven. Left to their own devices, they strive to change their reality, lacking a broader perspective that applies to themselves and their society as a human unit, which is alive and capable of change. Syrians lose their shaky faith in themselves and the entire social system—a system that failed them at the first challenge.

Syrians are not taught leadership skills or believe they have what it takes to lead. Domesticated, molded, and meticulously devoted to dependence, they see it is safer to follow everyone. This qualifies Nawãri individuals for Asch's[227] famous experiment, where death with the group is merciful[228].

---

[227] In psychology, the Asch conformity experiments, or the Asch model, were a series of studies directed by Solomon Asch. It studied whether individuals yielded to or defied a majority group and the effect of such influences on beliefs and opinions. Its most significant finding was to prove the tendency of individuals to conform to the group's opinion, even if they had doubts about the validity of this collective opinion.

[228] Referring to a famous Arab proverb that prefers dying with one's group than staying alive by themself.

And if a calamity befalls, the herd falls into a stupor without a compass or a plan, unprepared and inexperienced in these situations, and not because of laziness. Running a familiar race for obedience, Nawāri people follow superiors and elders of knowledge and authority who introduce unchallenged postulates for the herd to consume. In this race, they spent a lifetime putting forth their utmost to rank first, as if it were a strong bond with the obedient people. In reality, the intellectual or emotional bond with obedience is weakly founded, and they question the validity of these postulates to which the herd gravitates. Despite their disbelief in salvation in Jesus the Savior and the descent of Mahdi (Guided), or the redeemer, they still associate with a group that upholds these values, seeking comfort and safety. Though disapproving of these ideas, the number of their supporters and believers vouches for their validity and credibility. Hence, repeatedly judging that postulate is pointless and a waste of time. To follow the group's footsteps and race them to the first row takes precedence. Maintaining what one of prophet Mohammad's hadith dictates, "My nation will not unite on misguidance," whoever agrees with that postulate must be the nation with which to identify. Consequently, whenever the nation unanimously agrees on a postulate, then it is correct. Nobody knows how many skeptics share the same opinion because no one openly discusses what would jeopardize their position as a member of that system or group. Essentially, each person believes they are the dissent, for each doubts their opinions kept hidden from the crowd and masses.

Passive neutral

Nawāri individuals constantly apprehend the exacerbation of crises, problems, and surrounding tragedies and deny any signs of change that indicate danger and an upcoming eruption of events. As a rule, change is unappealing for Nawāri societies that refuse whatever might imbalance their critical reality. Any risk leads to different, unforeseen results, no matter how small. Regardless of how bleak the Nawār community's reality is, the unknown future always seems darker in comparison. At the very least, they believe it is tangible and bears known damage, with which they can deal and adapt.

Affliction and adversity take the vast majority by surprise, despite multiple red flags of their imminence. Change is associated with misfortune and ordeal in a society that is adamantly opposed to it. Positive change is the outcome of appropriate action and a solid foundation. In the seemingly united and intrinsically selfish Nawãr society, change is widely assumed to bring the cracked foundation of the social and moral crisis crashing down. Worse, everything that was and is being built during that rigid stage is on shaky ground, whether it is infrastructure, political systems, national unity, or religious identity.

Nawãri individuals have no memory of positive change in their society, present or past, so if they are to expect any, likewise, it must be the worst. Usually, their surroundings are not a source of inspiration for success stories and positive and constructive changes, even if they are contemporary and nearby incidents. Future lessons and change are derived from their personal and peer histories. Protecting positive change from envy and the evil eye is done through concealment and discretion. In contrast, disasters are to be discussed and circulated for years. However, Nawãri individuals certainly have beacons of light in their history, but the closest is several centuries in the past. These beacons are shrouded in sanctity and perfection, to the point where they are believed to be irreproducible. Hence, those nations and their victories are beyond reach.

Positive change is contextualized in two double-edged dimensions in the Nawãri mindset: temporal and sacred. First, a time-bound myth is created for Nawãr people to deal with their glorious past mythically. Second, those legends revolve around historical heroes and icons detached from their environment and society. They are deemed omnipotent, timeless, and absolute entities, devoid of personal interests or human weakness. As immortals and defiant of time and space, their achievements are irreproducible, whether this idolized icon is a prophet, a companion or an apostle, or an ancient scholar. Put on a pedestal for boasting and esteem, their experiences, details, facts, and reasons for success are not empirically studied or explored. Worse, if that historical glory's decline is examined, it only concludes that barbaric foreign aggression ravaged and undermined that pure, innocent icon. Accordingly, the Ottoman Sultanate collapsed because the Germans implicated them in a war as part of a Western scheme to destroy that righteous caliphate. Western interests are attributed to religious enmities and to settling old and modern scores, such as the Crusades or controlling Jerusalem. Nawāri people perceive their history apart from what internally contributed to the Ottomans' fall. They disregard—even disacknowledge—the role of poverty, injustice, and the systematic consolidation of underdevelopment imposed by the repressive policies of the Sublime Porte within the Empire's controlled countries. Accusations of starvation and economic exploitation are unacceptable despite making those countries backward and lacking creativity and civilizational factors. Similarly, this perspective applies to the fall of Andalusia, Malta, and other territories they boasted of once being under their control.

The Nawāri vision of change is also connected and resonates with historical events lacking direct experience to acquire a different perspective. The inexperience in forming an alternative vision and society leaders' inability to formulate one led to transforming history into ready-made models of what has been dubbed "ignorance sciences" to fill the void. Consequently, the spiritual distance from and factual disobedience to Allah—mirrored in the disconnection from and disobedience to leadership and authority—led to the Ottoman Empire's dissolution. These were the fatal flaws in the loss of that once-glorious status. To illustrate, Nawāri individuals recognized the Great Arab Revolt as a betrayal of the caliphate, bringing about the loss of the Ottomans' overwhelming glory. This is not a human-initiated change; it is the result of a divine will or a just punishment that befell those people and translated into these events. What primarily triggered this punishment could even be irrelevant. The cause-and-effect relationship is unnecessary because there is an external trigger uninvolved in the equation that directs the scene. That external influence might be the Israeli state, foreign imperialism, or divine providence.

This perspective that rejects a cause-and-effect relationship is demonstrated in the status quo of Syrian and Arab scene evaluation in terms of the initial outcomes of the Arab Spring. Hence, it validates their extrapolation of history. Under this understanding, if people had gathered around Bashar al-

Assad, a resistance symbol; Morsi[229], a post-revolution success symbol; or whoever won or had the upper hand, serious troubles would have been avoided, saving the country from destruction and dispersion. The precariousness surrounding the symbol brings its doom, not the contradictions or legitimate demands. In the case of Bashar, the popular risings led the country to its collapse, not his brutal suppression or the retaliatory military action carried out against his people. The protests against Morsi became a counterrevolution symbol, making the demands of the 2011 demonstrations unjustified and destroying the Egyptian revolution's achievements. The revolution—and the counterrevolution in Egypt—were just an external conspiracy that brought this strong country to its knees. In addition, the divine will was responsible for the lost lives of innocent people and not the tyrants' oppression or the decision-makers' failure.

This perspective, popular among neighboring countries and peoples or negligent participants in the scene, indicates a mentality that blames the victim for suffering and champions oppressors and tyrants. Provided that the oppressor promises to prevent change—Nawãr people's worst nightmare—the revolution is a non-normal and non-rational individual act in which the masses have no role or interest. The "injustice" is a mythical heavenly will beyond control, and it is impermissible to transgress this cosmic system or take matters into one's hands. Hence, passive neutrality is Nawãr individuals' safety-motivated dimension, a far-removed dimension from change that submits to the fait accompli and exists outside the borders of their destiny.

Nawãr individuals, embracing a passive neutrality perspective, set three obstacles to change. First, they remove themselves from the change equation to remain entirely neutral and thus unable to effect change. Second, they cling to purity, detached from this change, or probable change, by keeping away from their surroundings and the social system undergoing or about to change. They may even participate in obstructing change if offered

---

[229] Mohamed Morsi, the Muslim Brotherhood candidate, won Egypt's presidency in its first free elections. After popular protests erupted against him, the Egyptian army stepped in and deposed him in a coup d'état, whereby its leader, Major General Abdel Fattah El-Sisi, assumed the presidency. He died in detention on June 17, 2019.

a chance. Third, regardless of what the ongoing authoritarian tyrant inflicts or might inflict, Nawār individuals identify with them to remain in power.

Syria: Allah is its protector!

A religious reference and sanctity must back all efforts to prevent change, this sacred stagnation, and a heavenly obligation Allah preserves. In one of his speeches years before the revolution, Bashar al-Assad said Syria's protector was Allah. It later became a frequently chanted slogan and rang out once more on Syrian streets as the events of the revolution escalated. The "no-change" supporters forcefully and persistently chanted it in marches. They were backed by the repressive regime that had long impoverished and repressed them, although the rising change aimed to improve their conditions. It was reiterated on mosque pulpits and churches to affirm the heavenly message upon which they pivot their position on the movement roaming the streets of some cities.

"This bunch of riffraff and Nawār executes foreign plots to destabilize the country" was the unanimous verdict among Nawāri cultural venues. It indicated the exclusionary mentality rooted in a society that suffered centuries-long religious, national, and military dependencies. Syria's Protector Is Allah slogan was a response to the Syrian People Are One slogan, which was the essence and goal of the peaceful movement erupting among Syrian youth. The Nawāri community overwhelmingly rejected it, determined to stay as distant from the action as possible. They maintained a safe distance from a tornado of events that spared none. The passive, neutral side was their escape from a world-threatening earthquake. It did not matter who supported this movement or whether its demands were justifiable, just, or beneficial to them and everyone. All that mattered was that the sacred stability is not to be jeopardized; this was a divine commandment and a heavenly action ensuring that change never occurs. Thus, Allah protects Syria from the future and from getting exposed to its faults and those on its land, whereby the sacred divine will is followed and paid due respect.

In response to this shock after the eruption of the revolution, helpless Nawāri individuals only complain and abide by a neutral approach, hoping it ensures the promised protection to reach ground zero of current events. Barely a few of them participated in putting down the revolution, engaged in counterdemonstrations, joined the popular committees, or reported on the activists' and demonstrators' whereabouts after fleeing. All they wanted was for Syria to have Allah as its protector, for the wrongdoers' destruction at the hands of the wrongdoers, and to come out of this affliction safe.

Nawãri Syrians fully realize their impotence to affect progress or change, let alone stand in the face of a yelling army soldier at a checkpoint or a glowering guard at a government directorate gate. They believe their air weight cannot tip any scale; therefore, they fear a storm might come their way. Hence, they feel inadequate years before taking an exam and do not want to take it, regardless of how this changes their destiny. Having full knowledge of an upcoming exam, they feel unfit to prepare for and pass it. Syrians have a popular joke about someone carrying a basket full of eggs, and upon noticing a banana peel on the sidewalk, they shudder and say, "O God, there goes my eggs!" Syrians find it funny because this youth can avoid stepping on that banana peel. Yet, did they presume they could have avoided their downfall and tragedy?

Despite supplications and prayers for the tsunami to pass by or subside and to survive it, despite all self-assurances that remembrances protect them, defiant against plights, Nawãr people fall into a bottomless abyss again. They had long heard and seen it but had never believed it until the sure fall. In a déjà vu moment, "sly" Syrian society falls victim to major events, reliving what their ancestors experienced when the Crusades knocked down their gates and the Mongol invasion washed the streets with their blood. Anyhow, an army coup is not far behind in history.

Multiple concocting signs before the revolution foretold a new calamity spread over land and people of the Nawãr—the worst, deadliest, and unprecedented calamity. It was surprising, despite indications of its imminence. Unsurprisingly to Nawãri people, they felt it crawling upon them and prayed it would pass their time. Then came the moment of truth and confrontation, and their final position must be declared. They hoped remaining silent would spare them from being drawn into the vortex. It seems Heaven betrayed their dreams and prayers, as they felt.

We all witnessed Nawār catatonia[230] against the wave of the revolutionary popular movement ten years ago. When disaster struck, Syrians realized their wishes would not save them from a destiny cooked in front of them and in their hands. They fled to their cantons, where they were raised. Nawāri people believed themselves to be a sly part of society, of one nation, bound only by fear and greed. Suddenly, it dawns on them that fear and greed bind them. Stupefied, they stand in their cantons, chanting together, Syria's protector is Allah, and praying, May Allah extinguish it with His light.

By referring work and responsibility to metaphysical powers, Nawāri people accomplish two things. First, submit to inaction to confront change—a matter of undesirable consequences in Nawār reality, as aforementioned. Second, assign destiny responsibility, and inaction is relegated to the metaphysical. In the manner of the Quran verse, "Why should we feed those whom Allah could have fed if He wanted to?"[231] It refers to how disbelievers respond when ordered to provide for the poor and needy. They answered that their inaction fulfills Allah's command, so if Allah had willed, He would have provided for and fed them from His provision. Then, they conformed to Allah's will. Similar reasoning applies to Syria's Protector Is Allah slogan. When another value substitutes the actor from the Allah, Syria, Bashar slogan, this develops utter learned helplessness. From the Nawār viewpoint, non-action is the best of all actions.

Non-action was our deadliest sin in the monumental 2011 popular uprising. We, the Nawār masses, renounced taking a stand or "committing action" when it was due. This catatonia was among the most essential tools the regime used and supported to kill the revolution. Individuals are undeniably helpless. Yet, we, the Nawār group, deemed this deficiency on a collective scale a natural reaction, which defined us as a group. Acceptance of inaction exhibits our belief in helplessness. It is a fatalism-based acceptance of how things happen. Depriving people of their ability to act denies them this right.

---

[230] Catatonia (abnormal movement) is a state of increased muscle tone that leads to immobility and rigidity. It is usually associated with psychiatric syndromes such as major depression or schizophrenia.
[231] Surah Ya-Sin: Verse 47.

This super-positional process begins with believing we do not own our destinies and ends with denying our right to change them. Thus, helplessness transforms from being an individual choice to a collective will, from which none has the right to escape.

2-Infallible

Our social dealings reveal an inability to admit and take responsibility for a mistake. We can devise countless interpretations and excuses for denying a mistake and shifting responsibility. People who make mistakes are more likely to be mistaken overall, which increases their capacity to disregard accountability and place the blame elsewhere. Furthermore, the extent of resentment towards the outside world and abundant external excuses are integrated into pretexts to blame others. In Nawãri communities' isolated bubbles, an error becomes less burdensome and easier to justify. It gradually becomes familiar and acceptable to attribute blame for unfortunate events to other reasons and be absolved of responsibility. This behavior spreads and transforms into a frequently applied and acceptable approach without any questioning or objection.

Nawãr are never in error. It could be a matter of bad luck, the weather, the powder[232], or fate—never their mistake. With a stock of justifications up their sleeves, responsibility can be evaded. This shield safeguards them against taking responsibility at any time and under any circumstances. Keeping away from confession and accountability is necessary for Nawãri individuals' survival. Besides, how can they be held responsible for a reality they cannot change? And how can they be solely responsible and not those other actors and non-actors?

The passages that follow show how Nawãri people reject accountability for their actions and deny wrongdoing in every situation. I explore the meaning and implications of error in Nawãri reality.

---

[232] "The problem is in the detergent powder" is a widely spread phrase in Syria. It is a punchline in a joke about a technician unable to fix a washing machine; so he put the blame on the detergent powder as the root cause of the malfunction. Afterward, it was widely circulated.

A mistake worth all of one's life

All actions are interpreted as aggressive-motivated in a society oppressed and under repression. Following the authoritarian's trail of oppression in all actions, the oppressed Nawāri individuals interpret actions that may influence them as an attempt at extreme aggression. This is particularly true if they turn out to be harmful. All that happens to them is an atrocious event intended to inflict personal harm. Why not, given that they are always victims of constant oppression?

Suffering due to the ups and downs of life, natural disasters, or terrible accidents is ruthless, urgent, and sudden. Consequently, it is more dangerous than authoritarian oppression, which is slow, general, continuous, expected, and avoidable. Hence, it is better and safer. The same applies to errors. It is forbidden to make a mistake against us, the Nawār masses. Isn't all this insufferable injustice enough? Work and intentions are inconsequential; intentions always have ulterior motives, which is sufficient proof of condemnation. Whoever has a hidden motive is accordingly evil. Every mistake must be intentionally harmful. Thus, sloth and resistance to change are connected to inaction to stave off error, especially when an error is deemed a sin. People have multiple motivations to avoid accountability for error; this is understandable in a repressive society where the authority exercises tyranny for no reason. People always have their reasons for evading responsibility. Their helplessness on various issues undoubtedly relieves the burdens of uncontrollable issues. However, generalizing this as an absolute judgment creates a problem because all "powerless" Nawār s' actions become involuntary and even forced, at least from their perspective.

In the Nawāri tradition, error equals sin. In this sense, whoever errs against Nawāri people must be an unforgiven criminal worthy of the maximum penalty. These are among the repercussions of identifying with oppressive authoritarians. Given this, Nawāri people are constantly urged not to admit fault and to assign others the blame.

Therefore, Nawāri people are always correct without an inclination to err or bear the consequences. Filling in the role of inaction solely saves them from facing the music and grant them solidarity with the oppressed. Nawār masses are ever united under the slogan, "We don't know who we are, but you are all against us."

I don't act, therefore I don't err

Repudiation of error is only the tip of the iceberg. Nawãri individuals, being helpless and slothful, cannot make a mistake. Instead, they refrain from making one as if infallible. How can they make a mistake when doing so requires action? How does one err while being a non-doer? Learned helplessness is a gateway to being faultless.

In Nawãri understanding, helplessness means a lack of action, even if arguably inaction is in itself a conscious and directly effective act, and that inaction signifies irresponsibility. They believe that no error is produced by inaction; it is the simplest option, so one doesn't err! Poorly capable Nawãri individuals fail to make a mistake. How can they commit one when they don't even act? How can they make a mistake when both the action and the result are beyond their control? These are not correlated. The result is entirely independent of the action in Nawãris' mind!

Nawãri non-doers do not err. Making no mistakes creates infallibility. In this sense, non-action is useful in abdicating responsibility. By practicing non-action, Nawãri individuals found refuge against making mistakes.

The dilution of responsibility

Eventually, action is inevitable, regardless of the Nawãri people's efforts. Action produces a right or wrong outcome, and a sinful mistake is unavoidable. If an error exceeds the low tolerance limit and the low threshold of society's forbearance, dealing with error enters its second stage. This is when individuals resort to diluting responsibility as the second step to evade accountability or the duty to change and reform. Playing the everyone-does-it card comes next—a process of dealing responsibility cards to everyone. It boils down to not being the only one to be blamed for or having committed a mistake or fault. An error is a "shared ownership" without identifying the parties involved. Whoever tries to incriminate one party for a deed must do so for everyone else committing it. This is a just method of judgment. If anyone denies that, they are prejudiced. Instead of targeting joint action and reform, shared responsibility is utilized as a tool for individual evasion of accountability.

It takes a short journey from "They all do it" to "It's not my fault." The transition from diluting responsibility to its complete renunciation is more accessible when someone else is to blame. Disclaiming responsibility is effortless when Nawāri individuals have no obligation or responsibility, have no position or power, and are therefore not accountable.

Attempting to shift responsibility to other parties facilitates evading it for the entire Nawār people since what is external is uncontrollable and for which they cannot be blamed. Disease, hurricanes, oppression, and death are ungovernable, predestined, ordained, and unpreventable events. External and irreversible matters do exist. Yet, adopting this rule as a base eliminates accountability, whether that of the unjust for their injustice, the authoritarian for their oppression of people, or the doctor for the death of a patient. External parties will always bear our faults and absolve us of our misdeeds!

Damned be the Devil!

This title speaks volumes about Nawārs' convictions about error and responsibility. It is common when someone commits an error or a sin to reflexively shout out "Cursed be the Devil" as a sign that this error happened because of the devil's whisper. The collective consciousness figured out how to deflect blame for minor mistakes in a day-to-day context. "Cursed be the Devil" represents numerous concepts in Syrian society about relationships with the surroundings, the external, and the metaphysical or the unknown. This hackneyed cliché is not merely a subconscious utterance in cases of a mistake, such as forgetting to buy a grocery item or handing over a required work task on time according to schedule. This marks the first sign of evading responsibility that someone has to bear. This action or reflexive saying is not just jargon. It indicates a deep conviction of being free of responsibility for the smallest and simplest remediable mistakes. Gradually, those small errors creep into socially accepted norms, having ready-made justifications of external origin. Therefore, they are increasingly granted social acceptance for being uncontrolled and preordained. In the case of excuses not approved yet, the "damned be the devil" response is always good enough.

All events are external and uncontrollable, without causation or reasonable sequential reasons. Instead, there is an action and an outcome that may or may not have a cause to explain it. Having no causation is preferable because it reduces the possibility of assigning liability. Conclusions such as "it is written in the stars" and "there is no escaping fate" are more straightforward and reliable. However, if pressed into naming an actor in such sayings, the best alternative would be, "As you are, you are ruled." An in-depth study of the reasons reveals unwished-for consequences. It is more feasible not to oversimplify what is complex, as long as this helps in preventing accountability.

Superstitious Nawãri people surrender to and never address circumstances. Fate is a law regulating an unpredictable universe without explaining it. What matters is not to blame this wretched person and find someone else to relieve them of their misdeeds.

3- Selfish

Selfishness and egoism are two different concepts that are often confused. Their difference is not about the centrality of the self or egoistic thinking but rather how the ego or the self is perceived. While egotism is interrelated to self-love, selfishness is associated with self-preservation and self-prioritizing without entertaining love for it. Selfishness and self-hatred may even go hand-in-hand is some instances.

A reasonable dose of egoism is undoubtedly healthy and necessary, in contrast to the self-centricity corresponding to pathological selfishness. In truth, under the right circumstances, selfishness is not only a natural and appropriate reaction but also necessary to preserve one's happiness and self-worth. It stimulates positive action to remedy bad situations, particularly when it is undirected by denying the other and disregarding their rights. Selfishness may then be a way to achieve the golden rule, "treat others the way you want to be treated yourself," or take guidance in the hadith of "love for others what you love for yourself, hate for others what you hate for yourself."²³³

Nawāri's selfishness chiefly demonstrates two aspects. First, excessive self-interest; second, complete denial of others or their needs and utter disinterest in anyone. Selfish people ignore all those around them in their circle of interaction. The self-hatred associated with selfishness gives a sense of justice to a Nawāri mind driven by a Darwinian survivalist perspective in a constantly threatening environment. Selfishness is a practical manifestation of transitioning from exclusion and isolation to self-denial for Nawāri people, whether or not they hate themselves. It is not out of self-love and pampering but a biological process for survival and self-preservation.

"May they be granted what they wish for me "is a third aspect of Nawāri character selfishness. While its surface meaning of wanting justice for enemies and friends alike seems reasonable, its ill-wishing perspective is prominent. Its call is not rewarding goodness with a good deed and meeting a bad deed with a bad one, let alone repaying a good deed for a bad one. The denoted concept is to what extent selfishness and greed have penetrated the mindset of Syrian society. The tables are turned. Instead of initiating a good deed and avoiding harm, goodness is restricted to Nawāri persons receiving it. It follows the "scratch my back, and I will scratch yours" module. Initiating a good deed is pointless; it is reciprocated only if others initiate it. Similarly, the others and enemies must suffer Nawāris' ordeal. Selfishness is a borderline between a person and their enemies. Hence, the mutual interactions among Nawār people are militarized.

Is the ego/others classification exclusive to the enemies of society? In what class does the existential enemy fall? The issue is no longer limited to egoism and adopting and promoting positive opinions about oneself; a fourth dimension must be probed. I discuss in the following section some features of Nawār selfishness, especially in line with Syrian reality.

---

[233] It is a prophetic hadith narrated by Imam Ahmad in his Musnad No. 22130. Its verifiers deemed it authentic to others."

Syria is the homeland of 23 million lone persons

This section is not about immersing the Syrian identity in individualism[234]; Nawrāna is not founded on self-love; there is a denial of the individualistic, higher self that seeks transcendence. The pivot point orbits around selfishness (altruism), governing the Syrian person's thoughts and actions. Selfishness, or altruism, is to favor oneself over others. The egoist is engrossed in their self-interest as a being or a thing, not as an individual in a human group. Heedless and oblivious to the public good and the benefit of others, the egoist may harm others to deny them access to an interest they deem their exclusive prerogative.

Nawãri society has predominantly lost faith in being a human group and having rights and duties. Nawãr people do not share a destiny or a common cause. Repression and authoritarianism experienced in the Nawãr social system eliminated any frameworks for joint action except for the minimum requirements for that working individual to survive. Human interactions are individually motivated; they do not go beyond the minimal requirements that are largely individually based, such as gaining money, taking up a position, or achieving fame. Always floundering in fear of others, Nawãri heads play only one broken record on repeat: "They are green with envy. That is a wicked person! May they be granted what they wish for me!"

Nawãr learn to work individually rather than collectively from a young age, believing teamwork deprives them of credit and exposes their work to exploitation. They have to protect themselves from this cheating and injustice. In the early school years, a fierce rivalry among classmates nurtures selfishness. Syrian children—as a rule—do not work in groups on school assignments because the required homework needs only a notebook and a pen. It is absurd how someone would benefit from another's work when a group collaborates on a task; one would respond while the others received theirs on a silver platter. Besides, group thinking is cheating, which is a punishable act. Interaction is a competitive battlefield in Nawãr society. Its schools do not encourage teamwork but foster unhealthy competitiveness; they are not arenas for peers but for enemies and thieves greedy for others'

---

[234] Individualism regards the individual as the standard of everything.

work. Knowledge is monopolized and possessed, not shared or developed. No one expands on others' work because it is an exclusive property. Syrians play solo in group activities and only cooperate if they are in trouble and must cover up their mistakes.

In a profession or specialization, a Nawāri person is also a solo player with no inclination or desire to partner but leans toward receiving all the credit and reputation. To illustrate, some family-owned businesses or professions get broken up into single, identical modules at the hands of the siblings raised under their wings and from whom they gained experience. When a father establishes a thriving business or a retail store and then he dies, they almost always break up into five stores under the same name to provide the same service as the founder-established stores by all siblings. They become adversaries, thinking the other is trying to steal their name and reputation. This reoccurs in countless living examples, including dessert and electrical appliance stores; they embody Nawār selfishness in minute detail.

Selfishness has been exacerbated in Syrian society, particularly with the emergence of its consequences. This self-want to possessiveness overgrows while forbidding it on others. Evolving into a gravitating force and centrifugation at the heart of society, the closest object is the largest, heaviest, and most expensive, while all distant objects decrease in size and material value. The common benefit standard is no longer part of Nawār society's standards. The vulnerable have no place in Syrian society, being small in size and value and useless.

All or none

As aforementioned, the Nawāri community manufactures general societal values into molds for local consumption. The Nawār individual monopolizes justice, favor, and assistance; no one else gets credit and reward but them. If that is not the case, their surroundings must suffer the consequences. Interests do not align in the Nawāri medium. There is no compromise if there is no gain. Otherwise, deliberate sabotage occurs.

It is widely believed among political analysts that actions and behaviors prevalent in the Nawāri community are disconnected from reality, as is my perspective. To illustrate, revenge for al-Ḥusayn's death[235], fulfilling the Kurdish nationalistic dream, restoring Maronite political hegemony, consolidating Alawite rule in Syria, the majority Sunni group's right to rule, and others are oversimplified judgments and mass illusions, besides peremptory, unrealistic, and false statements. There is no evidence of unity of destiny or action within these specified groups; therefore, their work demonstrates no collective perspective. Yet they prefer to be identified within social, religious, national, regional, or class frameworks. Their sectarian identity is emergent; adhering to it is relevant to the appearance or lack of specific circumstances. These subgroup members do not have ideology-based clusters or maintain this affiliation, except if necessary. Besides, the definition and delimitation of justice in a society presupposes an existing collective will and, hence, a collective interest. Hopefully, this section explains why the Nawāri community exhibits no general interest in the first place.

Scrutinizing collective work methods among Nawār groups reveals aspects of their selfishness. Most prominently, it requires, if this oxymoron is correct, quotas rather than participation in decision-making. Herein, narrow affiliation (religious, sectarian, or tribal) is valuable for Nawāri interests. The Nawāri selfish viewpoint gains more clout by counting on a broader identity and a more clearly defined group. Subsequently, they gain legitimacy from an affiliation that was and is out of sight and mind. It is unfathomable how that Nawār individual feels entitled to represent that group. Ultimately, this quota supports the positions and interests of those selfish, Nawār individuals with more leverage, from which they benefit. The brotherly state Lebanon is a living model of this point, as is Iraq in the post-American invasion era.

In collective action, Nawār people do not muster to acquire interests. For them, action follows the zero-sum game[236]. Achieving others' interests

---

[235] Al Husayn bin Ali bin Abi Talib is the grandson of the prophet Mohammed and the second imam in the Shia tradition. He was killed by the Omayyad army in Karbala, Iraq. His death is commemorated annually, mainly by Shia Muslims.

[236] In game theory and economic theory, zero-sum describes a situation in which a participant's gain or loss is precisely equal to that of other participants. One party's

comes at the expense of Nawāri interests; following this reasoning, others' loss of interests is a personal gain! Therefore, Nawāri people work under the motto, "Either I am in, or all will have none." Hence, if I get nothing out of this, why let anyone else?

This selfish Nawāri individual barely observes the outcome, as it is a long-term result under a broad definition. This makes them almost impossible to work with or collaborate with, given they neither co-work for interests nor recognize an outcome related to a cause where their work has a direct influence. Conversely, what works for the public good causes them direct loss. In this view, they must see others suffer a loss for their benefit in a zero-sum game. The Syrian Negotiations Committee, the closed circle of the Assad regime, or any Syrian collective work all illustrate the work of Nawāri selfishness. They are only dunes waiting to be blown away, lacking vantage ground and the ties to keep them whole.

4- Harbook (Sly)

Intriguingly, the Arabic word harbook (sly) is frequently used to describe Syrian people, their behavior, and their approach to life. The slyness phenomenon primarily defines Syrian identity, boasted of and deemed distinctive and progressive among nations and peoples. Many think it is synonymous with intelligence or affectation, while it does not have positive connotations. I cannot stress enough how defining terms significantly reflect the importance of distinguishing between overlapping concepts. Affectation idiomatically denotes claiming more than one has of dexterity and skill, providing the pedantic with a false sense of power and superiority, and simultaneously influencing their targeted victims. Unlike the common connotation of harbaqa[237] (slyness), which denotes the "faculty" of wit, it lexically means spoiling the work! After all, the word does share a shade of meaning with its common use in work and interactions.

---

gain is the other's loss, and one party's loss is the other's gain. As for the non-zero equation, it allows two parties or more to equally gain and lose.

[237] Harbaqa is an Arabic word meaning to spoil work.

This so-called slyness is everywhere. If one observes a leaning wall, the builder simply remarks" It looks just fine to me!". A product with an apparent flaw is marketed as having a unique feature. The electricity cables are stolen from transportation lines to be used in houses. It goes beyond the downright lie and falsehood to penetrate work foundations, as we see how cheating in all forms has become part of any accomplished work.

Nawāri's work, with its form and founding values, is a recipe for failure. Their approach to all matters is to do the least possible and overstate it as much as possible. The Nawāri individual does not focus on how dexterous their work is as much as how well it is communicated. Syrians are not keen on coming across as adept; instead, giving the false impression of adeptness is the focus. Mixing this false adeptness with well-crafted lies and dressing them up, although disagreeable, aims to convince others. They equally manipulate their self-image to project superiority over others—a deliberate, deceptive enhancement. This deception extends beyond marketing the corrupt and self-glorifying; it shifts into a work methodology and intentionally deceives people for no reason. Thus, they feel in charge—that ability to control, power, and superiority of which Nawāri individuals are deprived in a world that shuns them. This is how the oppressed get their payback from the authoritarian holding them among the crowds of Nawār people and their ruins. This revenge is directed towards those who are incapable of responding to or anticipating aggression; it is the transmission of oppression and the passing of the sense of injustice.

Harbaqa (slyness) is often considered a coping and adapting mechanism for reality. Though this justification corresponds to the bitter dystopian reality, harbaqa was not the only way out. Since our reality is consumed with suffering, every attempt at adaptation or its elimination is classified as a form of creativity in our Nawār understanding. Agony does not generate creativity, but improvisation does; these are two separate matters. Confusing them perpetuates the intellectual blindness about what constitutes civilization and evokes solutions to problems that never should have arisen in the first place.

A sly person almost resembles the middle-of-the-road man described in Malek Bennabi's[238] book, The Conditions of the Renaissance: the one who accomplishes half-finished work with half-exerted efforts. This is the borderline and hard point between a person of instinct and a person of civilization. The Nawāri sly individual is a master of fraud as a means of work, an attitude, and a way of life.

Cheating is not realized as a defect to be concealed but as a source of pride in our society and a working framework governing the Nawāri community. This is a widely respected and acceptable framework; it even rules on its terms. Accepting that confusion incites society to approve of a minimum level of credibility and transparency without being provocative or resented by people. People are accustomed to accepting a minimum level of honesty and have settled for deception and cheating as part of the order of social interactions.

Harbaqa is a form of unconscious and indirect social power the public aspires to and seeks. It is an expression of identification between the oppressed and the authoritarian, and in this arena, the oppressed compete for dominance and superiority in strength and cleverness. This approach grants the oppressed control in a world they are familiar with as victims. Unfortunately, it comes at the price of overly tormenting their victims, who are no different than themselves and unable to master this approach. People's wrongdoing of others constitutes the general rule or the accepted and acknowledged social norms. It is a return to jungle law, in which the strong enslave the weak. The centuries-long social contract is no longer valid and is replaced with the rule "survival of the fittest."

Harbaqa is an openly opportunistic practice. It is a repulsive behavior to which some people resort, believing in their cleverness in manipulating and scamming others. However, this behavior is disclosed to the parties involved. The problem is that the victimized party does not resist or object to this form of harbaqa, believing it is satisfactory and desirable intelligence. Although society is generally the only victim of this practice, its members

---

[238] Malik Bennabi (1905-1973) was one of the pioneers of Arab Islamic thought and the Islamic Intellectual Renaissance in the 20th century.

find it not problematic. The blessing granted for slyness is the initial approval of whoever provides it to claim the right to practice harbaqa whenever an opportunity arises.

Slyness, then, is a reproduction of cheating. However, cheating is usually associated with an attempt at covert falsification, whereas harbaqah is a public falsification. Both the sly and the victim recognize it as an unrighteous act. Cheating mixes the fair with the foul to hide its maliciousness. Harbaqa, by contrast, is selling the foul without anything fair. Cheating is individualistically prompted and possibly associated with intentionally harming others. Conversely, harabaqa deliberately inflicts harm for a probable short-term personal benefit or none. It is closer to imposing and exploiting force to disdain the targeted person than an act for quick profit. A harbouq (sly) person emerges as superior, stronger, and smarter than those simpletons who fall victim to their power.

On the other side of the equation, the victimized society glorifies this practice and finds it proof of superiority. By identifying with the authoritarian, a harbouq person imposes the fait accompli on their victims who fall to their will. Hence, cheating is unconcealed in this game; it violates its rules. A sly person's superiority is based on imposing the fait accompli, or public falsification, even against the will of all. This superiority is a gift to be guarded for Nawāri individuals' survival. Consequently, people must follow the school of harbaqa, if not already sly, similar to crying when one direly needs a good cry.

It is like playing a trick on language! Cheating is not the issue as much as distorting the interaction with it. Harbaqa is granted acceptance rather than denouncement. It is even considered a desirable practice for those involved, especially if safeguarded from its direct adverse effects. What was condemnable and punishable metamorphosed into a source of pride and a role model. Tables are turned when evaluating and interacting with this practice, creating a sweeping collective desire to be sly. This act, usually abnormal, constitutes the collective identity and is among its most characteristic features. No society is without cheaters, yet our dealings and perceptions of cheating designate us as harbouq people.

Harbqa has been developed, incubated, and endorsed among the Nawāri community since childhood. Parents wish their children to excel in class and memorize the Qur'an and poetry. Equally, they take pride in the early signs of budding harabqa. The Nawār community promotes and nurtures traits like children's innocent lies to avoid embarrassing situations and the impressions of people around them. Yet the victims of this practice are the same society that takes pride in this trait. Utilizing slyness, bullies and cowards team up against the underdog, as will be illustrated later.

This behavior knows no geographic boundaries, though it is often found in urban areas. Generalizing misbehavior is a misplaced criminalization; besides, this description does not indicate the character of places or the characteristics of their people. Nonetheless, accepting such a practice is a voluntary blessing and establishes opportunistic behavior as one of the pillars of that social contract. Failing to address it signals a rupture of the social contract and emphasizes a defining feature of the Nawāri personality. Starting with confusing right and wrong, to the inclusiveness of harbaqa as a practical interpretation of "May the best hustler win," then consolidating the isolation of the one threatening "do your worst." Across these stops, harbaqa is positioned as the most crucial Nawāri practice worthy of examination.

The mawanah (provision) the Nawār's way

Mawanah (provision) is a term found in many dialects of Arabic vernacular that connotes preference and affection enough to be attentive to a beloved. Its origin is "provide," as in assuming the provision of and fulfillment of someone's needs, meaning to attend to their sustenance and maintenance. "You have mouths to feed" or "You are a provider; feel free to take whatever you want!" are said to acclaim and honor the benefactor—the sustainer and giver—who sustains provided-for persons, recipients of sustenance and support. Therefore, the provider has an impact on the provided-for persons. The provider wins the entitlement and respect based on their giving and the recipient of sustenance is the one to initiate acts of gratitude, often immaterial. The benefactor and those provided-for have a circulating relationship in which interests and rewards are exchanged on different levels. One party might provide financial support, and the counterparty's role is to return the favor with exceptional rewards, often symbolic. This is not an absolute form of business-based relationship. The parties involved exclusively interact through a unique preferential-based connection.

Gradually, the connotation shifted from the provider, breadwinner, or source of subsistence to a source of social influence. The provider denotes the one who influences the other party to respond to a request, even if support is not extended. This ranks higher across the human dealings ladder; the provider is entitled to a right without tangible merit. Moreover, the provider obtains this right in exchange for how much love the provided-for party holds.

In vernacular, "provision" connotes recognized social dimensions and is linked to a specific culture prevalent in society. It represents the existence of "providers" who influence the rest of society. This type is typically used to resolve a conflict and effect reconciliation. The provider is often a community leader who seeks no material or personal interest because the principal beneficiary of a request is often another person or others. In this case, the community leaders are the ones who position themselves as being requested; they are the providers who initiate requesting a provision from other parties. However, people do not find that problematic, based on the sort and purpose of the requested provision. There is no usurpation of a right or ratification of a falsehood. It serves only the general public.

Benevolence is usually met with gratitude, as the provided-for party expressly appreciates what they received, tangible or intangible. Gratitude is coupled with feeling good at work and in life. As a result, gratitude facilitates communicating with something bigger, whether other collective or the divine. Accordingly, the favor becomes a sublime act in the cause of Allah to be rewarded non-materially and in the future.

In this view, benevolence and provision are positive concepts that advance society. This material symbiosis is an unrequited love, a preference of others who recognize this favor with gratitude. Gratitude is not a commodity delivered for payment but a response to a gift. As a response to receiving a gift, it is a form of generosity that honors the other for an unremitted thing.

Provision is an instrument for unity of destiny and identity, in which the provider and beneficiaries produce a positive value and a stronger bond.

Only the name and the initiation of a provision request are shared between the Nawãri provision and the above-described actions. In Nawãri provision reality, someone, not a source of favor, initiates a provision request to gain an exclusive direct personal interest, who is none but a harbouq individual. Even if the benevolent party loses everything, it is still acceptable. The provision initiator—its receiver—has a provision merit to be collected from the requested party, making it a compulsory demand not to be refused. This provision is not a gift or an honor received from the requested party, but an unjust entitlement for the initiator. To decline means animosity. How outrageous to deny the dictations of the unjust initiator! As an entitlement, granting the "benevolence" and the demand is not appreciated. Given for the cause of Allah, the disapproving answer would be, "As if you're doing me a favor!" The requested party has no merit or right to a provision in return.

The mawanah (provision) phenomenon exhibits another side, gratitude is demanded in exchange for people's rights. Even if something is rightfully theirs, Nawãri individuals believe that it is the ultimate blessing to be given anything back, even when it is not theirs in the first palce. Rights are not protected, nor are there legitimate demands in Nawãr allies. One should be grateful when someone performs what is part of a good neighbor's duties, grants an inherent right, or is paid the wages due for work. This approach turns demanding rights into an exceptional act, not an established custom or an unnegotiable axiom. A pivotal foundation of social interaction is deemed a favor or benevolence that might have been otherwise dispensable. This perception facilitates the non-fulfillment of rights. It is another form of provision in the Nawãri way, echoing the response, Won't you cut me some slack?

Rather than establishing benevolence- and reciprocity-based social relations, the mawanah (provision) is transformed into an individual harabaqa (sly) practice, infringing others' rights. The Nawãri's mawanah is thus an unjust usurpation of rights to gratitude and appreciation. It is pressing another Nawãri person for a grant, where the mawanah owner asks for an exclusive

Fig. 4-2: Syrian actor Douraid Lahham, known for his character "ghawwar Ettosheh", and an iconic Sly in reality and in character.

material favor. It comes even at the expense of those requesting provision, with no societal benefit. On the contrary, the achievement or non-achievement of this provision leads to social disintegration.

5- Mkoleck (Sycophant)

Kowlakeh (sycophancy) denotes false flattery, hypocrisy, blandishment, obsequiousness, and adulation. I do not know its linguistic source in Arabic. It is commonly used in the Syrian colloquial dialect. Baize-wiping, synonymous with sycophancy, is groveling to upper-class people who were the first to wear baize trousers. Historically, the term traces back to the Turkish word Jokha dar, denoting someone who serves the ottoman by preparing, cleaning, and dressing their shoes and trousers. It later denoted those who closed and opened curtains in royal courts and ministers' palaces. The groveler's bowing of the head seemed like wiping people's trousers. I might have missed a better explanation, but its connotation is clear and intelligible. Synonyms for "sycophant" vary throughout Arabic dialects. For instance, in Jordan and Palestine, sahheej[239] (loud clapper) and in Egypt, mtabalati (drum banger) denotes sweet talkers.

The Kowlakeh description has four conditions to be met. Firstly, flattering someone must be for something they are not, as in praising a fool for intelligence and a miser for generosity. Secondly, the sweet-talker knows and is convinced they tell lies; this is adulation. Thirdly, the shameless groveling of a sycophant must have witnesses. Kowlakeh is a pretentious act publicly performed by the flattered one and the sweet talker; it is not a private show. Fourthly, this act aims to implore for a specific personal benefit, despite rarely ever being fulfilled.

The Kowlakeh must have an entreated benefit and an audience to watch this show, where the performers are often the upper class of masters and the lower class of followers or subjects. Our heritage profusely recorded sycophancy, attesting to millennia-long human practice. Similar to other Nawāri practices, sycophancy is not an accidental historical event, nor is it

---

[239] In Arabic, scrubbing means peeling through rubbing. In this context, it is a metaphor for excessive applause that the hands' skin is peeled off.

limited to Syrians or Arabs. Its most noteworthy historical consequences are praise poems, a distinct literary genre with well-known poets and figures.

In ancient times, people of wealth, power, and authority were the targets of praise and flattery as a means of social climbing and achieving undeserved gains. The sycophant may not have a supportive or adversarial predisposition towards these targets. Praise may be transformed into satire if the desired aspirations are unfulfilled. To illustrate what the poet Abū al-Ṭayyib Mutanabbi did with Kafur, the ruler of the Ikhshidid state who ruled Egypt and the Levant in the 4th century AH/10th century AD, Al-Mutanabbi generously praised Kafur. Celebrated eulogies gave way to the most scathing satirical poetry when he did not get his way. Modern-day sycophancy is not so poetic and is readily embraced and accepted, bearing little fruit and barely compensable. The compensation and composition of flattery are now futilely utilized for no specific circumstances or interests.

The motives of adulators and hypocrites are self-evident, with a likely grant or gift in mind and a position or status as their end goal. In any case, the purpose of that flattery is some reward or return. The sole beneficiary is the adulator. The better their sweet talk is, the greater their reward. Flattery is a selfish act to attain a personal interest, insensitive to cause harm to others.

It makes no difference for Nawāri Kowlakeh if its target is liked or disliked. It could be more influential if the target is hated. In the past, favors and gifts were the goals; now, Nawāri's Kowlakeh bears no significant benefit but is a voluntary act of self-humiliation for the hated and feared. This form of flattery does not achieve self-benefits but instead harms others.

Hand-picked by the regime, all people around the tyrant were sorted out and carefully chosen for this role. Why would Said al-Bouti[240], a world-renowned cleric, wail over the despot Hafez Al-Assad in his funeral and declare he sees his seat in heaven? Why engage in this sort of voluntary Kowlakeh? If out of fear of the despot's oppression, ask Allah to pardon and

---

[240] Muhammad Said Ramadan Al-Bouti (1929-2013) was a renowned Syrian Sunni Muslim scholar, writer and professor, where he was a staunch defender of the Assad and his crimes in Syria.

show him mercy, or go the extra mile with your oration of flattery and quote a situation worthy of praise. It is more disgraceful coming from a cleric!

Undoubtedly, the pioneer sycophant has a reserved place in Hell for devising "bloody fingerprinting" on ballot papers in Syria. What an inexplicable degree of hypocrisy! This bloody fingerprint is an icon of the Nawāri Kowlakeh. Because an imbecile foolishly stoops in this manner, millions were forced follow their step, or otherwise punished. How wretched we are!

In the previous chapter, I discussed totalitarianism and its fusion with oppressed people, besides their identification with the oppressor. I elaborated on how this process results in social disintegration and the rise of selfish people. Some observed practices proved harmful to society while being useless to the individual! Of these practices, harbaqa and Kowlakeh are the gravest Nawāri practices experienced.

Undoubtedly, the roots of this have to do, in part, with self-protection. Several psychologists widely believe that flattery and imploration are possible responses to psychological trauma to prevent conflict and shock. In the case of children, they fall victim to the "good child" syndrome to avoid an abusive or uncaring parent. In adults, this act is often observed among those in relationships that do not satisfy their needs, values, and rights. So, the traumatized adult resorts to flattery to abide by what they believe is expected of them.

Again, Nawār behavior predominantly reflects responses to what they suffered from oppression and violence. Investigating and exploring the scientific justifications and explanations for these phenomena proves this is a conscious and willful human act. If someone flatters a traffic officer or a security guard to avert harm, personal motives for Kowlakeh are clear. Accordingly, each case has independent circumstances and different reasons. Besides, each person can endure oppression up to a particular limit and a varying degree of dignity. Our patience and burdens certainly vary. The indifference to the adverse repercussions of our actions or the disregard for these practices has its reasons, yet it remains harmful.

Kowlakeh is ultimately a public spectacle with performers and a vast audience. In return, the interaction of the mighty person offered Kowlakeh is also part of the show. On their high and mighty stage, they are haughtily unresponsive to the offered Kowlakeh until a second, a third, and more join this performance. As time passes, they look around to see if anyone did not join the Kowlakeh parade, and if they are disobedient, they are punished.

Let it fall on me and my enemies

Kowlakeh is a show with an actor performing for someone and spectators. The scene opens with a mckolek, an actor, performing for the tyrant, the show's target, with the people as their spectators. The tripartite structure of the distribution of roles is dynamic. Shortly, these roles transform into an actor, an object, which is the people, and spectators. Exchanging spectator and actor roles, the mckolek and the tyrant compete and take turns harming the people. Sycophancy helps the mckolek to stand out from the oppressed crowds, at least for a short time. This dynamicity grants the mckolek an exclusive identification with the authoritarian, where both inflict humiliation on the rest. The mckolek is never elevated, secure, or immune. Finding the delusion of an imagined position of a temporary oppressor sufficient, they carry on this show.

The relationship between the tyrant and mckolek is comparable to that between the coward and the bully. Arduously groveling, the coward stays out of the bully's grasp by helping to inflict harm on a victim the bully chooses. The bully/tyrant and the coward/mckolek also share an attitude towards the vulnerable. The hope to escape those victims' fates dissipates as the coward immediately realizes they are another face in the bully's or tyrant's view. The despot is heedless of that groveling wimp, whether it is an actor, a university professor, or a street vendor. There must be stuntmen to play this dramatic role under their shadows.

Ultimately, the mckolek further submits to the despot and increases the humiliation and repression inflicted upon the oppressed groups. The kowlakeh shares some similarities with altruistic punishment, in which one party brings punishment on themselves to spread the damage inflicted upon another. Altruistic punishment usually focuses on inflicting harm and enduring self-damage to that end, whereas kowlakeh finds everyone fit for an offering. Besides, the harmed person suffering the loss resorts to inflicting the altruistic punishment, not those witnessing it. In this situation, the mckolek, the audience, engages in altruistic punishment to multiply the harm of the afflicted or oppressed, whoever that is. Most appropriately termed, altruistic punishment targets inflicting punishment on someone out of personal animosity. Driven by less logical and more basic motives, those adopting kowlakeh must first identify with the despot for the rest to follow suit. They wish all to be lost in the totalitarian horizon, where they are the pioneers savoring this favor. At least, this is their fantasy.

Whoever institutes an evil practice will have its sin and the sin of those who act upon it. Motives aside, voluntarily producing an act to harm others is a form of psychopathy perpetrated by someone not in their right mind. A society's foundations must have been inherently eroded to be thus infested. Probably, mckoleks do not act in this way to intentionally cause damage to others or give others any thought in the first place. Still, the fruits of their bad deeds remain the same.

Assad's torture chamber survivors' testimonies were featured on the television show "Hey, Freedom"[241]. Whoever saw it must recall how hunger and torture pushed those detainees to the extreme of reporting on and eating each other alive. Whatever they committed is justified and excused. To be starved for two years and never once know the feeling of being full is not to be judged from a distance. Suffering sleep deprivation and lice, being deprived of medicines, and being at the mercy of relentless executioners are matters beyond the utmost bounds of human reason. Still, they are far less harrowing and more logical than the atrocities voluntarily committed outside torture chambers.

---

[241] A famous program on Syria TV, an opposition leaning channel, where they interview ex detainees to talk about their life stories and experiences in brutal prisons.

Fig. 4-3: This is a screenshot of a video showing a child being severely beaten in school by people in military uniform, as they were forcing him to prostrate to Bashar al-Assad's picture. In that clip, they were hysterically yelling at him, "Who is your God?". The video was from Inkhil in Daraa, southern Syria, September 14th, 2011.

6- Antar

Antarah bin Shaddad's[242] epic poems and Abu Antar's[243] image offer a source of meaning for the modern Arabic term antaria and our perception of its connotations. It combines social traits, encompassing more than one behavioral practice on multiple levels and directions. Most accurately put, the Antari person embodies emotional outbursts, violence, and revenge. It is a range of Antarah bin Shaddad's courage and enthusiasm for battle and Abu Antar's violence and display of strength and power, besides the strong emotions exhibited in their violence. I believe "Antaria" distinctively identifies Nawāri behaviors for dealing equally with events and people.

I recall a memorable scene from "Our Beautiful Days," a Syrian television series from 2003. It is the "Kibbeh" scene in which actor Rami Hanna[244] is a poor young man; he comes home and finds his sister, the actress Karis Bashar, had brought some food from a house she works in as a housemaid. Infuriated, he beats her for stooping so low and bringing home food alms. She bursts, crying, out of the kitchen. A few minutes later, the brother is on the screen, nibbling on the kibbeh his sister brought, as his tears run down his cheeks and his injured pride[245].

Why the sister was pushed to tears was justified, but not what made the brother cry. It was also evident what angered that antari brother, but why he wept is inexplicable. In full Antar mode, offended Rami Hanna stole the limelight, indifferent to the context and his surroundings. Similarly, I focus on antarism as a behavioral practice for Nawāri people, apart from its triggers. The external observer usually overlooks the role oppression and ignorance play and considers antarism a psychological trait inherent in

---

[242] One of the most renowned pre-Islamic Arab poets for his poetry, adventurous life as a knight, and a notable hanging ode.

[243] A fictional character on television, the late Syrian actor Naji Jabr, was famous for performing it. He is a violent man who constantly harasses the vulnerable. He symbolizes the strongman or thug.

[244] [C] Rami Hanna (1972-) A Syrian TV actor. After he graduated from the Institute of Dramatic Arts in 1997, he started his professional career as an Actor in many TV Series.

[245] Go to the third episode, the 33rd minute, and then from the 43rd minute.

Nawãr people; this is not my perspective or approach. I seek to study Nawãr individuals who choose this behavior in response to oppression, given that antarism is not exclusive to them. Also, it is not commonly resented. Apart from Bollywood[246], Hollywood[247] is more into antarism than any other film industry center worldwide.

Antarism is a mixture of intense emotions, violence, and revenge. For a Nawãri person, their passion is openly and intensely communicated. Passion and violence are their default modes, varying in intensity. Nawãri violence takes multiple forms at different times. It could be subtle, as in domestic violence, or verbal or physical. It may also be psychological when the victim is completely neglected and treated as non-existent. Active violence is exhibited exactly like our mental image of it. Furthermore, external violence is discernible. Alongside other forms to be discussed later, multiple internal, self-inflicted types originate from psychological variables like self-hatred or behaviors like self-injury disorder.

The oppressed society is constantly under a torrent of subtle violence, exposed to detention, torture, and killing that are unexpected and incessant. Thus, this overhanging apprehension takes over their lives. Nonetheless, they are acutely aware of the impending intimidation. In schools, government departments, and shops, a Nawãri person moves around in an orbit of human interactions dominated by verbal or physical violence. If not, they are met with complete negligence in their surroundings and denied all verbal and physical interactions. They are entirely overlooked at home or school. A Nawãri individual practices subtle violence towards the authority or what represents it, for instance, throwing garbage in the street, vandalizing public facilities, especially by the employees, and being negligent at work. These typically exemplify subtle violence. Lethargy and unproductivity partly constitute their payback. Additionally, lethargy is an emulation of the authoritarian and the privileged.

---

[246] A term that refers to the famous Mumbai-based film industry in India, producing motion pictures in Hindi. Bollywood has one of the largest film production facilities in the world.

[247] It is a famous area in Los Angeles, US, and is one of the most important centers of cinema and visual art worldwide.

By contrast, active violence bursts into our minds with images of physical violence by injury or killing. It is outward, directed against the community. Or internally focused within domestic settings, and even self-inflicted. Antaria is a multifaceted and multidimensional practice. It is not limited to the iconic scenes of boiling cauldrons, hyper-masculinity, and the epics that literary and artistic works have consolidated regarding this concept.

Revenge usually fuels violence. Undoubtedly, some cases of excessive violence respond to an emergency that ignites its fuse. Yet, this moment of explosion necessarily requires gunpowder. It is produced through Nawār people's continuous exposure to the persecution and subtle violence of the authorities, which include political, social, religious, and economic. Aggressiveness is demonstrated in Nawāri individual counter-violence. However, antarism goes a mile further to being unguided and un-triggered violence. Nawāri violence is uncalled-for and not always a response to an event or threat. Its pattern is interactive, viewing the world from a different lens. Antarism, then, is continuous violence that does not differentiate between its targets, declaring war on all and everyone.

The relationship between subtle violence and active violence resembles gasoline and fire. To elaborate, subtle violent acts generate anger in the Nawāri victim. Not knowing how to respond constructively or because the tyrant denies them this ability, their overwhelming anger is articulated through physical violence. Family and kids stand as the first victims of this explosion, falling within its radius and lacking the power to defend themselves. Exceeding this close circle, it multiplies among people in indirect surroundings, such as at work, public squares, or neighborhoods. This subtle violence constructs the raw material on which active physical violence feeds.

The epic between individuals and public utilities is one of the master scenes of antarism. The oppression they suffer is projected at these facilities. Thus, their aggression toward them represents their victory and pride. Nawāri life is a duel between the individuals and the authoritarian, where all else is background detail like stage props and inanimate objects playing no part and unaffected by what happens on stage. The real tragedy is that Nawār people entirely fit these roles.

No wonder, under all challenging conditions, negligence is the driving force. It is common regarding the misuse of government infrastructure, breaking traffic regulations and rules, or public health issues, for example, during the COVID-19 pandemic and other earlier crises. Nawãri nihilism emboldens them to recklessly embrace and sink their teeth into calamities. While trying to shelter from authoritarian oppression and harm, they abide by reckless courage in the face of other dangers. This is particularly true in times of loud and clear dangers that require a public response. Covid-19? There is nothing to fear! The seat belt? It is useless! Welcome to death on stage! We antari Nawãrs fear none!

The Nawãr person acts in rage, retaliation, and violence by damaging public property. Directing this form of external violence towards public facilities gives them a sense of freedom from and identification with authority's indiscriminate oppression. Nawãri people emulate the official negligence of public and private property. Delinquent behavior and lawlessness are other ways for the Nawãr individual to escape the oppressed class and enjoy a fifteen-minute-of-rage moment. Laws and public facilities symbolize the state and are representative of the despot. In antari individuals' view, breaking the law and vandalizing schools and public transportation is a means of retaliation and restoring pride. It is insignificant to whom their acts harm. Proving their ability to regain their dignity takes precedence.

The Nawãri individual mimics the rich and powerful in appearance and food. The antari emulates top officials' sons, practicing a wreckless car drift and picking up fights with people at random. These, among other examples of Nawãri antarism, fall under unguided violence. It is their payback for the oppression they suffer. Eventually, other Nawãrs fall victim to this fury. It is the last thing on their minds, driven by an insatiable thirst for confronting those equal to or less than them. The usual verbal aggression includes swearing and insulting others. Verbal escalation forms are countless, and all have the same baseline: a verbal exchange, disagreement, threat, and, in conclusion, a clash. In the Nawãri community, the trigger for physical violence is highly light. I have witnessed endless fights that start with "What are you looking at?" for accidentally glancing at someone.

During the COVID-19 pandemic, domestic violence was exponentially exacerbated. Early in the pandemic, several impacted countries sounded the alarm about its effect on domestic violence. The Chinese police have stated that 90% of the causes of these latest cases can be attributed to the pandemic. In the United States, domestic violence incidents increased by a little over 8% during the first nine months of the pandemic. The American Journal of Emergency Medicine and the United Nations Organization for Women have found an increase in domestic violence cases since the pandemic's outbreak. They detected an increase of 300% in Hubei Province in China, 25% in Argentina, 30% in Cyprus, 33% in Singapore, and 50% in Brazil.

Among the possible causes of these dramatic impacts are the growing fears and anxieties about prolonged restrictions on movement, increased economic stress, and the depleted ability of the healthcare system to support survivors. It can be said that these factors constitute the daily reality of Nawãr, from cradle to survival or grave. In the Nawãr communities' states, no accurate statistics are reliable enough for a clear picture of reality and chart trends. Hence, seeking other alternatives to examine these global phenomena, personal experiences can convey the reality we underwent and are undergoing in the Arab region.

Observing several Arab states, particularly Syria, the precariousness of their situation is obvious, indicating a rise in homicide and suicide cases, which reflects the escalation of oppression and unavoidable failure. These murders signal an imminent explosion, which does not always have to be an uprising or revolution. However, antari Nawãri is a wide-open gateway to social violence directed at its most vulnerable, such as torturing animals, beating women and children, or many other similar examples. Similar to homicides, violence cases and divorce rates exacerbate in response to the escalation of tension and oppression. Numerous countries witnessed a spike in violence, matching increased poverty and economic crises, particularly in wartime.

Resembling external violence, the antari hyperbolizes illness primarily for its symbolism, besides justifying failure and defeat. Illness, another rival to violence for Nawãri individuals, represents a form of internal violence inflicted on their secretly hated selves and a declaration of protest against the bitter reality. Falling to illness is protesting against oppression and injustice without fighting it. It could be a hysterical public show of how Heaven chose them to endure hardships. Hence, they are incomparable to none, and only they are selected for good and bad fate. They embrace the slogan that resolutions, merits, and adversities are measured according to those who take them. Being submissive to injustice is because Heaven ordained its will to be accepted and unchallenged. Accordingly, treating or preventing disease is unacceptable. How can anyone reject being selected for an affliction? How can anyone get rid of what Heaven has ordained and chosen?

Passive, neutral Nawãri individuals fear adverse ramifications. They discard and rebel against anything unusual. They interpret change as a disaster. Every invention is misguided and bound to meet its fate in hell. Fearing envy and the evil eye, good fortune must be concealed, but misfortune is exhibited. In this manner, change is reinforced as another form of calamity. Treachery is declared, loyalty is obscured, and only evil prevails. This explains why the antari displays another form of violence harbored toward change and the future. Their aggressiveness towards the world makes its mark on their perspective on life. Past times represent only the good old days and righteous predecessors, unlike the bitter present and corrupt generation. This trend is based on refusing the future before it happens—not only that but anticipating it would carry the worst. Following this logic, Nawãri people always expect failure at the end of every path before even taking it or reaching the finish line. Seeing life through this dark lens, they wage war on everything, significant or insignificant. Powerless, the mckolek person takes out their anger on the vulnerable around them.

Antari Nawãri people become oppressive and bully cudgels against Nawãri people. Interchangeably, the despot's antarism and oppression are sharpened. Besides, each uses the other as a pretext. Within this vicious circle, violence and aggression fuel all forms of violence—subtle and internal. Lost in this circle, the authoritarian ruler's violence becomes a prerequisite to controlling barbarianism, terrorism, or sabotage, according to the geographical and temporal coordinates.

Fig. 4-4: Actor Rami Hanna in the iconic scene described in this chapter.

A mute, blind, deaf, and broken-winged human form is how we picture the oppressed. Without a voice to speak their mind, their eyes are kept down, and their tail is between their legs. Hence, if a screaming voice echoes in the distance, it is certainly not them. Likewise, the needy person must be broken and subservient. So, their poverty is denied if they carry their heads high or appear angry and sulky. The oppressed people vent their anger on themselves and their loved ones, who are the first to pay the price for this explosion.

Conclusion

The One Nawãri I Know Well

I make no claims to being a neutral party in the oppressed-and-oppressor relationship. I am one of the Nawãr group. I stand by us and am not against us. Our rapidly deteriorating situation in the past decade is an extension of a decades-long demolition process. I am a Nawãri. I share many habits with what this book recorded—it is a self-examining book with a lot of self-elucidation. I am on a journey to become my best self. I am not alone; we—the Nawãr—are a herd grouped around fear. Eventually, we must group around more than fear. We can and are bound to be better.

The word Nawãr used to describe our group stems from a common and unconscious habit about a matter's propriety or impropriety. This habit might be related to the bourgeoisie in Syrian cities. In another context, I found the word "peasant" to differentiate from the other uptown city dwellers, whether a habit or taste in fashion. In rural areas, the word "Bedouin" describes the low job of shepherding. Yet, we use the word "Nawãr" to deny something and refer to the adversary who is not us. Though we have never met one Nawãri in person, we can spot the aspects of "nawrãna: and a Nawãr person from miles away.

Nawrãna is an acquired character, identity, and features. It is all we are not, or at least what we do not wish to see in ourselves. This enticed me to champion the Nawãr group. I describe our unifying oppression aspects, which constitute our nawrãna, despite our disgust at the Nawãr and anything relevant to them. Ascribing them with hateful speech and actions and projecting all sorts of shortcomings onto them, I equally attribute all of this to myself and us. I seek atonement for the racism and repression practiced against a group we did not try to know adequately. This emulates what we, the oppressed masses, experienced and are experiencing. What we unconsciously attribute today to the Nawār concept is an attempt to pass on some of what is attributed to us. Addressing these intellectual phenomena is superficial. This book does not adopt external impressions of slave morality[248] or general observations supposing that oppressed people are morally degenerate[249]. I wanted to delve beyond the outward scope of these concepts and constructs. My efforts study this intellectual system's formation, its behavioral features, and how these ideas and practices contributed to developing the dystopian reality we experience.

"Gratuitous death" looming upon us has long been brewing. We first made some successive concessions. Then, the act of death sealed our fate, with barrel bombs dropped on us and in the intelligence torture chambers. Reorganizing the oppressed masses marked the operation of a killing machine, which took time to complete. Over a long and unwinding road, society's rock turned into chaff blown away in the wind. Reducing power to a toy in the tyrant's hands was forcibly and submissively achieved. Numerous factors carved out this bitter reality.

The human race is ever-rejuvenating. The threat of its eradication has now diminished. However, society's death and the decay of civilization occur

---

[248] Master-slave morality is a central philosophical theme of Friedrich Nietzsche's works. He argues that slaves developed morals to help them endure slavery, vulnerability, and poverty and nurture their hope of being rewarded in the future or after death.

[249] This phrase is attributed to Ibn Khaldun. The text is an extract from an introduction to a book he authored. It goes as follows:
> Whoever among the educated, the Mamluks, or the servants suffered oppression and injustice, their souls were debased, and their vigor changed. They became lethargic and were pushed to lie and show malice, pretending to be what they were not. Fearful of tyranny's cudgels, they were taught deception and deceit until adopted as habits and manners. The sense of humanity in terms of socializing and civility was corrupted. They became dependent on others to defend them or their houses. Unwilling to acquire virtues and fine morals, they lacked purpose and became devoid of humanity. This way, they relapsed and fell to the lowest of lows. Consequently, this is the fate of every nation that fell into the grip of oppression and suffered injustice.

gradually, similar to that of living species. A species may go extinct when its origin disappears, whereas its mutated images would survive. I wonder how the great-grandfather of dogs lived before being domesticated. Is this substitution necessarily undesirable? We do not know. We assume that mutation and change would be for the better. As the famous quote by Antonio Gramsci goes, the old is dying, and the new struggles to be born.

We must agree that moral standards are still lacking. My reference here is not to what some believe to be the phenomenon of moral decline, a favorite topic for mosque imam sermons. Instead, I indicate the unnamed effects of these phenomena that we witness. They match the outcomes reflected in slave and oppressed morality. Therefore, we must create a new set of ethical and moral standards, but first, several prerequisites for what is or is not moral must be identified. To define these "unethical morals," I follow my approach to non-civilization as a path to escape decadence.

Defining what something is not helps us understand some unclear concepts before adopting this approach. It differs from defining the opposite. To clarify, miserliness is the opposite of generosity; "not to be a miser" does not make one generous, and vice versa. Also, to be unvirtuous is not necessarily to be vicious, yet some elements negate the existence of virtue. These are fatal gaps that our intellectual heritage has failed to fill to this day. For instance, what Muawiyah did to Imam Ali and his family (both were the Prophet's companions) flaws our concept of virtue, necessary to achieve advancement. Bringing up this example is not intended to ignite a sectarian clash. The fact that it is a contentious point is what I mean by hiding intellectual and moral gaps. Without detecting these gaps that we have in and around us, we are doomed to an abyss of history and the bottom of underdevelopment. They are hard to identify, but they are significant. Still, several intellectual and practice principles supporting them can be traced once defined. This has been this book's goal since its inception.

Our consciousness is worst afflicted by the mantra "none of my business." We established it as an approach to reality and a philosophy governing our actions and restraining our thoughts. Our withdrawal from the public sphere allowed tyranny to usurp our lives. The inaction that we cling to is our deadliest sin to this day. Our downfall will seal our fate if we do not change.

The Arab Spring has taught us the harsh lesson that an acre lost to tyrants is paid for with rivers of blood to regain it. Also, when the time for construction passes, the demolition machines go first. I wish we had repaired our pillars before this day came.

This book does not call for an ideology of social regulations and protocols that shape individual consciousness. I refuse to mold rigid stereotypes. This is not a list of requirements; instead, its message is that we must identify the cognitive gaps, or else they will be our doom as individuals and as a human group. While these activities could seem like self-preservation strategies, I hope I can show how they horrendously worsen rather than reverse our fate.

I wrote these final lines just a few days after the idiotic "Butcher of Damascus" delivered his alleged victory speech for a fourth term as president in 2021. He threatened neutral people who did not declare their loyalty to the regime built by both him and his father—a fear-and-oppression construction built with skulls and rubble. This is not a surprise ending, as there is an urgent and permanent need to have an enemy, that other, and an adversary! An adversary does not even have to declare their antagonism or opposition to the totalitarian oppression system. The system takes care of this imperative role, even if performed by an extra. "The Police and People" TV program, featuring public interrogations of petty criminals, is unforgettable for Syrians. The totalitarian regime must constantly have enemies or invent them out of nowhere. How can the conspiracy theory illusion exist without an evil foe who is victoriously crushed and defeated? The "adversary" enemy crucially constitutes the totalitarian framework; otherwise, it is lacking.

No longer providing rights or services, the homeland has nothing to promise but a blessing of safety and security. Empty-handed, what it offers at best is to be kept hostage without being killed, submissively playing hostage or scapegoat. Sooner than later, each scapegoat meets its inevitable day of sacrifice. These mob homelands bargain with people over keeping them alive and taking their lives. They rob people of the ability to live, prosper, and enjoy freedom and dignity in exchange for survival. It is time for those standing on neutral ground to know this fact, whether in Syria, among its Arab neighbors, or anywhere else. These bankrupt countries offer only one broken record on repeat: a security and safety chant. They invent illusionary enemies, wage imaginary wars, and defeat unreal conspiracies. However long it may take, someone will find themselves enemies of this state who will be conquered. This homeland always overcomes that sort of "foe."

The Arab Spring has yet to come. It feels a lot like the Arab region before 2011. July 25, 2021, marks the inevitable end of that season, when Qais Al-Said, the Tunisian president, dealt a massive blow, announcing a coup. A dark and dreary winter is ahead of us. Why not! Tens of thousands took to the streets to support Al-Saeed's coup against the Tunisian constitution, similar to Al-Sisi's coup in Egypt in 2013. Understanding the motives of these masses' behavior contributes to better comprehending how tyrants become the invaders' bridge.

Oppressive regimes are not an Arabs only phenomenon. My argument immensely intersects with the black citizens' reality in the US and poor white people from the rednecks and any social hierarchy based on a controlling group and maintain inequality. What propelled Donald Trump—and many others worldwide—to be the president of America in 2016 is similar to what keeps Bashar al-Assad and others in authority. They are the same intellectual shortcomings and human "un-virtues"; it is the global "none of my business." In the book's English translation, I use both words "Nawãr" and "savage," to which many readers would relate other equivalents with similar connotations.

At the end of the book, nothing can explain how we reached the point where a doctor in a hospital performs torture or how Ahmed Hassoun[250], the last Mufti of Syria, faces his dirty soul. Hopefully, the book sheds some light on intellectual and behavioral aspects to help us understand how these people and their likes emerged through some ethical gaps. I have recounted some stories and jokes to illustrate a lesson and provide proof. The last is about Ibn Khaldun, the great scientist and founder of sociology. Al-Muqaddima (The Introduction), his most well-known work, concentrates on human

---

[250] Ahmad Badreddin Hassoun (1949-) was the Grand Mufti of Syria from 2005 to 2021, after which the post was abolished. He is anothe staunch defender of the regime's crimes.

civilization and sociology. Researchers and historians overlook that Ibn Khaldun was in Damascus during its siege by Timūr Gurkānī (Tamerlane). In the first meeting, Ibn Khaldun was summoned into the ruthless conqueror's presence and kissed his hands. Ibn Khaldun gave him a detailed report on Damascus, along with a complete description of the Maghreb countries, Tamerlane's next destination of invasion. Ibn Khaldun was keen on meeting Tamerlane and asked him to join his entourage. He persuaded the people of Damascus to surrender to Tamerlane, promising them safety. Afterward, everyone above the age of five was killed, and women were ravaged in front of their families. Damascus was entirely ransacked and plundered for twenty days. Mamluk Sultan Nasir-Ad-Din Faraj's army did not disappoint Damascus. Conversely, the illustrious scientist Ibn Khaldun and a crowd of scholars and jurists went to Tamerlane's camp early to avoid his atrocities. Historical Miniatures, the late Saad Allah Wannous's play, immortalizes this story. Upon reading it, Abd al-Rahman Munif was provoked to immediately investigate its authenticity. He found more gruesome details, which need not be mentioned at this stage.

In a society lacking sound equations for its moral system, it is unknown how to position scholars and intellectual figures within its societal context or what role they play toward their people. It is worth emphasizing that one's guilt multiplies with knowledge, power, and status. Hence, I confidently list and rebuke these names, dead or alive. We must re-extrapolate our reality and create maps of interaction to list all the actors involved. Thus, everyone would be assigned their own responsibilities, including ours. In this manner, our deserved losses would be equally distributed among us, with the hope that someday gains, and good fortune would replace them. Searching for individuals' roles in what transpired in Syrian reality and the change equation, in general, is not out of bullying the weakest despot. My sole quest is to uncover what we committed. On this justice scale, hopefully, one of us can add weight in favor of the oppressed. One will not affect the outcome, but if slighter, more people join, the odds will be stacked in their favor. Not only that, but the tyrants' scales will also be thrown into a bottomless abyss to meet their deserved fate.

This book is finished, though incomplete. I maintain my right to complete it if my understanding of what I wrote is altered. I reserve the right for my ideas to mature and my views to develop. I will add any necessary ideas for its completion. Finally, despite the dark nature of this book, I must stress that the world is full of Noor[251] (light); we only need to look closer.

---

[251] Nawar and Noor are spelled exactly the same in Arabic (with different diacritization), yet the meanings are extremely different.

- THE END -